THE TRINITY

Understanding God's love,
His plan of salvation,
and Christian relationships

WOODROW **WHIDDEN** ◆ JERRY **MOON** ◆ JOHN W. **REEVE**

REVIEW AND HERALD® PUBLISHING ASSOCIATION
HAGERSTOWN, MD 21740

The authors assume responsibility for the accuracy of all facts and quotations as cited in this book.

This book was
Edited by Gerald Wheeler
Copyedited by Delma Miller and James Cavil
Cover designed by Trent Truman
Cover illustration by Terrill Thomas
Interior designed by Toya M. Koch
Electronic makeup by Shirley M. Bolivar
Typeset: 12/15 Bembo

PRINTED IN U.S.A.

06 05 04 03 02 5 4 3 2 1

R&H Cataloging Service
Whidden, Woodrow W. 1944-

The Trinity: understanding God's love, His plan of salvation, and Christian relationships, by Woodrow Whidden, Jerry A. Moon, and John Reeve.

1. Trinity. I. Moon, Jerry A. II. Reeve, John. III. Title.

231.044

ISBN 0-8280-1684-4

Dedicated to the memory of the late

Otto H. Christensen,

who deeply cared about these Trinitarian issues.

CONTENTS

SECTION TWO

The History of the Trinity Doctrine From A.D. 100 to A.D. 1500

SECTION THREE

Trinity and Anti-Trinitarianism From the Reformation to the Advent Movement

SECTION FOUR

The Doctrine of the Trinity and Its Implications for Christian Thought and Practice

INTRODUCTION

Have you ever had a knock at the door unexpectedly interrupt a relaxing Sunday afternoon? You break away from whatever you are doing and answer the door. Suddenly you realize that it is not some old friend making a surprise visit. Rather, it is an intense couple representing the local Kingdom Hall and the Watchtower Bible and Tract Society—the publishing arm of the Jehovah's Witnesses.

You swallow hard, knowing that if you invite them in, it will put your grasp of basic Bible knowledge and doctrine to a rather trying test. Further, it generally takes only one encounter to realize that one of the first items for discussion will be a strong challenge to the doctrine of the Trinity.

But the greater surprise in my life and ministry has not been so much in dealing with zealous Jehovah's Witnesses on the Trinity—rather, it is now having to meet essentially the same anti-Trinitarian arguments coming from fellow Seventh-day Adventists. And they are raising this issue with an intensity not too far removed from the zeal of the Watchtower representatives.

WHY A NEW BOOK ON THE TRINITY?

Some might question the need for a new book on the subject of the Godhead, or the Trinity, at this time. Since the church has seemingly settled the issue with clearly Trinitarian positions in its 27 fundamental beliefs, why reopen the question?[1] The answer is basically threefold.

A Revival of Anti-Trinitarian Thought

First, as already referred to above, new challenges to the doctrine of the Trinity have arisen both from inside and outside of Adventism. Various reports and observations suggest that my own personal experience with this issue fairly reflects the current situation.

When dealing with the subject of the Godhead and the Trinity, I had always told my Seventh-day Adventist congregations and Sabbath school and college religion classes something like the following:

Whereas Arianism[2] and anti-Trinitarianism were very strong among many of the pioneer Adventist leaders,[3] the Trinitarian view of the Godhead had become the standard view by at least the 1940s, if not earlier. In fact, the view is now the position duly voted in our official statement of the Fundamental Beliefs of Seventh-day Adventists. The most recent action took place at the General Conference session of 1980 in Dallas, Texas.

I had heard about important teachers and denominational leaders who had lived into the 1950s and 1960s while holding strongly anti-Trinitarian views.[4] Since my college and seminary years in the mid- to late 1960s, however, I was also fond of telling my Adventist audiences, "I have not met an Adventist anti-Trinitarian or Arian in my lifetime." It was not just dramatic rhetoric on my part, but the honest truth.

Yes, I was really telling the truth—that is, until the early years of the 1990s. I distinctly recall a pleasant afternoon walk across the campus of Andrews University, when two young men passing out pamphlets on the steps of the James White Library suddenly greeted me. Being the curious person that I am, I accepted their material, began looking it over, and asked, "What is it that you are promoting?"

To my great surprise, they proceeded to inform me that they had made a wonderful recovery of precious truth—they had rediscovered what they claimed were the teachings of the Adventist pioneers on the Godhead. Now they promoted ideas that denied the full and eternally preexistent deity of Jesus and the personal deity of the Holy Spirit.

Later I found out from acquaintances around the country that the young men were not an isolated phenomenon. Not only are there increasing reports of pockets of anti-Trinitarian revival in various regions across North America, but via the Internet its influence has spread around the world. As this grassroots Arian or anti-Trinitarian movement gains ground, local churches increasingly find themselves drawn into debate over the issues.

The Relative Theological Neglect of the Godhead

The second factor that has raised our interest in the issue of the Godhead is a rather universal, though benign, neglect of the issue by both Adventist scholarship[5] and the leadership in local Adventist conferences and churches all across the world. The church has widely accepted the Trinity, but reflected little upon the teaching for many decades. As a result, we feel that the time has arrived for a fresh review of the subject.

A New Awareness of the Pioneer Views

The third and final factor in the present revival of interest in the subject of the Godhead is the convergence of Ellen White's counsel to reprint and study the works of the early Adventist pioneers and their availability on CD-ROMs. The explosion of electronic technology has empowered laypersons (with little investment of time or money) to have immediate access to all the early pioneer statements by simply typing in appropriate words and/or phrases. To put it quite simply, we now have a renewed awareness of the wide-ranging anti-Trinitarian views of the pioneers of the Advent movement.

Our Target Audience

The authors of this book seek to speak to the members of the local church as well as to busy pastors (or administrators) and college students who have faced questions about the Trinity. Indeed, although we will seek to speak from the base of the best scholarship on the issue, it is our purpose to present them in a way that will appeal to all believers, young and old, in Sabbath school classes, college classes, and the pews and pulpits of the local churches around the world.

How Shall We Answer Questions Raised by the Trinity?

Can we answer the questions that swirl around the issue of the Trinity from the Scriptures (our primary authority), the writings of Ellen G. White, sanctified reason, and Christian experience? Is it proper for Seventh-day Adventists to go against the majority of its pioneer thinkers, who were clearly anti-Trinitarian? Upon what grounds can we continue to officially embrace and profess a teaching that has a long history of support and development not only in Eastern Orthodoxy and Roman Catholicism, but also in Protestantism? Would not that involve accepting the traditions that compose the great apostasy called "Babylon"? Would it not be better to follow the lead of our courageous and truth-driven pioneers?

The Bible, Our Primary Authority

In the spirit of the pioneers of the Seventh-day Adventist Church, the authors of this book firmly hold the following conviction: if we cannot support any teaching biblically, we do not want it.[6] We humbly take up this project in the spirit of John Nevins Andrews (1829-1883), one of the most able of our pioneer scholars, who exclaimed, "I would exchange a thousand errors for one truth."

And how shall we know what is the truth about the Godhead and the Trinitarian claims of the majority of Christians? Primarily the truth will emerge from a careful, prayerful search of the Written Word of God.

Furthermore, we claim the promise of Jesus that "if anyone wills to do His will, he shall know concerning the doctrine, whether it is from God or whether I speak on My own authority" (John 7:17, NKJV). He promises that those who are willing to follow God in obedience can know the "doctrine" of God. And where shall we go to settle this issue? Again Jesus is very clear: "Sanctify them by Your truth. Your word is truth" (John 17:17, NKJV).

The reader must also recognize that the settled conviction of the authors of this book is that whatever the expression "Your word" covers, it at least includes the 66 canonical books of the Holy Bible. We believe that this Written Word contains revealed messages that are sufficient to give us doctrinal clarity on any controverted question—including the issue of the Trinity.

We will be very candid with our readers—if it is not biblical we do not want it, even if the vast majority of authorities in the religious world endorse it (including Adventist pioneers and the theologians of "Babylon"). Thus this book will begin with the biblical evidence.

The Organization of the Book

The first chapter will open the discussion by marshaling the strongest evidence that we have been able to locate regarding the questions of (1) the full divine and eternal nature of Christ, (2) the personhood and deity of the Holy Spirit, and (3) the profound unity or oneness of what Ellen White refers to as the "three living persons of the heavenly trio" (Ellen G. White, *Evangelism,* p. 615).

After the initial presentation of the strongest, most straightforward biblical evidence (the author is Woodrow Whidden), we will proceed in succeeding chapters with more detailed presentations of the biblical evidence from the Old and New Testaments (again, the author will be Whidden).

After the biblical evidence, the next sections will trace the history of the development of the Trinitarian doctrine and the teachings of its opponents throughout church history. The historical survey will fall into two main sections: (1) developments from the early second century to the sixteenth century (the author is John Reeve), followed by (2) the unfolding of ideas from the Reformation of the sixteenth century up through the history of Trinitarian and anti-Trinitarian thought in Seventh-day Adventist history (the author is Jerry Moon).

After the historical survey, the book will reflect on the theological implications of our biblical and historical discoveries (the author is Woodrow Whidden). In other words, the opening section will deal with the question *What* is the biblical doctrine? The next two major sections will deal with *how* Christians came to express these doctrines. Finally, however, we must address the question of *why* they are important for Christian thought and experience. In other words, what are the crucial implications of the beliefs that we might hold about the nature of the Father, Son, and Holy Spirit and Their relationship to one another?

The Key Questions to Address

What then are the key questions we need to deal with? What issues have divided those who accept the doctrine of the Trinity and those who deny it?

First of all, there appears to be no one involved in the current debate who denies the full and eternal deity of the Father God, the first person of the Godhead. Thus the three remaining areas of contention that cry out for biblical answers are as follows:

The Deity of Christ

This issue concerns the question of whether Christ possessed a divine nature that was, in substance, the same as the Father God. In other words, was the Jesus who was the Son of God just as much God as the Father? Or was He some sort of semideity having a qualified or partial divinity? Did He truly exist as a divine person from all eternity past? Was He not only the "preexistent" but also the "self-existent" Son of God about whom the Bible "assures us that there never was a time when He was not in close fellowship with the eternal God" *(ibid.)?* Did such "self-existence" mean that He really had a divine nature whose life was "original, unborrowed, underived" (White, *The Desire of Ages,* p. 530)?

The Personality and Deity of the Spirit

The second central issue deals with the questions of the personality and full divinity of the Holy Spirit as a definite "divine person" (White, *Evangelism,* p. 617). Is the Holy Spirit "as much a person as God is a person" (*ibid.,* p. 616)? Does this Holy Spirit truly "walk" among humanity as a "person" who "beareth witness with our spirits that we are the children of God" *(ibid.)*? Does the Holy Spirit's "witness" manifest the "power of God" that can hold "in check" the "power of evil" and do this great work as the "third person of the Godhead" (*ibid.*, p. 617)?

The Oneness of the Godhead

Finally, are there "three living persons of the heavenly trio" (also referred to by Ellen White as the "three great powers—the Father, the Son, and the Holy Spirit" [*ibid.*, p. 615]) into whose "name" those who receive Christ by living faith are baptized? Furthermore, are these "three great powers" truly divine, personal beings who "cooperate with the obedient subjects of heaven in their efforts to live the new life in Christ" *(ibid.)?* Can we honestly confess that Christ "was equal with God, infinite and omnipotent" *(ibid.)*? Dare we declare that Jesus the Son "is the eternal, self-existent Son" *(ibid.)?* Are these "powers" ("the three highest powers in heaven" [*ibid.*, p. 617]) also referred to as "the eternal heavenly dignitaries—God, and Christ, and the Holy Spirit" (*ibid.*, p. 616), truly one in Their divine nature, possessing "all the fulness of the Godhead" (Col. 2:9)? What saith the Scriptures?

A Helpful Note to the Reader

At the beginning of each section we have placed a glossary of key terms that we will employ. We realize that some of the terminology we use is somewhat technical. Thus we want to make it easy for the reader to quickly clarify what we mean when we use the specialized words and terms that often accompany any discussion of the Godhead. As far as possible we have sought to keep technical or insider jargon to a minimum. Furthermore, the context will explain many of these key terms, and if not, we will give brief explanations in the endnotes of each chapter.

ENDNOTES

[1] The key Trinitarian statement of belief appears in the Fundamental Beliefs of Seventh-day Adventists, number 2, with numbers 3-5 providing additional positions on the Father, Son, and Holy Spirit. Statement 2 declares: "The Trinity: There is one God: Father, Son, and Holy Spirit, a unity of three co-eternal Persons." You will find the 27 fundamental beliefs in the *Seventh-day Adventist Church Manual* (issued by the General Conference of Seventh-day Adventists, Silver Spring, Maryland), and the *Seventh-day Adventist Yearbook*. The semiauthoritative volume *Seventh-day Adventists Believe . . . A Biblical Exposition of 27 Fundamental Beliefs* (Hagerstown, Md.: Review and Herald Pub. Assn., 1988) also lists them. Produced by the Ministerial Association of the General Conference of Seventh-day Adventists, this volume provides fairly concise expositions of each one of the 27 fundamental beliefs.

[2] An Arian is a person who, following the teachings of Arius of Alexandria, who lived in the early fourth century A.D., denies the eternal preexistence of Jesus. "There was a time when Jesus was not," Arius declared. In other words, Arius and his followers held that Christ did not exist before the Father brought Him into existence. Furthermore, they have consistently denied the personhood of the Holy Spirit. We will explore more on this later when we discuss the history of the debates regarding the Godhead in the early church.

[3] Among the notable Arians or semi-Arians were James White (1821-1881), Joseph Bates (1792-1872), J. H. Waggoner (1820-1889), Uriah Smith (1832-1903), and E. J. Waggoner (1855-1916). James White ultimately confessed the full deity and eternity of Christ, and Uriah Smith evolved from an Arian to a semi-Arian position. E. J. Waggoner, a semi-Arian, came very close to confessing the full deity of Christ. A number of his twentieth-century admirers strongly deny that he was a semi-Arian. The evidence, however, seems quite clear that he was. We will more fully address the Arianism of the "pioneers" in section three below.

[4] Probably the most well known of the later prominent anti-Trinitarians were longtime college religion teacher W. R. French and religious liberty advocate and editor Charles Longacre (1871-1958). Roger Coon tells the story of an alumni weekend at Pacific Union College in the mid-1960s when the retired W. R. French, who had been asked to give a brief vesper presentation, promptly proceeded to deliver a strong one and a half-hour discourse in defense of his anti-Trinitarian views.

[5] While occasional articles on the Godhead have appeared in both church journals and books devoted to Adventism's basic beliefs (usually expositions of the 27 fundamental beliefs), until recently there was no book-length treatment of the subject since Otto H. Christensen's *Getting Acquainted With God* (Washington, D.C.: Review and Herald Pub. Assn., 1970).

[6] Among the "pioneers" we would include Ellen White. The strong emphasis on the final authority of the Bible that we hold to does not in any way diminish the importance of Ellen White's contribution to our thinking on this subject. If we are to take her seriously as our most authoritative pioneer writer, we must obey her when she tells us that we are to test every teaching by the Bible.

SECTION ONE

The Biblical Evidence
for the Full Deity of Christ,
the Personality of the Spirit,
and the Unity and Oneness of the Godhead

Glossary for Section One

Apocalypse—that which is revealed or unveiled. Thus the Greek transliterated title of the New Testament book of Revelation.

Apocalyptic—the type of literature best represented by the biblical books of Daniel and Revelation. This literary form features picturesque symbolism, a cosmic conflict between the forces of good and evil, and covers great sweeps of time that climax with the end of the world.

Arian—any person or position that basically subscribes to the teaching of Arius of Alexandria, an early fourth-century A.D. thinker and writer who denied the eternal preexistence of Jesus Christ. "There was a time when Jesus was not" was Arius's classic declaration. In other words, Arius and his followers held that Christ did not exist before the Father brought Him into existence. Arians have also consistently denied the personhood of the Holy Spirit.

Arianism—the theological emphasis that supports the basic teachings of Arius and his followers.

Canon and Canonical—technical terms referring to the books that came to make up the authoritative list of works known as the Bible. Protestants, Roman Catholics, and the Eastern Orthodox tradition disagree as to which books to include in the authoritative "canon." The major point of controversy has to do with the "apocryphal" books of the Old Testament.

Case—the grammatical expression that seeks to identify whether the word in question functions as subject, object, indirect object, and so forth in a sentence.

Deity—having the nature of God. Transcendent, as opposed to that which is earthbound, infinite as opposed to finite. The key issue in Trinitarian discussion is whether we are dealing with full deity or only its trappings or selected characteristics. Refers to any "being" who is declared to possess the nature of deity. They should be self-existent from all eternity past to all eternity future and have an existence unborrowed or underived.

Emanation—a coded message sent from otherworldly regions to humans; usually involves secret knowledge of a magical or spiritistic nature. The Gnostics in the early church claimed that they had special knowledge from the spirit world. Such views were of particular concern to the apostle Paul in his Epistle to the Colossians.

Godhead—a theological term often used to refer to the Father, Son, and Holy Spirit. It can be used in either a Trinitarian or non-Trinitarian sense, depending on whether the person employing the term is Trinitarian or not.

Inanimate—being in an inert, incommunicative, or lifeless state. It is often used to refer to that which is inorganic as opposed to the organic. Used in this book mainly to refer to lifeless subjects or substances.

Incarnation—the experience of God becoming human. Comes from two Latin words that literally mean "in the flesh." Usually used theologically to refer to Christ, the divine Son, coming to earth to take upon Himself human nature.

Lexicographer—a person who studies the meaning of words; usually used in biblical studies to describe a scholar who develops Greek and Hebrew dictionaries so that those who do not know the ancient languages can best understand what the meaning of a particular word is in a modern language. In the English-speaking world, a Greek or Hebrew lexicographer would be a scholar who seeks to clearly define Greek words with their English meanings.

Magisterial—the truly authoritative or most influential leader in any field of endeavor. Normally employed to refer to the person's signature work.

Modalism—an ancient Christian teaching that held that there exists only one God who has successively manifested Himself as Father, then Son, and finally as Holy Spirit. The teaching denies the Trinity of three coeternal Persons who have always existed in a profound personal oneness of nature, character, and purpose.

Monotheistic—the belief in and worship of one God as opposed to many divine beings (polytheism).

"Omega"—a term used by Ellen White to describe Satan's last great delusion before the end of the world. It most likely will have something to do with philosophical views that almost totally depersonalize God.

Omnipotent—the ability to exercise unlimited power, a trait that Christians believe is unique to God.

Omnipresent—the ability to be everywhere at the same time. Also a trait deemed by Christians to be a unique characteristic of God.

Omniscient—the ability to know everything, a trait traditionally understood by Christians to belong to God alone.

Oratorio—a sacred musical composition similar to an opera, but does not have acting in it. The most famous oratorio is George F. Handel's *Messiah.*

Pantheon—literally means in the Greek "all gods." Originally used by classical Greeks and Romans to refer to buildings in which they kept images of all their gods on display.

Parody—a piece of music or writing that imitates another in such a way as to make fun of it.

Person—a being who is rational, self-conscious, able to make choices and moral distinctions, build relationships of affection, and can communicate in ways that are not only concrete but also abstract.

"Pioneers"—an expression used in Adventist studies to refer to those leaders of Sabbatarian Adventism who helped establish the Seventh-day Adventist Church and shaped its doctrinal message. The time frame for the pioneers is generally from 1844 until the death of Ellen G. White in 1915.

Polemics—the activity of any person who seeks to defend what they believe to be truth over against the perceived or real falsehoods of a fellow believer. Apologetics involves the activity of Christians defending their understanding of truth over against the conflicting claims of non-Christians.

Polytheism—the belief that more than one God exists. Persons or groups that are polytheistic worship many divine beings who inhabit the universe and affect life in this world. Polytheism is the opposite of monotheism, the belief in one true God.

Preexistent—the key issue that this term addresses is whether Jesus had a divine existence before He took on human nature, or became incarnate. Almost all Bible-believing Christians assume that Jesus had self-conscious existence before He came to earth, but the key issue deals with the question of whether He was co-eternal with the Father in His preexistent state.

Reformation and Reformers—terms normally used by Protestants and Roman Catholics to refer to the major religious reformatory figures and movements of sixteenth-century Europe. Protestants most often use the term Reformer to refer to their major founding leaders, such as Luther, Calvin, Zwingli, and so forth.

Sabellianism—an important variation of the ancient teaching of modalism.

Self-existent—a term to describe any being who is divine and whose existence is understood to be not dependent on any other divine being.

Semi-Arianism—the teaching that while the Father and the Son are not coeternal persons, They do share divinity in that the Son was "begotten" by the Father in the sense that Jesus was generated out of the divine nature of the Father in some sort of "amoebic split." Thus, while there was a time when Jesus as a separate and identifiable person did not exist, the divine nature of Jesus was alleged to have derived from that of the Father.

Septuagint—a second-century B.C. Greek translation of the Hebrew Old Testament. This expression literally means the version of the "seventy," supposedly produced by 70 Hellenistic (Greek-speaking) Jews in the Egyptian city of Alexandria. The writers of the New Testament often cited it.

Tetragrammaton—a technical word used by Bible scholars to refer to the most often used name or title applied to the God of the Old Testament: YHWH, most likely pronounced "Yahweh," and usually translated as Lord or Jehovah.

Transliterate—to take the letters of words from one language and express them in the equivalent letters of the alphabet of another language. For instance, the Greek word for "god" is transliterated into the English letters as *theos*.

Trinitarian—a person, group, school, or church that confesses the doctrine of the Trinity.

Trinity—the Christian belief that the Godhead consists of three divine, coeternal persons (the Father, Son, and Holy Spirit) who are "one" in nature, character, and purpose. There are not three Gods, but one God manifest as three persons.

Unitarian—any person or group that denies the Trinity doctrine by suggesting that there exists only one God, the Father. Unitarians consistently deny the full deity of the Son and the personhood of the Holy Spirit.

Chapter 1

THE STRONGEST BIBLE EVIDENCE FOR THE TRINITY

One person who recently shared his struggles over the Trinitarian version of the Godhead on the Internet found himself so troubled by the alleged pagan and papal origins of the doctrine that he concluded that its acceptance by Adventism could possibly be the "omega" of deadly apostasy foretold by Ellen White.

He did, however, appeal to his fellow Adventists to approach the issue with the seriousness and sincerity of the "fair-minded" (NKJV), or "noble" Bereans (KJV)[1] described in the book of Acts. They "received the word with all readiness, and searched the Scriptures daily to find out whether these things were so" (Acts 17:11).

In the spirit of the "noble" Bereans, this first chapter will seek the clearest, most straightforward scriptural answers to the following questions:

Is there sufficient biblical evidence in support of the Trinitarian claims of the vast majority of the Christian tradition and contemporary Seventh-day Adventism at least to merit serious consideration of these claims? Or is it so sketchy as to suggest that the doctrine is simply one vast piece of deception that has come straight out of pagan polytheism and has been mistakenly "baptized" by apostate Christianity (and thus unwittingly by Seventh-day Adventists)?

We invite the reader to carefully follow the lines of biblical evidence brought forward in the following pages and then ask yourself this question: Is the evidence sufficient that we should honestly consider the Trinitarian claims of the majority of Christians in general and contemporary Seventh-day Adventists in particular?

In other words, what we are attempting to do is marshal the most obvious, compelling biblical evidence in favor of the Trinity. At the risk of needless repetition, we want to make it clear to the reader that we are not demanding that anybody swallow the whole package in one gullible gulp. We only urge that you honestly ask yourself if the evidence is sufficient to pursue the issue with further Bible study and prayerful reflection.

So let's proceed to Scripture. Try to picture yourself as a baptismal candidate who has joined a pastor's Bible study class to prepare for church membership. The pastor now proceeds to give the best biblical evidence in support of the church's Trinitarian statements of belief. We would remind the reader that the basic issues to be biblically tested are:

(1) the full, eternal deity of Christ,

(2) the personhood and full deity of the Holy Spirit, and

(3) the unity in nature and character of the alleged three persons of the Godhead.

Two Important Clarifications

1. Before we begin the direct interpretation of the biblical data the reader should know what we mean when we say things like "divine nature," or "fully divine in nature." All Bible-believing Christians, both Trinitarian and anti-Trinitarian, seem to agree that when the Bible describes the Creator God (in contrast to false gods or creaturely beings) He has the following distinctively divine aspects:

God is by nature:

(a) personal, but everywhere present (omnipresent) in His created universe (Ps. 139:7-12);

(b) all-knowing (omniscient—Ps. 139:1-4);

(c) all-powerful (omnipotent—Matt. 19:26);

(d) from "everlasting to everlasting" (eternal—Ps. 90:2);

(e) unchanging in His nature and character (immutable—Mal. 3:6);

(f) all-righteous and good (goodness—Ps. 145:9; 19:7-9);

(g) a being of love (perfect, selfless love—1 John 4:8).

Therefore, if any of these divine traits are missing, we are not talking about the great God of the Bible.

2. While the Old Testament uses a number of names and titles (such as "El," "Elohim," "Adonai," and the most often used expression, "Yahweh") to refer to God, it seems clear that when the Bible wants to talk about the true God, any one of these names can appropriately apply to Him. Yet, as will soon become apparent, sometimes the New Testament makes it clear that certain Old Testament passages have either the Son, the Father, or the Spirit more specifically in mind. Thus any one of the Old Testament names for God can speak of God in His unitive oneness (Deut. 6:4) or more particularly to the discrete person of either the Father, the Son, or the Holy Spirit.

Some anti-Trinitarians (the Jehovah's Witnesses) try to restrict the term *Lord* (YHWH, Yahweh, or Jehovah) only to God the Father, while others (feeling the force of the evidence we are about to present) try to limit *Lord* only to the Son. The evidence, however, clearly supports the fact that from the New Testament perspective the term *Lord* in the Old Testament can refer to either one of the members of the Trinity or to all three in Their profound oneness.

For instance, John 8:58 clearly interprets the Lord of Exodus 3:14, 15 as being Jesus Christ. Yet Revelation 4:8 regards the "Lord God Almighty" of Isaiah 6:3 as the Father "who was and is and is to come." Thus the Lord (Yahweh) can refer to both the Father and the Son.[2]

THE FULL DEITY OF JESUS CHRIST

The key question that confronted the early church was Could they retain their strong view of God's oneness (inherited from Judaism) and yet affirm the full, eternal deity of Jesus Christ?

The Epistle to the Hebrews

This challenging book obviously has in mind converts with a strong Old Testament and Jewish background. It is saturated with citations from the Old Testament and assumes that the readers have an intimate familiarity with the Jewish Temple/sanctuary and its services.

The very first chapter includes three rather striking lines of evidence (it has others, but we will present only the strongest here) that powerfully suggest that the Jehovah God of the Old Testament included in His identity the person of Jesus of Nazareth.

One of the major themes of the entire Epistle is to demonstrate from the Old Testament the superiority of Jesus Christ to the angels, Moses, and the Levitical priests. Finally, the author will demonstrate the superiority of Christ's once-for-all sacrifice compared to the numerous and repetitive offerings made at the earthly sanctuary. Chapter 1 deals with the angels who are the subject of the first comparison.

The author's basic argument is that the angels are great beings, "ministering spirits sent forth to minister for those who will inherit salvation" (Heb. 1:14). They, however, cannot begin to compare with the importance and dignity of the Son of God. The conclusion is that Jesus is "better" than the angels. Let's carefully trace the writer's argument.

In verses 5 and 6 the author asks his readers if any angel has ever been set forth as an object of worship. Did the Father, who "brings the firstborn into the world," ever say to an angel, "Let all the angels of God worship Him"? The obvious answer is a resounding no! The clear implication is that Jesus, the "begotten" and "firstborn" Son of the Father,[3] receives worship from the "angels of God."

What does this suggest about Jesus? The inescapable conclusion seems to be that the "Son" (Jesus Christ) is God, since only God in the monotheistic Old Testament is worthy of worship by creaturely beings (see Ex. 20:2-4; cf. Rev. 19:9, 10 and 22:8, 9). The implication of verses 5 and 6, however, becomes quite explicit in the succeeding verses:

In Hebrews 1:7, 8 the writer goes on to say that while God made the angels to be "spirits and His ministers a flame of fire" (verse 7), "to the Son He says: 'Your throne, O God, is forever and ever' " (verse 8). Here the author of the book of Hebrews unquestionably uses Psalm 45:6 to speak of Jesus Christ, the Son of God. It is actually the first of seven direct New Testament applications of the Greek word for "God" *(theos)* to Jesus. The others, to be dealt with in subsequent chapters, occur in John 1:1, 18; 20:28; Romans 9:5; Titus 2:13; and 2 Peter 1:1 (Hatton, pp. 42, 43).

Such thoughts must have come as a stunning revelation to the early Jewish believers—that they could address Jesus as God! Yet there appears not one shred of evidence in the New Testament that anyone, either Jewish or Gentile convert, ever protested such a shocking conclusion.

Once more, let's be very clear as to what is going on here. The New Testament writers are referring to Jesus as "God" and interpreting the Old Testament through applying to Jesus a psalm originally addressed to the God of the Old Testament. And make no mistake about the grammar of Hebrews 1:8—the expression "O God" is clearly in the Greek grammatical case of direct address (called the vocative case). To put the issue in very plain English, the authors of the Bible are clearly calling the Son of God by the title God. The case, however, gets even weightier.

Let's now turn our attention to verses 10 through 12. Carefully observe that the Bible writer is continuing to exalt the Son above even the privileged status of the angels. He does so by applying Old Testament passages to the Son that clearly laud the Son's divine status. The next Old Testament passage used for the Son is Psalm 102:25-27. The portion cited begins with "You, Lord, in the beginning laid the foundation of the earth, and the heavens are the work of Your hands" (Heb. 1:10).

What are we to make of the biblical writer's use of Psalm 102? The first thing that we need to point out is that in this instance the author is again saying, as He already has in Hebrews 1:2, that Jesus is the Creator Lord who made the earth and heavens. This, in and of itself, is certainly powerful support for the full deity of the Son, but the evidence becomes even more striking when we turn to Psalm 102 and look at the first verse of this chapter. There we discover that the entirety of the psalm is a prayer addressed to the "Lord."

Think about this for a moment: This Lord is none other than the

Jehovah God of the Old Testament. Whenever you see the word "Lord" in capital or small capital letters in such English translations as the King James Version (KJV), the New King James Version (NKJV), and the *New American Standard Bible* (NASB), you can always know that it is a translation of the most sacred word in the Hebrew language for God—the "tetragrammaton," transliterated from Hebrew as either JHVH or YHWH. Furthermore, Bible scholars normally translate the word as either "Lord" or "Jehovah."[4] Now, what are we to make of all this?

The amazing thing in this context is that the author of the Epistle in Hebrews 1:10-12 is taking an Old Testament prayer addressed to the Lord (Jehovah or Yahweh God) and is applying it to none other than Jesus Christ! The issue seems to be quite straightforward—the writer of this extremely Jewish Epistle is strongly suggesting that the Jehovah God of the Old Testament is none other than the Jesus of the New Testament.

Biblical evidence such as is found in Hebrews 1 provides a ready response that Christians often give when approached by the zealous Jehovah's Witnesses: "I can forthrightly confess that I too am a 'Jehovah's Witness,' since I witness for and to Jesus who is 'Lord' Jehovah in the mind of the New Testament writers."

The Book of Revelation

The book of Revelation also offers evidence for the full deity of Christ similar to that found in Hebrews 1:8-12. In Revelation 1:12-17 we have a vision of Jesus as the glorified high priest in the heavenly sanctuary. The reader should particularly notice verse 17 in which Jesus says to the fearful, fainting prophet, "Do not be afraid; I am the First and the Last."

A quick look at the marginal references or notes of any good study Bible will tell the reader that John the revelator here draws on Isaiah 41:4; 44:6; and 48:12. Isaiah 44:6 declares: "Thus says the Lord, the King of Israel, and his Redeemer, the Lord of hosts: 'I am the First and I am the Last; besides Me there is no God.'" What are we to make of this terminology that the revelator reports as coming from the mouth of our glorified high priest?

Is it not obvious that John quite comfortably tells us that Christ, our high priest, is none other than the Lord (YHWH, Yahweh or Jehovah) of the Old Testament prophet Isaiah? Can we not then reasonably conclude that the Lord who is the "First" and the "Last" of Isaiah is the "Lord Jesus" who is the central subject of the book of Revelation?

Furthermore, it is interesting that this designation of Christ as the "First and the Last" echoes a similar title clearly applied to God the Father in this very same opening chapter of the book. Revelation 1:4 describes Him as "Him who is and who was and who is to come" and in verse 8 has Him proclaiming Himself as "the Alpha and Omega [first and last], the Beginning and the End, . . . who is and who was and who is to come, the Almighty."

Are not such similar titles referring to YHWH in the Old Testament when applied to both the Father and the Son in the book of Revelation strong evidence that the Son is equal to the Father in divine nature? This, however, is not the end of the matter regarding the expression "the first and the last" in the book of Revelation.

In Revelation 22:12, 13 we find John reporting the following declaration: "And behold, I am coming quickly, and My reward is with Me, to give to every one according to his work. I am the Alpha and the Omega, the Beginning and the End, the First and the Last." Which person of the Godhead is speaking here? The Father or the Son?

It is not absolutely clear from the context, but it seems more likely that it comes from the mouth of Jesus. Please carefully note that what immediately precedes verses 12 and 13 is a quotation in verses 9 through 11 from the angel whom John mistakenly "fell down to worship before" (verse 8). This quotation ends, and immediately, with no clear identification as to who is speaking, come the great "first and last" declarations of verses 12 and 13. Certainly the statement, which claims titles that could apply only to Jesus or the Father, could not be coming from the mouth of the angel, who has just rebuked John for treating him as "God" (who alone should be worshiped)! Quite obviously the one who claims in these verses to be "coming quickly" and "the Alpha and the Omega, the Beginning and the End, the First and the Last" is none other than Jesus!

Furthermore, while it is not clear that the following verses (14 and 15) originate with Jesus, the context strongly suggests that they do, and then comes a key clue as to the identity of the speaker in verse 16. It plainly identifies Jesus as the one speaking by claiming that it is "I, Jesus." Moreover, verse 20 makes it extremely clear that the one who says "I am coming quickly" is not God the Father, but the "Lord Jesus!" "He who testifies to these things says, 'Surely I am coming quickly.'" Then comes the report of an "Amen" benediction followed with a heartfelt, prayerful appeal—"Even so, come, Lord Jesus" (verse 20).

What should we make of this remarkable use of the titles "Alpha and Omega, the Beginning and the End" that have, up to this point of the last chapter in the Revelation, been applied only to the Father?[5] We would simply suggest to the reader that the terminology is clear evidence that whatever is common to the divine nature of the Father the divine Son also possesses.

Additionally, we should note that these expressions are some of the most powerful vehicles the Bible uses to express the eternal preexistence of both the Father and the Son.

Finally, we should point out that the most likely reason that Jesus employs "Alpha and Omega" and "Beginning and the End" as self-descriptive titles is that here for the first time the book of Revelation describes both "God and the Lamb" as fully sharing "the throne." Note very carefully how Revelation 22:1 and 3 clearly label "the throne of God" as the "throne of God and of the Lamb." No longer is Christ the "Lamb" pictured as before the throne of God (cf. Rev. 5:6, 7); He now sits on the one throne with the Father as a fully equal coruler over the redeemed universe.

The Gospel of John

Many consider this Gospel to contain the strongest possible testimony to the full, eternal deity of Christ in the New Testament.

One of the most often cited passages used to prove the full deity of Christ is John 1:1, especially the last phrase in the verse—"the Word was God." I would like to suggest that the verse does present strong support for the Word (Jesus) as a divine person. Since, however, a credible interpretation involves some rather technical grammatical considerations, we will deal with it in more depth in chapter 3. Suffice it to say, this verse and its detailed grammar clearly testify that Jesus, the Word, is a being with full deity. The most clear-cut and incontrovertible evidence, however, comes from John 8:58.

John 8 reports a serious dialogue with the Jewish leaders in which "Jesus said to them, 'Most assuredly, I say to you, before Abraham was, I AM' " (verse 58). Some astonishing points leap out at us from His declaration.

First, the overwhelming majority of Bible students acknowledge that when Jesus said "I AM" He is clearly referring to Exodus 3:14 and applying it to Himself. In this famous Old Testament passage Moses asks God what he should tell the children of Israel when they ask him to name the God sending him to lead them out of Egyptian bondage (verses 11-13). God plainly answers Moses, " 'I AM WHO I AM.' And He said, 'Thus you shall say to the children of Israel, "I AM has sent me to you." ' Moreover God said to Moses, 'Thus you shall say to the children of Israel: "The Lord God of your fathers, the God of Abraham, the God of Isaac, and the God of Jacob, has sent me to you" ' " (verses 14, 15).

Jesus' application of these verses to Himself offers compelling evidence of His full deity. Christ was plainly appropriating to Himself the very expressions used by the God of the Old Testament Exodus to identify Himself to the enslaved children of Israel. Furthermore, not only does Jesus present Himself as the God who refers to Himself as the "I AM," but also the deity who refers to Himself as "the God of Abraham, the God of Isaac, and the God of Jacob," the one who is "The Lord God of your fathers" (verse 15). Jesus is most obviously claiming to be none other than the God of the Exodus, the Lord (YHWH, Jehovah) God of the great founding patriarchs of the nation of Israel.

Did Jesus' audience grasp the thrust of what He was claiming?

They most certainly did! Clearly they understood Him to be saying that He was none other than the God of the Old Testament, the Lord of the patriarchs and the Exodus. And how is it that we know that they recognized His claims? The very next verse reports that the people "took up stones to throw at Him" (John 8:59). Why? Because it was the appropriate Jewish response to any human being who made claims that they considered blasphemous! And what is blasphemy? It is a human claiming to be God (cf. John 5:18).

Now we acknowledge that some consider that Jesus' use of the "I AM" terminology in John 8:58 speaks only of a limited preexistence rather than an eternal preexistence. Max Hatton has provided some helpful comments:

"It should be pointed out that if Jesus simply wished to say that He was in existence prior to Abraham, He could have said *Ego En* (I was). Instead He used the term *I Am* in the absolute sense. The expression is used with a clarifying noun in other places—for example: I *am the good shepherd.* But here Jesus abruptly said *'I Am'* without any further clarification:

"Exodus 3:14: 'I AM WHO I AM. This is what you are to say to the Israelites: "I AM has sent me to you."'

"It should be evident that the second 'I AM' is an abbreviated form of the name given in the first instance. 'I AM THAT I AM' in the Greek Septuagint translation of the Old Testament is 'EGO EIMI HO ON.' Referring to John 8:58 the great New Testament Greek scholar, Archibald Thomas Robertson, says: 'Undoubtedly here Jesus claims eternal existence with the absolute phrase used of God'" (*ibid.,* pp. 45, 46).

To put the issue as candidly as it can be, Jesus was what He claimed to be in John 8:58 or He was either (1) deranged or (2) one of the most blasphemous persons in human history!

John's Gospel contains additional evidence for the full deity of Jesus as one equal in nature to the Father. We will, however, leave that until chapter 3.

THE PERSONHOOD AND DEITY OF THE HOLY SPIRIT

On this issue, the testimony of Scripture is not as extensive as it is for the full deity of Christ. The evidence, however, is nonetheless quite suggestive (at the very least), if not downright persuasive. The most striking support appears in Acts 5.

Acts 5

The first part of this chapter deals with the tragic case of Ananias and his wife, Sapphira. The early Christians had made a vow to God to donate the full proceeds from the sale of their property to the needs of the struggling church. The story turns on the fact that the couple secretly "kept back part of the proceeds" for themselves. When they came in to lay the partial offering at the feet of the apostles, they died.

Carefully note Peter's telling explanation for their summary execution by God's power: "But Peter said, 'Ananias, why has Satan filled your heart to lie to the Holy Spirit and keep back part of the price of the land for yourself? . . . Why have you conceived this thing in your heart? You have not lied to men but to God' " (verses 3, 4).

Let's reflect a moment on the implications of this rather straightforward report.

First of all, Peter is saying that we can lie to the Holy Spirit. It is quite apparent that only a "person" or personality can be lied to. One cannot lie to an inanimate thing, only to self-conscious beings with the ability to personally communicate and relate responsively to other persons. I can lie to my computer all day and it will not affect the computer one whit in the way that it would the reader if I proceeded to tell you a proverbial pack of lies. Only personal, relational beings capable of meaningful communication can be lied to in ways that have moral consequences.

Second, Peter not only reports to Ananias that he had lied to the "Holy Spirit," but then goes on to further explain that he had "not lied to men but to God" (verse 4). The obvious implication is that the Holy Spirit is God! I ask the reader, Is there any other conclusion that we can come to?

Ephesians 4:30

A similar type of evidence for the personality of the Holy Spirit appears in Ephesians 4:30. Paul admonishes his readers to "not grieve the Holy Spirit of God, by whom you were sealed for the day of redemption." Can we grieve an "it" or a "thing"? Of course not! Only persons can be grieved. Grieving here means to bring to the point of deep regret or disappointment. It is a sensation that only personal beings with senses, feelings, and caring propensities can experience. Inanimate or impersonal things do not have the ability to be "grieved."

THE TRIUNITY OF THE ONE GOD

Here we confront one of the deepest mysteries about God. While we have some human illustrations of powerful unities that can transpire between discrete personalities (marriage, friendships, teams, etc.), the concept that underlies the Trinitarian vision of God is the most profound. What is the best evidence that the Godhead is not simply unitary, but consists of a united plurality of divine Persons?

Matthew 28:19

Probably the strongest clues to such a divine triunity occur in the famous gospel commission that Jesus gave the church in its baptismal formula: "Go therefore and make disciples of all the nations, baptizing them in the name of the Father and of the Son and of the Holy Spirit" (Matt. 28:19). Please note that it declares the three members of the Godhead to have a "name" (singular, not plural), strongly suggesting that They are one in personal character and nature. In the Bible the concept of "name" includes character or nature. Here Scripture suggests that the Holy Three are one in name since They share the very character of divinity.

This verse, along with 2 Corinthians 13:14, offers a striking insight to the life of the early apostolic church. The passages present the apostolic greetings and Christ's own formula for the rite of initiation (baptism) into the family of God in triune ways. Both suggest the unity of the three great Persons who are operative in redemption and the life of the church.

Matthew 3:16, 17

Another interesting evidence of the unity of the Godhead arises out of the presence of the Three at the baptism of Jesus. Carefully observe Matthew 3:16 and 17: "Jesus, when He had been baptized, came up immediately from the water; and behold, the heavens were opened to Him, and He saw the Spirit of God descending like a dove and alighting upon Him. And suddenly a voice came from heaven, saying, 'This is My beloved Son, in whom I am well pleased.'"

What is truly remarkable about the incident is that as Jesus formally begins His public ministry of redemption, all three members of the Heavenly Trio are present. The newly baptized Jesus stands on the banks of the Jordan, the Spirit descends on Him like a dove, and the Father audibly speaks words of divine approval and identity from heaven. This scene powerfully portrays the oneness of purpose held by the Godhead. Furthermore, it clearly evidences the distinctness of each divine being. Matthew does not present the Spirit and the Son as simply different manifestations or personifications of the Father, but as distinct personalities in concert with the Father. Yet They give every appearance of oneness in purpose and character as They focus on the redemptive mission of the Son.

OLD TESTAMENT EVIDENCE

Is this conception of a plural unity within the Godhead typical only of the New Testament? Certainly not.

What is striking is that the great passage always recited to open the synagogue services and which powerfully confessed the Jews' belief in the one true God strongly suggests that the God of Israel was a multipersonal, yet profoundly one God.

Deuteronomy 6:4 and Genesis 2:24

Commonly referred to as the Shema, Deuteronomy 6:4 says: "Hear, O Israel: The Lord our God, the Lord is one!" This famous passage has a number of points to teach us about our subject. First of all, the God of Israel is none other than the Lord (YHWH). Second, Jehovah God is the Lord who is "one." What is striking about this important word translated as "one" in English is that it is the Hebrew word *'echad.* It "means 'one [among others],' the emphasis being on a particular one. . . . The possibility of there being others is inherent in *'echad,* but *yachîd* precludes that possibility" (Christensen, p. 69). Another way to explain *'echad* is that it refers to the oneness that results from a unity of numerous persons.

Now Moses most certainly had the Hebrew word *yachîd,* which he could have employed if he had wanted to describe the Lord God of Israel as an exclusively unitary being. In contrast to *'echad,* the word *yachîd* "means 'one' in the sense of 'only,' or 'alone'" *(ibid.).* To put it another way, it refers to one in the unitary, not the plural sense. Moses, however, employed the plural *'echad* (one among others in a joined or shared oneness).

It helps us understand more fully the meaning of *'echad* when we remember that Scripture employed it to describe one of the most profoundly human unions: "Therefore a man shall leave his father and mother and be joined to his wife, and they shall become *one* flesh" (Gen. 2:24). Here the word *'echad* describes the marriage union between two self-conscious, loving, relational beings.

Genesis 1:1-3, 26

Our reading of the book of Genesis leads us to the final lines of evidence for the personal unity of divine persons in the Godhead. Genesis 1:26 reports the Creator God as saying, "Let *Us* make man in *Our* image, according to *Our* likeness." The passage has God speaking of Himself with plural references. When we place this kind of evidence alongside two other key facts in verses 1-3, we have strongly suggestive evidence of the profoundly unitive nature of the Godhead:

(1) Genesis portrays God working in conjunction with "the Spirit of God" that hovered over the "face of the waters," and

(2) the repeated declarations of the New Testament that the active agent in creation is none other than Jesus, the Son of God. Here, the Godhead creates humans in "Our" image—the Father, Spirit, and Son forming a creative, loving, and personal plurality.

Furthermore, when God did create humanity in "Our" image, He established a plurality of two individuals, distinct from each other, yet capable of becoming "one" (Gen. 2:24). These verses strongly portray the historical fact that the plurality of oneness involves the image of God.

Summary

So here we have some of the clearest biblical evidence for the full deity of Christ, the personality and deity of the Spirit, and the deeply personal union of the Godhead. We ask: Is this evidence persuasive enough for the reader to give consideration to further Bible evidence for the Trinitarian claim that we should understand the Godhead as a profoundly united personal threesome? We hope so.

Although we have presented some of the most straightforward evidence, there is much more to come. If you are willing, let's now turn our attention to other lines of evidence from the Bible.

ENDNOTES

[1] Unless otherwise noted, all biblical citations in this chapter are from the New King James Version.

[2] We find another illustration of this point in the following passages: compare Genesis 17:1, 35:11, and 48:3 with Exodus 6:2, 3 and 3:6, 13, 14. In Genesis 17:1 the "Lord" *(Yahweh)* introduces Himself to Abram as "Almighty God." Then in Genesis 35:11 "God" *(El)* speaks to Jacob and refers to Himself also as "God Almighty" (compare Gen. 48:3). Exodus 6:2, 3 has "God" *(El)* speak to Moses and clearly identify Himself as "Lord" *(Yahweh)* and "God Almighty." The most well-known of these passages is Exodus 3:6, 13, 14, which Jesus plainly applies to Himself by claiming the title "I AM." In other words, the Old Testament applies both the titles "God" *(El)* and "Lord" *(Yahweh)* to the God of Israel, the God whom Jesus claims to be in John 8:58. Furthermore, the God of the Old Testament, whom Jesus presents as being Himself, is also called "Almighty God." This proves interesting later when we consider the Trinitarian evidences from the book of Revelation. Even though Revelation never directly applies the term "Almighty" to Jesus, it is very clear from the above texts that Jesus, along with the Father, bears this title also as a part of His divine description.

[3] We will explore further the meaning of the expressions "begotten," "only begotten," and "firstborn" in a later chapter.

[4] The authors of the book *Seventh-day Adventists Believe* . . . have given the following succinct comment about YHWH or Yahweh: "Yahweh is 'a conjectural transliteration' of the sacred name of God in the Old Testament (Ex. 3:14, 15; 6:3). The original Hebrew contained the four consonants YHWH. In time, out of fear of profaning God's name, the

Jews refused to read this name aloud. Instead, wherever YHWH appeared they would read the word *Adonai.* In the seventh or eighth century A.D., when vowels were added to the Hebrew words [there are no vowels in the Hebrew alphabet, only consonants], the Masoretes [Jewish textual scholars] supplied the vowels of Adonai to the consonants YHWH. The combination produced the word *Jehovah,* which is used in the KJV. Other translations prefer the word *Yahweh* (Jerusalem Bible) or *Lord* (RSV, NIV, NKJV). (See Siegfried H. Horn, *Seventh-day Adventist Bible Dictionary,* Don F. Neufeld, ed., rev. ed. [Washington, D.C.: Review and Herald, 1979], pp. 1192, 1193.)" (p. 26).

[5] It is true that Jesus uses these titles in Revelation 1:11 in the King James and the New King James versions. The vast majority of more recent versions, however, do not record Jesus as employing the titles, since the manuscript evidence for them is very scant in this verse.

Chapter 2

THE FULL AND ETERNAL DEITY OF CHRIST

—PART I—

The New Testament Epistles, the Old Testament, and the Gospels

Like most of you, I used to dread grammar in my high school English and foreign language classes. The whole thing seemed so technical and dry. As most of us mature, however, we come to realize the importance of grammar as a necessary tool for clear communication. This more technical side of written communication is also an important tool to employ when we are called upon to interpret important passages of Scripture that speak to the issues of a proper understanding of the Godhead.

2 Peter and the Epistle to Titus

In Titus 2:13 we have a very interesting and well-known reference to God. We will cite the fuller context of verses 11-14: "For the grace of God that brings salvation has appeared to all men, teaching us that, denying ungodliness and worldly lusts, we should live soberly, righteously, and godly in the present age, looking for the blessed hope and glorious appearing of *our great God and Savior Jesus Christ,* who gave Himself for us."[1]

The key phrase involving the deity of Christ is the "glorious appearing of our great God and Savior Jesus Christ." The fundamental question is Does the expression "great God" refer to Christ or to God the Father?

We can answer our question through an explanation of the grammar employed by the apostle Paul. In the original Greek the expression "our great God" has a definite article and the expression "Savior Jesus Christ" does not. So, the reader may ask, what is so significant about a definite article? The answer to this question proves quite enlightening.

Greek grammar has a well-known rule formulated by Granville Sharp (way back in 1798). The rule, simply stated, declares that when a conjunction such as "and" (*kaí* in the Greek) connects two nouns of the same grammatical case (both are in the genitive case, the case of ownership), and a definite "article [the] precedes the first noun and is not repeated before the second noun, the latter [or second noun] always refers to the same person that is expressed or described by the first noun" (Metzger, p. 79).[2]

Thus the expression "Savior Jesus Christ" does refer to "our great God," and the New King James Version has correctly translated it as "our great God and Savior Jesus Christ." To put it plainly, the "Savior Jesus Christ" is the "great God."

Furthermore, we must point out that Titus 2:13 is not the only instance in which a biblical writer employs this type of grammar and terminology. In 2 Peter 1:1 we have a very similar expression: "To those who have obtained like precious faith with us by the righteousness *of our God and Savior Jesus Christ."*

Bruce Metzger concisely makes the case: "All that has been written [with reference to Titus 2:13], including the judgment of the grammatical authorities cited . . . applies with equal appropriateness to the correct rendering of II Peter 1:1. Accordingly, in this verse also there is an express declaration of the deity of Jesus Christ, '. . . of our God and Savior Jesus Christ'" *(ibid.).*

Romans 9:5

Nor is Titus the only place Paul clearly applies the word "God" to Jesus Christ. He also does the same thing in Romans. When expressing his great burden for the salvation of the Jews, his "brethren" and "countrymen according to the flesh" (Rom. 9:3), he goes on to declare that "Christ," a Jew "according to the flesh," "came" as "the eternally blessed God."

Could words be plainer? Paul here plainly declares Christ to have come not just as a Jewish man, but as "God"! The great apostle, however, cannot leave it there—he feels compelled to define Christ as "the eternally blessed God." Here is simply powerful testimony not only to the deity of Christ, but to His nature as an eternally, ever-existing "God" (cf. Isa. 9:6).

The Epistle to the Colossians

Not only can grammar prove to be important in interpreting certain biblical texts, but also the further clarification of the meaning of important words can prove to be helpful. As we have seen in chapter 1, the meaning of words such as the Hebrew *yachîd, 'echad* (one) and YHWH (Yahweh, Lord, Jehovah) have been very decisive to a sound interpretation. The same is true of Greek words. In Colossians, the meaning of the Greek word translated as "Godhead" is pivotal if we are to get a full understanding of the deity of Christ.

In Colossians 1:19 Paul refers to Christ as the one in whom "all the fullness should dwell." The question immediately comes: "all the fullness" of what? We get the explicit answer in Colossians 2:9: "For in Him [clearly referring to Christ] dwells all the fullness of the Godhead bodily." The word translated "Godhead" in the KJV and the NKJV is the Greek *"theotēs."* The word means the very face of God, His express image, the very transcript of His being.

Now what proves interesting and instructive is that Paul did have another, very similar Greek word at his command to express the "fullness" of Jesus' divinity—he could have used *"theiotēs."* It also refers to divine characteristics (see Romans 1:20, in which Paul employs the same terminology). But similar as the words are in spelling and meaning, they are not the same.

The anti-Trinitarian Greek lexicographer[3] Thayer has this to say about *"theotēs": "Theotēs* (Deity) differs from *theiotēs* (divinity) as essence differs from quality or attribute" (Thayer, p. 288). In other words, in Romans 1:20 Paul is clearly suggesting that certain "invisible" qualities, attributes, or trappings of deity *(theiotēs)* are "clearly seen, being understood by the things that are made." In Colossians

2:9, however, the apostle declares that in the person of Christ Jesus we have the very "essence" of the nature of deity revealed "bodily."

What is interesting about the context of the Epistle to the Colossians is that the so-called Colossian heretics were calling into question the very essence of Christ's deity. These false Christians were trying to bring Jesus down to the level of the angels or certain impersonal emanations that allegedly had the power to reveal to humanity some secret knowledge.

Paul's response to such heretical teachings was to proclaim Jesus as neither some mere angelic being nor an emanation from some impersonal spirit world, but as the one in whom "dwells all the fullness" of the essence of, or the express image, of God. Jesus bodily bears the very nature or transcript of a divine being.

We would humbly suggest that this word usage, in the context of the challenges faced by the church at Colossae, is simply powerful testimony to the full, eternal deity of God the Son.

Philippians 2:2-8

One of the most interesting traits of Scripture is the way profoundly theological issues often pop up in contexts that deal with highly practical issues. Philippians 2 is one such instance.

Paul begins by appealing to the believers in Philippi to be "like-minded, having the same love, being of one accord, of one mind" (Phil. 2:2) and to do "nothing . . . through selfish ambition or conceit, but in lowliness of mind let each esteem others better than himself. Let each of you look out not only for his own interests, but also for the interests of others" (verses 3, 4).

Then Paul exhorts his readers to "let this mind be in you which was also in Christ Jesus" (verse 5). It is at this point of concrete practicality that the great pastor proceeds to set forth one of the most profound expressions of the full deity of Christ to be found in Holy Writ. Christ, "who, being in the form of God, did not consider it robbery to be equal with God, but made Himself of no reputation, taking the form of a bondservant, and coming in the likeness of men. . . . He humbled Himself and became obedient to the point of death, even the death of the cross" (verses 6-8).

The key terms that express Christ's deity are "being in the form of God" and not considering "it robbery to be equal with God."

What does Paul mean when he says that Christ came in the "form of God"? The Greek word *morphē* (form) denotes "all the essential characteristics and attributes of God. . . . Whatever form that manifestation has taken, it was possessed by Christ, who thereby existed as one with God. This places Christ on an equality with the Father" (*The Seventh-day Adventist Bible Commentary,* vol. 7, p. 154).

Millard Erickson comments on the meaning of *morphē* that "this term in classical Greek as well as in biblical Greek means 'the set of characteristics which constitutes a thing what it is.' It denotes the genuine nature of a thing. The word *morphē* contrasts with *schēma,* which is also generally translated 'form,' but in the sense of shape or superficial appearance rather than substance" (Erickson, *Christian Theology,* p. 350).

Now, what about the meaning of the phrase "did not consider it robbery to be equal with God"? Here the NIV translation gives a better sense of what the Greek is seeking to communicate: "did not consider equality with God something to be grasped." What Paul is here saying is that one who was equal with the Father was willing to give up "the *status* and *privilege* that was his in heaven" (Grudem, p. 551). He did not rescind His divine nature, but in manifesting His self-sacrificing, redemptive attitude, neither did He consider the privileges of "equality with God something to be grasped" or "clung to for his own advantage" *(ibid.).* It led Him to take "the very nature of a servant, being made in human likeness" for the suffering of death—"even death on a cross!" (verses 7, 8, NIV). In other words, it was not Christ refusing to grasp after the "form" or essence of deity, but rather His willingness to release His "grasp" on its privileged status. Once more, Erickson's comments prove insightful:

"Some have argued . . . that Jesus did not possess equality with God; the thrust of this verse is, then, that Jesus neither coveted nor aspired to equality with God. Thus, *harpagmon* ('a thing to be grasped') should not be interpreted as 'a thing to cling to,' but 'a thing to seize.' On the contrary, however, verse 7 indicates that he 'emptied himself.' . . . While Paul does not specify of what Jesus emptied himself, it is apparent that this was an active step of self-abnegation, not a passive declining to take action. Hence equality with God is something he antecedently possessed. And one who is equal with God must be God" (Erickson, *Christian Theology,* pp. 350, 351).

To sum up, what this passage is really saying is that Jesus Christ was truly "equal with God" and thus He did not have to grasp for or cling to His divine equality. Such an "equality" gave Him a divine status or privilege that was His to lay temporarily aside for redemptive purposes. The truly stunning point of this remarkable passage is that Christ did not have to grasp at or cling to "equality with God" because of one simple, yet profound fact—He inherently possessed the essence or substance of the divine nature or "form."

Have you ever noticed that it is the petty government officials who are constantly feeling the need to posture about their presumed powers and prerogatives? The people with the real power are calm in their privileges and status. They seem to feel no need to demonstrate their power credentials. It was thus with our Lord Jesus Christ: He could serenely lay down His divine status because He was fully aware of His divine credentials as an equal with the Father.

Hebrews 1:1-3

Before we directly interpret these verses, a more extensive explanation of the monotheistic backgrounds of the first-century Christians might prove helpful. The reason for doing this is that if the apostolic writers were teaching something contrary to their cherished monotheism, the New Testament would certainly have recorded somewhere a reaction against it. Did early Christians protest the abandonment of monotheism? Before we answer, let's further clarify the theological makeup of the early Christians.

All three of the major groups that composed the majority of the early Christians (Jews, Gentile "converts" to Judaism, and the "strangers" at the gate) had been nurtured either in or attracted to

Judaism because of its high moral tone, its Scriptures, and its worship of the one God who spoke through the Old Testament prophets. In other words, one of the major attractions of Judaism was its monotheism, which stood out clearly against the rampant pagan polytheism of the times.

Let's consider more closely the latter two groups of early Christians. The "converts" (also called "proselytes") were Gentiles who had gone all the way and become members of the local Jewish synagogue through the rite of circumcision. The "strangers at the gate," however, while strongly attracted to the Jewish religion, had not had the courage to receive adult male circumcision.

Now whether the early Christians were religious Jews, Gentile "proselytes," or "strangers at the gate," all of these earnest believers in Christ were strongly partial to Jewish monotheism. Most certainly if the apostles were pushing a new brand of polytheism on them they would have strongly resisted.

With these comments in mind, let us return to some further considerations of the deity of Christ in the book of Hebrews. We need to remember that this book was the most Jewish and Old Testament-saturated of the Epistles of the New Testament. Certainly, if the apostles were teaching something contrary to the monotheism of the Old Testament, it would have shown up here. What, however, the author of the Epistle to the Hebrews immediately proceeds to do is to argue for the full deity of Christ and the fact that He was the active agent in creation.

Carefully ponder Hebrews 1:2, 3: "[God] has in these last days spoken to us by His Son, whom He has appointed heir of all things, through whom also He made the worlds; who being the brightness of His glory and the express image of His person, and upholding all things by the word of His power, when He had by Himself purged our sins, sat down at the right hand of the Majesty on high."

Please note the strong statement that declares that Christ bears "the express image of His [God's] person." While some might debate that "express image" refers only to God's character rather than to His essential divine nature, the context strongly suggests otherwise.

First of all, I would remind the reader that the subsequent verses in Hebrews 1, discussed in the previous chapter, clearly addressed Jesus in verse 8 as God, and then in verses 10-12 the author applies to Jesus an Old Testament psalm directly speaking to the Lord (Jehovah or Jahweh God), strongly implying that Jesus is the Jehovah of the Old Testament.

Second, the phrase in verse 2 that declares that Jesus was the being "through whom also He [God the Father] made the worlds" merits close attention. What the author of the book of Hebrews is saying here is that Jesus, the divine Son, is the active agent in the creation of the universe. It is very similar to claims made by numerous other New Testament writers (see John 1:3; Eph. 3:9; and Col. 1:16).

Such assertions provide strong testimony for the full deity of Christ. Can we really say that the One who was the active agent in the creation of the universe is some sort of derived deity? Such a question takes on particular urgency when we recall the great claims of the Old Testament authors that what really identifies the true God is His ability to create.

Isaiah 40 celebrates the great "Lord God" (verse 10) as the "Holy One" (verse 25) of God's people (Judah). In verses 25, 26, and 28 the Holy Lord lays down a challenge: "'To whom then will you liken Me, or to whom shall I be equal?' says the Holy One. Lift up your eyes on high, and see who has created these things, who brings out their host by number; He calls them all by name, by the greatness of His might and the strength of His power. . . . Have you not known? Have you not heard? The everlasting God, the Lord, the Creator of the ends of the earth, neither faints nor is weary. His understanding is unsearchable" (Isa. 40:25-28, NKJV).

When we place the testimony of the "Holy One," the "Lord God" of the prophet Isaiah, beside Hebrews 1:2 and the numerous other passages of the New Testament that proclaim Jesus as the active agent in the creation of the universe, it becomes pretty hard to say that He is some sort of semideity. Once more, the New Testament testimony that Christ is the Creator and the Old Testament claim that this Creator is none other than the Lord

Jehovah make it pretty clear that Jesus the Creator is none other than the Lord God, Jehovah Creator of the Old Testament.

Hebrews 7:3

From Hebrews 4:14 to 8:2 the writer continues his theme that Christ is "better." Having shown that Christ's ministry is "better" than that of the angels and Moses, he now seeks to demonstrate that Christ's high priesthood is superior to that of Aaron and the Old Testament Levites. He does this by suggesting that Christ's priesthood is after the order of Melchizedek, not that of Levi. And why does he consider Mechizedek's priesthood to be superior? The key answer comes in chapter 7.

Using methods of interpretation typical of the rabbis, the writer sees Melchizedek as a type of Christ for a number of reasons. The one, however, that concerns us here has to do with the fact that Scripture not only calls the ancient ruler " 'king of righteousness,' and then also king of Salem, meaning 'king of peace' " (Heb. 7:2), but also that Melchizedek was "without father, without mother, without genealogy, having neither beginning of days nor end of life" (verse 3). In other words, since the Genesis story of this king makes no reference to a father, mother, a human genealogy, or his having a beginning or end to life, therefore Melchizedek becomes a wonderful type of Christ, "a priest forever according to the order of Melchizedek" (verse 17). But in what particular sense? The answer is clear in verse 3: Melchizedek was "made like the Son of God" who "remains a priest continually." And how is it that Christ can minister continually? It is because our Lord Jesus and high priest (like His type Melchizedek) had "neither beginning of days nor end of life."

Hebrews 7:3 indicates that Jesus has eternally preexisted, with no "beginning of days" to recall and "no end of life" to anticipate. The characteristics of eternal preexistence from the past and unending life in the future can reside only in a fully divine person.

We find not one hint in the book of Hebrews or in the rest of the New Testament that the early monotheistic Christians found themselves uncomfortable with these mighty testimonies to the full deity of Christ. To the contrary, the testimony of John, Paul, and Peter is so straightforward that there seems to be no controversy at all except that from the unconverted Jewish opponents of Jesus. Certainly if there had been a monotheistic reaction to the apostles' declarations of the full deity of Christ, we would see it reflected somewhere in the New Testament documents. Think about the great debates that erupted over the circumcision question that we find so strongly reflected in Acts and the Pauline Epistles of the New Testament. We discover nothing of a similar nature regarding the apostolic claims for Jesus' deity.

Qualities Common to Both the Father and the Son

Countless writers have noted that Scripture ascribes numerous qualities, activities, and attitudes toward Christ that the Bible also shares with or applies to God the Father.[4]

First of all, Paul speaks of qualities to Christ that the Old Testament applied specifically to God: sanctifier (Ex. 31:13 and 1 Cor. 1:30), peace (Judges 6:24 and Eph. 2:14), and righteousness (Jer. 23:6 and 1 Cor. 1:30).

Second, in his writings "a number of interchangeable statements appear, in one place ascribed to God and in another to Christ" (Johnson and Webber, p. 123). Carefully note the following: (1) the gospel of God in Romans 1:1 and the gospel of Christ in Romans 1:16; (2) the power of God in Romans 1:16 and the power of Christ in 2 Corinthians 12:9; (3) the peace of God in Philippians 4:7 and the peace of Christ in Colossians 3:15, NIV; (4) the church of God in Galatians 1:13 is spoken of as the churches of Christ in Romans 16:16; (5) the "Spirit of God" in 1 Corinthians 2:11 and Romans 8:9 is also referred to as the "Spirit of Christ" in Romans 8:9; (6) the "kingdom of God" in Romans 14:17 is called "the kingdom of the Son of His love" in Colossians 1:13.

Third, Paul describes God and Christ carrying on a number of common works or activities in the church and the world: (1) the grace of God in Galatians 1:15 and the grace of Christ in 1 Thessalonians

5:28; (2) God saves us in Titus 3:4 and Christ saves us in 1 Thessalonians 5:9; (3) forgiveness from God in Colossians 2:13 and from Christ in Colossians 3:13, or forgiveness coming from God for Christ's sake in Ephesians 4:32; and (4) revelation derives from God the Father in Galatians 1:16 and from Jesus Christ in Galatians 1:12.

Fourth, Paul's attitude to both Christ and God is one and the same: (1) boast in God in Romans 2:17 and boast in Christ in Philippians 1:26; (2) "faith in God" in 1 Thessalonians 1:8, 9 (NIV) and "faith in Jesus Christ" in Galatians 3:22.

What are we to make of so many common qualities, ascriptions, and activities shared by both God and Christ? Is this not strong evidence "that while Paul knew that Christ and God were distinct, yet in his mind they were equal and one" *(ibid.)?*

We now will turn our attention from the Epistles of the New Testament to the prophecies of the Old Testament and how the Gospel writers saw them as fulfilled.

Isaiah 43:10, 11

Here we have the great banner text of the most well-known anti-Trinitarians of our times—the forthrightly Arian Jehovah's Witnesses. This passage is to them what Revelation 14:6-12 is to Seventh-day Adventists. What is ironic about it, however, is that it is one of the strongest refutations of their attempts to make the Christ of the Scripture some sort of created or derived semigod. It is the most compelling piece of Old Testament evidence that we can cite for the full deity of Christ. " 'You are My witnesses,' says the Lord, 'and My servant whom I have chosen, that you may know and believe Me, and understand that I am He. Before Me there was no God formed, nor shall there be after Me. I, even I, am the Lord, and besides Me there is no savior' " (Isa. 43:10, 11).

Here Isaiah is obviously quoting the words of the Lord (YHWH, Jehovah), who plainly says to the people of God that they are His "witnesses." And who is the Lord? He is the everlasting Creator-God and declares that before Him (in time) "there was no God formed, nor shall there be after" Him (verse 10). In other words, the Jehovah God of the Old Testament plainly tells us that there was never any God "formed" either before or after Him.

Think about this for a moment. If the Arians deem Jesus to be some sort of created or derived God, then how can this passage be true? Here the Unitarians and Arians, who want to suggest that Jesus was some sort of semi- or demigod brought forth by the Father sometime during the long lost ages of an ancient past, directly contradict the plainest testimony of the Jehovah God.

The only sensible explanation for the meaning of this text, if we are to take seriously the clear testimony of the New Testament writers that Jesus is God, is to conclude that whoever the Lord, YHWH, or Jehovah who speaks in Isaiah 43:10, 11 is, His identity must include that of the Jesus of the New Testament who claimed to be in some sense the Jehovah of the Old Testament.

Furthermore, the case becomes even more compelling when the Lord goes on to say that "besides Me there is no savior" (verse 11). When the New Testament writers declare Jesus to be Messiah, the one who would "save His people from their sins" (Matt. 1:21), it must mean that the Messiah Jesus of the New Testament is the Lord Jehovah of the Old Testament prophet Isaiah.

Now, some Arians might reply to this interpretation by acknowledging that the Lord here speaking is indeed the preincarnate Jesus. They then go on to interpret the passage as teaching that Jesus was "formed," or created, by the Father, and that there was never any other "god" either before or after Him. The problem with this interpretation is that the Lord is not here describing His origins so much as He is contrasting His person with that of the numerous other false gods—the idols that so many Israelites of Isaiah's time were worshiping. Clearly, the issue in this chapter is to distinguish the eternal self-existing Lord of Israel from the false gods of the nations.

Isaiah 7:14 and Matthew 1:23

Matthew clearly applies this prophecy of Isaiah to Christ: "Behold, a virgin shall be with child, and bear a Son, and they shall call His name Immanuel" (Matt. 1:23). The Gospel writer straightforwardly declares that the birth of Christ to Mary and Joseph "was done that it might be fulfilled which was spoken by the Lord through the prophet" Isaiah (verse 22). Not only does Matthew cite Isaiah 7:14, but he takes the liberty to interpret the passage by translating the title "Immanuel" as "God with us" (verse 23). The New Testament author is quite comfortable with simply saying that the name that Isaiah gives to Jesus is that of "God"—the God who has come to be the incarnate Son of God.

Isaiah 9:6

This well-known and beloved prophecy of the coming Messiah of Israel has thrilled the hearts of both Jews and Christians for more than 2,700 years. The words of this text provide one of the best-known passages from Handel's great oratorio, *The Messiah.* So deep is the association of these inspired words of Isaiah with "The Messiah" that every time Christians read this passage they almost spontaneously break forth in musical expression—"For unto us a child is born unto us a son is given: and the government shall be upon his shoulder: and his name shall be called Wonderful, Counsellor, The mighty God, The everlasting Father, The Prince of Peace" (KJV). Quite possibly, the reader has already started quietly singing these memorable words that have gladdened Christmas celebrations for more than 250 years.

What is truly striking about this stirring passage is that it refers to Jesus as "The mighty God, The everlasting Father." It is a strong prophetic declaration that Jesus has and will continue to have an "everlasting" existence. Also it is interesting that Jesus can prophetically be referred to as "Father." Obviously Isaiah is not trying to tell us that Jesus and the Father of Jesus Christ are one and the same person. What the great prophet is most likely trying to convey is that part of being a "mighty" and "everlasting" God is that Christ is our Father in both creation and redemption. The same basic message appears in the Messiah prophecies of Micah.

Micah 5:2

Matthew 2:6 sees this great prophecy as finding its fulfillment in the birth of Christ. It clearly pinpoints the geographic locale of our Lord's birth and provides explicit evidence for His eternal preexistence. Note carefully the full resonance of this inspired foretelling of the coming forth of Israel's "ruler": "But thou, Bethlehem Ephratah, though thou be little among the thousands of Judah, yet out of thee shall he come forth unto me that is to be ruler in Israel; whose goings forth have been from of old, from everlasting" (KJV).

It is the last, sublime description that speaks so tellingly of the eternal preexistence of the Babe of Bethlehem—"whose goings forth have been from of old, from everlasting." Could the prophetic writer have been clearer that Christ's "goings forth" are from time immemorial?

Summary

Repeatedly the Bible presents Christ in His deity as our "great God and Savior" (Titus 2:13), the uncreated Creator (Heb. 1:1-3), and the one Paul declared as He in whom "all the fullness of the Deity ("Godhead" in KJV, or essence of divine nature) lives in bodily form" (Col. 2:9, NIV).

Furthermore, the Jehovah, or Lord God of the Old Testament, declares Himself to be the one before whom and after whom no other God came into being. Thus the Jesus of the New Testament, announced as "God with us" (Matt. 1:23), must be the Jehovah (Lord, Yahweh) of the Old Testament. If He were a formed or "created" as a lesser god, how could the Lord in Isaiah 43:10 be speaking truthfully when He says that no God was formed either before or after Him?

Finally, of what human being, except the incarnate Christ, could it be truly stated that "who, being in very nature God, did not consider equality with God something to be grasped" at or clung to (Phil. 2:6, NIV)?

What do you think? Is the biblical case solid enough for us to say with humble confidence that Jesus is just as fully divine as is God the

Father? Can we really charge the Trinitarians with being grossly unbiblical in their claims for the full and eternal deity of Jesus? Does the weight of evidence suggest that Jesus was more than a mere human being or some sort of created, derived semigod?

If you still need more evidence, we again appeal to you to hang in there with us. We have yet more testimony from the Word of God. In the following chapter we will turn our attention to the witness of the writer who, probably more than any other, testifies that Christ's divine nature is "equal" to that of the Father God. Of course we are referring to John the beloved and his sublime Gospel.

ENDNOTES

[1] Unless otherwise noted, biblical citations in this chapter are from the New King James Version.

[2] Metzger goes on to point out that the translations, based on Sharp's grammatical rule, contained in the KJV, RSV, and the NKJV are supported by "such eminent grammarians of the Greek New Testament as P. W. Schmiedel, J. H. Moulton, A. T. Robertson, and Blass-Debrunner. All of these scholars concur in the judgment that only one person is referred to in Titus 2:13 and that therefore it must be rendered, 'Our great God and Savior Jesus Christ' " (p. 79). Further, in more recent times the detailed study by Daniel B. Wallace has strongly confirmed the validity of Sharp's rule. He has conveniently summarized his findings in his *Greek Grammar: Beyond the Basics,* pp. 270-287. Wallace presents a brief biographical sketch of Sharp, how he discovered his "rule," and a very detailed study of how it reveals itself in the New Testament. The Trinitarian interpretation of Titus 2:13 rests on a very secure grammatical foundation.

[3] A lexicon is a Greek word dictionary and thus a lexicographer is a scholar that seeks to clearly define Greek words and their English counterparts.

[4] The following points I have drawn from Alan F. Johnson and Robert E. Webber's *What Christians Believe: A Biblical and Historical Summary,* pp. 123, 124, and Max Hatton's *Understanding the Trinity,* p. 38.

Chapter 3

THE FULL AND ETERNAL DEITY OF CHRIST

—PART II—

The Gospel of John

In any court case, the leading evidence for a proper verdict normally centers around the testimony of key "witnesses," especially the person referred to as the "star" witness. As already presented in chapters 1 and 2, we have many important biblical witnesses to the full and eternal deity of Christ. If we, however, had to pick the primary witness for the deity of Christ, our vote would have to go to the testimony of the "beloved" disciple, John.

In his Gospel and the book of Revelation we have the most compelling witness for Christ's divine nature. Thus this chapter and chapter 5 on the book Revelation will seek to present John's testimony regarding Christ's nature, especially what he reports concerning Christ's own self-understanding and claims about His relationship to the eternal Father.

The "I Am" Statements of Jesus

In chapter 1 we examined the most striking of Jesus' "I am" statements—"Before Abraham was, I AM" (John 8:58).[1] Please recall that what Jesus was unmistakably claiming is that His preexistence is that of the "Lord" of the Exodus. Jesus is clearly identifying Himself with the great "I AM" God of the Old Testament (Ex. 3:14), who commands Moses to say to the people of Israel that no less than the eternal "Lord God" of Israel's "fathers, the God of Abraham, the God of Isaac, and the God of Jacob" (verse 15; see also verse 16) was sending him.

Not only is Jesus claiming "preexistence" before Abraham, but that He is also the eternally existent "Lord God" of Israel. To put it bluntly, it was a bold claim to be God. Did Jesus' hearers clearly understand what He was claiming? It is quite apparent that they did, since John reports that they immediately broke off the conversation and "took up stones to throw at Him" (John 8:59)—the appropriate measure to mete out to blasphemers.

What is interesting, however, is that it is not the only instance in John's Gospel that reports Jesus as making "I am" statements. In fact, it is rather remarkable that John records seven other statements using the "I am" terminology to describe Jesus. As we trace these "I Am" statements it becomes apparent that they reflect different metaphors or symbols that illustrate various aspects of Jesus' saving work as the great divine "I AM."

The first statement occurs in John 6:35 (cf. verse 48): "I am the bread of life." What is truly astounding about this claim is that Jesus goes on to say that "if anyone eats of this bread, he will live forever" (verse 51) or "has eternal life" (verse 54). Obviously He is declaring that He can impart "eternal life" to those who trust in Him. The ability to give "eternal life" uniquely resides in deity (1 Tim. 6:16). Thus Jesus' claim to be the "I am" of the bread of eternal life strongly suggests His own self-understanding as a divine person.

The second claim appears in John 8:12: "I am the light of the world." It echoes and elaborates the testimony of John the Baptist (reported earlier in John 1:6-9) that Jesus "was the true light that gives light to every man coming into the world" (verse 9, NIV). Later on in 1 John 1:5 the disciple comments that "this is the message which we have heard from Him and declare to you, that God is light and in Him is no darkness at all." When one looks carefully at the context of 1 John 1:5 it is not clear if the pronoun "Him" points to the Father or His Son. What is clear, however, is that when John uses the metaphor of "light" it refers to "God." The disciple's writings strongly imply that Jesus' claim to be "the light of the world" is one to divine being or nature.

The third instance is from John 10:7: "I am the door of the

sheep." (See also verse 9.) The context indicates that it is one more way for Jesus to declare that the only way that the "sheep" can "have life, and . . . have it more abundantly" (verse 10), is through Himself. Once again, this abundant life refers primarily to eternal life that dwells, or naturally abides, only in God.

Closely related to the "door of the sheep" metaphor is the fourth "I am"—"I am the good shepherd" (verse 11). Plainly, the metaphor also refers to the "life" everlasting that is the unique gift of God. Notice how Jesus speaks of the gift of "life" that is His very own prerogative: "Therefore My Father loves Me, because I lay down My life that I may take it again. No one takes it from Me, but I lay it down of Myself. . . . I have power to take it again" (verses 17, 18). Is it going too far to suggest that Jesus here alludes to Psalm 23—"the Lord is my shepherd"? Could it be that Jesus is claiming to be none other than the life-giving Lord Yahweh of King David in the Old Testament?

All that we have said so far about Jesus as the source of eternal life is summed up in the fifth, sixth, and seventh "I am" claims of Jesus: "I am the resurrection and the life" (John 11:25), "I am the way, the truth, and the life" (John 14:6), and "I am the true vine" (John 15:1).

Most certainly the repetitive sevenfold use of the "I am" claims in the Gospel of John augment and highlight Jesus' stunning claims to be one person of the Godhead of the Old Testament who has now come as the life-imparting Savior of the New Covenant.

John 1:18

We encounter one of the more overlooked evidences for the deity of Christ in the writings of John in this verse. Many commentators recognize that it is the climax of the Prologue, the introductory section of the fourth Gospel. The reason that it often gets overlooked results from the fact that, along with the King James Version and many other earlier versions, the verse reads as follows: "No one has seen God at any time. The only begotten *Son,* who is in the bosom of the Father, He has declared Him" (NKJV). The expression "the only begotten *Son"* is, however, replaced in most contemporary English versions with either "the only begotten God" (NASB) or "God the One and Only" (NIV).[2] The reason for this more striking testimony to the deity of Christ is that the most reliable and ancient Greek manuscripts of the New Testament have the reading *monogenes theos* ("only begotten God" or "one and only God," or "unique God") in place of *monogenes huios* ("only begotten Son" or "one and only Son" or "unique Son").

While the above translations of *monogenes theos* are perfectly acceptable, quite possibly the rendering suggested by well-known Bible-believing New Testament scholar Leon Morris best reflects the sense that John is trying to convey: "It is possible that we should punctuate with a comma after 'begotten,' thus giving us three titles of Christ: 'Only-begotten, God, He who is in the bosom of the Father' " (Morris, pp. 113, 114).

If the witness of the most reliable Greek manuscripts support the term *theos* ("God"), rather than *huios* ("Son"), what we have here is one of the few direct, uncontested applications of the term "God" to Jesus in the New Testament (such as John 1:1, Phil. 2:6, and Heb. 1:8).

John 5

This striking chapter reports the healing of the paralytic by the Pool of Bethesda on the Sabbath. The incident greatly incited the opposition of the Jewish leadership. Verse 16 reports that this Sabbath healing was the "reason the Jews persecuted Jesus, and sought to kill Him." In His response Jesus made a very important claim: "My Father has been working until now, and I have been working" (verse 17).

Many commentators have pondered its meaning. It, however, appears that the next verse plainly gives its meaning: "Therefore the Jews sought all the more to kill Him, because He not only broke the Sabbath, but also said that God was His Father, *making Himself equal with God"* (verse 18).

The Jewish leaders obviously understood what Jesus was getting at—He was pointedly rejecting their false views of Sabbathbreaking, and the Gospel writer reports in no uncertain terms, He was "making Himself equal with God." Since they rejected Christ's claim, it is no wonder that they sought to kill Him. In their eyes, His claim was blasphemy, and the only appropriate remedy was execution by stoning.

Jesus, however, did not back off. He further explained His claim to "equality" by asserting: "For as the Father raises the dead and gives life to them, even so the Son gives life to whom He will. For the Father judges no one, but has committed all judgment to the Son, that all should honor the Son just as they honor the Father" (verses 21-23). Here Jesus supports His claim to equality with the Father by declaring that He has inherent life in Himself and that He deserves the same honor as the Father, since "all judgment" has been committed to Him.

This last phrase—"that all should honor the Son just as they honor the Father"—is powerful evidence for the equality of the Father and the Son. How could Jesus have been more explicit in His claim that He should be honored in a manner characterized with the expression "just as," or in the exact same manner, as the Father? No wonder the "Jews sought all the more to kill" Christ!

John 10

Not only did the religious leaders accuse Jesus of blasphemy in John 5 and 8, but He also made claims in chapter 10 that triggered the same charges.

In John 10:27-30 Jesus continues to explain His claim to be the "good shepherd" (verse 11): "My sheep hear My voice, and I know them, and they follow Me. And I give them eternal life, and they shall never perish. . . . No one is able to snatch them out of My Father's hand. I and My Father are one" (verses 27-30). It is quite apparent that the last sentence stirred the Jews not only to charge Jesus with blasphemy, but actually to "[pick] up stones to stone him" (verse 31, NIV). When Jesus asked them which of the "many great miracles from the Father" do you stone Me? (verse 32, NIV), the religious leaders answered, "We are not stoning you for any of these,

. . . but for blasphemy, because you, a mere man, claim to be God" (verse 33, NIV).

The Jews definitely understood what Jesus was claiming, and He does nothing to correct them. Jesus, however, does not plead guilty to their charge of blasphemy. In fact, in the succeeding verses, He unquestionably defends His claim to be "God's Son" (verse 36, NIV) and that "the Father is in me, and I in the Father" (verse 38, NIV).

Both expressions offer further descriptions of His relationship to the Father that support His explicitly stated and perceived claim that He "and the Father are one" (verse 30, NIV). Did His opponents get the point? It is abundantly apparent that while they did not accept Christ's testimony, they fully understood what the Master was getting at. John goes on to report that "again they tried to seize him" (verse 39, NIV).

The Confession of Thomas: John 20:28

John not only presents evidence for the divinity of Jesus through his reports of Jesus' confrontations with His opponents, but he also makes his case by relating the way His disciples came to regard Him. Probably the most remarkable testimony to the deity of Christ from the twelve comes from a most unlikely but convincing source—"Doubting" Thomas. In fact, Thomas's amazing turnaround constitutes what amounts to a telling, final testimony to the divine lordship of Jesus in John's Gospel.

The setting is a gathering of the disciples a week after Jesus' resurrection. On the evening of the Resurrection Jesus had appeared to His disciples, but Thomas had not been present. When told about the appearance of Jesus, the reluctant believer had boldly declared that "unless I see the nail marks in his hands and put my finger where the nails were, and put my hand into his side, I will not believe it" (John 20:25, NIV).

At the fateful gathering that occurred seven days after the Resurrection Thomas was present, and Jesus directly addressed His reluctant follower and his perplexingly painful skepticism: "Put your finger here; see my hands. Reach out your hand and put it into my side. Stop doubting and believe" (verse 27, NIV). Thomas responded by forthrightly declaring to Jesus that He was "My Lord and my God!" (verse 28, NIV).

His proclamation of faith was remarkable enough in and of itself, but even more striking, however, was that Jesus made absolutely no effort to correct the now exultant believer's spontaneous testimony that the Savior was both Thomas's "Lord" and "God." In fact, Jesus followed up the episode with "many other miraculous signs in the presence of his disciples" (verse 30, NIV). He gave the signs not only to enable the disciples, but also all who have been attracted to Him to "believe that Jesus is the Christ, the Son of God, and that by believing you may have life in his name" (verse 31, NIV).

John 1:1

It seems a bit strange to save the treatment of the first verse of John until last. We, however, felt that we could best approach the complexity of properly translating and interpreting it after we have clearly established an overall understanding of the deity of Christ revealed throughout the Gospel. While we briefly addressed the interpretation of this verse in the first chapter of the book, we have now reached the setting for a more in-depth treatment.

Some Preliminary Observations

In language that surely echoes Genesis 1:1 ("In the beginning God") John introduces his Gospel by declaring, "In the beginning was the Word, and the Word was with God, and the Word was God" (John 1:1). Before we attempt to interpret the wording and grammar of the key phrase "the Word was God," we should consider the following contextual and theological observations. First of all, it might be beneficial to establish what the expression "the Word was God" *does not* refer to. In this context the "Word" certainly does not have in mind God the Father. The reason is simply this: the earlier part of the verse said that the "Word was with God" in the "beginning." Thus the person called "God," whom the "Word" was "with" in the "beginning," must certainly be God the Father.

Therefore it would be highly unlikely that God the Father is the God referred to in the last phrase of John 1:1. Furthermore, if the "Word" refers to the person of the Father, then we fall into the trap of the ancient Christian heresy of modalism (also called Sabellianism).[3]

Second, it is also clear what the word "God" in the last phrase of the verse *does* refer to. Commentators almost unanimously agree that it speaks of some sort of divine nature in the person of Jesus.

Even the Jehovah's Witnesses acknowledge some version of the deity of Christ when they argue that the Father God is the "Almighty," whereas Jesus is only the "Mighty" God. They, however, are not supporting the full deity of Christ. Thus it should not surprise us that their New World Translation then proceeds to support their distinction between the deity of the Father and that of the Son by declaring that the Word was "a god."

Furthermore, other anti-Trinitarians also want to make essentially the same point—that Jesus is not merely a human being, but some sort of semi- or demigod who in some sense derived His divine nature from the Father somewhere in the dimly comprehended ages of eternity past. Such concepts about Jesus reflect the classic thinking of Arianism.[4]

Thus we can state with some assurance that practically everyone who has ever pondered the question of the deity of Christ in the context of interpreting the verse (both Trinitarian and anti-Trinitarian) readily admits that "Word" refers to Jesus Christ (see John 1:14). The key question, however, is what sort of divine nature does John attribute to the person of Jesus? Was it fully equal to that of the eternal Father, or was it some sort of semideity, derived from that of the Father?

Important Grammatical Considerations

As suggested earlier, grammar seems to play a vital role in answering the above question about Christ's deity. Without going into all of the details of the grammar involved, I believe that we can best understand the last phrase of John 1:1 as "and the Word [Jesus] was God" (not God the Father, but Jesus, who is God in the sense that He possessed all the *qualities* of the divine character and nature of the Father).[5]

In other words, John opens his Gospel with the clear declaration that Jesus is a being with all the eternal and divine qualities possessed by the eternal Father. Thus John 1:1 and 20:28 are like sturdy bookends at each end of the bookcase called the Fourth Gospel, a bookcase that contains "volumes" of "star witness" testimony to the fully divine nature of Jesus!

Summary

We ask the reader, What do you think? Can it be truly said that John the beloved is the star witness of the New Testament in giving the "testimony of Jesus" to the full eternity and equality of the Son with the Father?

While we will present further Bible evidence for the full and eternal deity of Christ from the writings of John (more evidence will come from the book of Revelation), we now need to turn our attention to the biblical evidence for the second and third key components of the Trinitarian expression of the Godhead.

What about the case for the personhood, or distinct personality, of the Holy Spirit as the alleged divine third living person of the "heavenly trio" (White, *Evangelism,* p. 615)? Further, is there credible evidence to support the profound unity alleged to exist among the three persons of the Godhead? It is to these questions that we turn in chapter 4.

Supplement to Chapter 3

GRAMMATICAL EXPLANATION OF JOHN 1:1: *"The Word Was God"*

Colwell's Rule

It appears that a well-known grammatical rule discovered by Professor E. C. Colwell (in the 1930s) offers some compelling evidence as to the most appropriate translation and interpretation of the expression "the Word was God." Scholars have appropriately named the concept "Colwell's Rule."[6]

The following discussion is a bit technical, but readers should be able to follow the argument if they can remember some basic high school English grammar used in diagramming sentences.

The key issues that Colwell's Rule addresses involve the following basic factors of sentence structure:

(1) The *subject* (the key idea, concept, or person); (2) *intransitive verbs* (that is, verbs that qualify or define a subject rather than show some action carried out by the subject); (3) the *predicate nominative* (usually consisting of a noun or an adjective that defines, identifies, or qualifies the subject); and (4) the significance of *definite articles* or their absence in a sentence (words such as "the" that clearly identify the subject or specify the predicate nominative). With these basic factors in mind, we can now directly deal with Colwell's famous rule.

Here is what it says:

"Definite predicate nouns [predicate nominatives] which precede the verb usually lack the [definite] article . . . a predicate nominative which precedes the verb cannot be translated as an indefinite or a 'qualitative' noun solely because of the absence of the article; if the context suggests that the predicate is definite, it should be translated as a definite noun" (Wallace, p. 257).

Before we seek to apply this rule to John 1:1, it might prove helpful to lay out the key phrase of the verse in both Greek and English. First of all, we will give an exact citation of the phrase as transliterated[7] from the Greek into the English letters *kaí theos ēn ho logos.*

Next, please consider the following (1) translation (in quotation marks) and (2) explanations of the grammatical significance of the words placed in parentheses following each Greek word and its English translation: *kaí* ("and," a conjunction); *theos* ("God," the predicate nominative without a definite article that comes before the verb); *ēn* ("was," the intransitive verb that connects the subject, *ho logos,* or "the Word," the nominative noun, to the predicate nominative, *theos,* or "God"); *ho logos* ("the Word," the subject or nominative noun of the sentence).

The Application of "Colwell's Rule"

Daniel Wallace has argued persuasively that Colwell's Rule allows for three possible translations.[8]

What follows is a digest of Wallace's presentation of the three options and his appraisal of their respective strengths and weaknesses (*ibid.,* pp. 256-270):

(1) THE "INDEFINITE" OPTION:

As previously noted, the most well-known example of this option appears in the Jehovah's Witnesses' New World Translation—"the Word was *a god.*" While Colwell's Rule would allow for such a translation (if the context calls for it), both the grammar and the context make such a translation doubtful.

The first problem with the "indefinite" translation is that the grammatical argument is weak, with little if any evidence to support it. Paul Stephen Dixon might overstate the case, but his point is basically valid when he contends that if *theos* were "indefinite" in John

1:1, it would amount to the only instance of its kind in the Gospel of John (*ibid.*, p. 267).

The second complication has to do with the inconsistency of those who support such a translation. The New Testament has 282 places where *theos* appears without the definite article, and the New World Translation employs the "indefinite" translation (a god, god, gods, or godly) only 16 times. Thus the Jehovah's Witnesses' translators apply the "indefinite" principle only 6 percent of the time. Clearly it is an arbitrary and inconsistent pattern of translation—most obviously driven by their theological presuppositions and polemical concerns.[9]

The third objection involves not only the theological burden of the Gospel of John (John 17:3), but also the rest of the Bible. The theological implications of the translation "a god" would amount to some version of polytheism! Surely such a translation would strongly suggest that Jesus is only a secondary or semigod inhabiting some pantheon of multiple deities—a concept quite at odds with the overall message of the Bible!

(2) THE "DEFINITE" OPTION:

Colwell's Rule "definitely" allows the noun *theos* ("God") to be translated as if it had the definite article. Furthermore, even though the Greek has no definite article, the implied article need not be translated (the way the KJV and the NKJV render it—"and the Word was God").

While this option is grammatically possible, the context would certainly dictate caution if the translation implied something like "the God." As previously noted in our preliminary observations, the "God" whom the "Word" was "with" in the first part of John 1:1 is clearly God the Father. Therefore, if we translate the last phrase of the verse as "the Word was the God," such a rendering would make "the God" be God the Father, thrusting us out of the pit of Arianism into the ditch of Sabellianism or modalism.

(3) THE "QUALITATIVE" OPTION:

The predicate nominative *(theos)* can be translated in a more "qualitative" manner. If we take this approach, the noun functions more like an adjective and seeks to translate some key quality or characteristic that more clearly defines the subject *(logos)*. Examples would include Bible versions that translate *theos* as either "divine" (Moffatt) or as "What God was, the Word was" (NEB).

This option appears to be the most satisfactory. Wallace offers the following judicious comments: "[This] option stresses that, although the person of Christ is not the person of the Father, their *essence* is identical. . . . The *idea* of a qualitative *theos* here is that the Word had all the attributes and qualities that 'the God' [mentioned earlier in verse 1] had. In other words, he shared the *essence* of the Father, though they differed in person. *The construction the evangelist chose to express this idea was the most concise way he could have stated that the Word was God and yet was distinct from the Father*" (*ibid.*, p. 269).

We could illustrate Wallace's point this way: My wife and I have been spouses since "the beginning" of our marriage. We share the very same essence of "married humanity" (I have dubbed it "human spousehood") while maintaining our personal distinction as male and female and husband and wife. While we are different in our gender and spousal roles, we still share the same essential "human spousehood." Thus the following illustrative paraphrase of John 1:1: "In the beginning of our marriage the woman [my wife, the human spouse] was with the man [me, the husband, the human spouse] and the woman [my wife] was of the same 'human spousehood' essence as the man [me, the husband]."

Most obviously John is not saying that Jesus, who possesses divinity, is simply "a god." Neither is he suggesting that we should equate Jesus with the person of God the Father. To the contrary, John is here employing carefully chosen grammar to express his conviction that Christians, along with the disciple Thomas, can truly confess Jesus as "My Lord and my God" (John 20:28). John is most plainly declaring that "God" can be used as a "qualitative" predicate nominative to describe Jesus as one who shares the full essence of the divine nature of the Father God.

ENDNOTES

[1] Unless otherwise noted, biblical citations in this chapter are from the New King James Version.

[2] Even the New King James Version has a footnote that reads "only begotten God," taken from the Greek text of Nestle-Aland.

[3] This heresy teaches that there is only one God who successively manifests Himself as Father, then Son, and then Spirit. In more recent times the United Pentecostals, popularly referred to as the "Jesus only" people since they believe that Jesus is the only true God who has manifested Himself as Father and Spirit, have taught this concept. Modalism completely denies the Trinity of three coeternal persons in a profound personal oneness of nature, character, and purpose.

[4] Arius of Alexandria presented the classic formulation during the late third and early fourth centuries He taught that "there was a time when Jesus was not." In other words, Arius and his followers claimed that Christ did not exist before the Father brought Him into existence. See the fuller treatment of Arius and his teachings given below by John Reeve in chapter 9.

[5] For those interested in a fuller, detailed explanation of the grammar involved in this "qualitative" interpretation of "the Word was God," please see the "Supplementary Grammatical Explanation of John 1:1" at the end of this chapter.

[6] For those interested in a more detailed discussion of the meaning, history, and application of Colwell's Rule, see Daniel B. Wallace, pp. 256-270.

[7] The word "transliterated" means to take the letters of the words in Greek and transpose or put them into the equivalent letters of the English alphabet. It is duplicating the sound of the word, not translating it.

[8] Of course, Wallace assumes the proper application will emerge when we have thoroughly investigated the rule in all of its uses in the New Testament and let the literary and theological context of the Gospel of John guide us.

[9] Polemics refers to the activity of Christians seeking to defend what they believe to be the truth over against the perceived falsehoods of other Christian opponents. Apologetics involves Christians seeking to defend their understanding of truth against the claims of non-Christian opponents.

Chapter 4

THE PERSONALITY AND DEITY OF THE SPIRIT AND THE TRIUNE ONENESS OF THE GODHEAD

The Personality of the Spirit

In the first chapter we presented some evidence for the personality of the Spirit. What follows will be further Bible support for the Holy Spirit's personality and deity.

Many sincere people understand the Holy Spirit to be some sort of electrical current or force hooked up to the throne of God or a celestial Internet seeking to provide some impersonal phone line for God to communicate with us. Yes, the Holy Spirit is certainly a great channel of communication! The overwhelming Bible evidence, however, suggests that He is a person, a self-aware member of the one true Godhead.

For those of us who are not very mechanically inclined, written directions are often not as helpful as the personal guidance and encouragement of another person who really knows mechanics. I recall my childhood and the passion that my brother Ivan and I had for model planes and ships. Every chance we had, we would haunt hobby shops looking for the latest scale model replicas of the great military aircraft and naval vessels of the day. I loved putting them together. There was, however, one problem—I had an extremely shaky hand and not a lot of physical dexterity. My brother, however, was blessed with a steady hand and wonderful spatial insight.

When I simply went by the printed directions alone, I did not make much progress. To be perfectly honest with you, I usually botched up the job quite badly. When, however, Ivan worked with me, giving guidance, encouragement, and an occasional steady hand on the trickiest jobs, I was able to produce some rather lovely models.

The biblical evidence strongly suggests that the Holy Spirit is a profoundly sensitive, helpful, and powerful personal presence to guide and direct. Only His business is molding us into wonderful models of transforming grace.

We have already pointed to the fact that the Spirit can be lied to (Acts 5:3, 4) and grieved (Eph. 4:30). We find, however, even more evidence for His being an interactive personality.

Matthew 12:31, 32

These well-known verses clearly speak of blaspheming the Holy Spirit. Now it is clear that only God can be blasphemed. Any Bible-believing Christian recognizes that if blasphemy is directed either at the Father or the Son it has as its target a divine person. Why then should it be any different with the Holy Spirit? Clearly, blasphemy is an intensely personal sort of insult directed at God. Not only are these verses evidence for the personhood of the Spirit, they also compellingly indicate the Spirit's deity. As noted above, only God can be blasphemed, and thus it is easy to conclude that the Spirit is a personal God, not some impersonal force.

1 Corinthians 12

One of the truly striking aspects of the New Testament's description of the workings of the Holy Spirit is the way that it portrays the Spirit of God as having a "will," or the ability to make choices. This is quite apparent in Paul's discussion of spiritual gifts found in 1 Corinthians 12:11. The apostle declares that "the same Spirit works all these things [His gifts], distributing to each one individually as He wills."*

Now I do believe that all should readily recognize that machines (such as computers and calculators) do not have wills. They are simply impersonal, passive instruments under the control of rational, self-conscious personal beings. The spiritual gifts are the ministering talents that the Holy Spirit distributes to each person in the body of

Christ. He, however, does so through the exercise of a self-aware will—as He chooses! The ability to will is one of the most profound traits of personal beings.

Romans 8

Paul gives a further, closely related description of the Holy Spirit in Romans 8:14-16 and 26. First of all, in verses 14-16 he depicts the Spirit as leading (verse 14) the sons of God and bearing "witness with our spirit that we are children of God" (verse 16). Both leading and bearing "witness" are actions with intensely personal overtones. Verse 26, however, is possibly the most powerful evidence of the personality of the Spirit in the letter to the Romans: "Likewise the Spirit also helps in our weaknesses. For we do not know what we should pray for as we ought, but the Spirit Himself makes intercession for us with groanings which cannot be uttered."

The whole phenomenon of "intercession" implies willing, active intervention between two personal beings. Furthermore, the "groanings" that cannot be "uttered" strongly suggest an emotional element in the intercession of the Spirit that is also typical of personal beings, not impersonal electronic technology.

1 Corinthians 2:10, 11

This passage presents one of the most important indications of the personal deity of the Spirit. Note carefully its language. Following the well-known verse that declares that "eye has not seen, nor ear heard, nor have entered into the heart of man the things which God has prepared for those who love Him" (1 Cor. 2:9), Paul assures his readers that they may have a knowledge of the "things which God has prepared for those who love Him" (verse 9). And how is such knowledge possible? "God has revealed them to us through His Spirit" (verse 10). And how is it that the Spirit is privy to such knowledge? Answer: "The Spirit searches all things, yes, the deep things of God. For what man knows the things of a man except the spirit of the man which is in him? Even so no one knows the things of God except the Spirit of God" (verses 10, 11).

What is Paul saying? First of all, we must point out that he here describes the Spirit as having the ability to "search" out "the deep things of God" and to "know the things of God." While it is true that our personal computers have "search" capabilities, it is not some sort of a "word search" that Paul has in mind—it is rather an intensely personal exploration of "the deep things of God." This strongly suggests an intimate, personal communion between the Spirit and God the Father. And what is its result? It is most certainly a deep knowledge of "the things of God."

Furthermore, what this passage seems to imply is that if you want to know the "things of a man," you cannot gain such knowledge unless ("except") you possess in you "the spirit of the man." To put it quite simply, to really know a man, you must be a man—"it takes one to know one"!

This, however, is true not only on the human-to-human level, but also on the level of deity. "Even so no one knows the things of God except the Spirit of God" (verse 11). Once more, only a divine person can truly know what is in the mind and heart of another divine being. As on the human level, so it is on the divine—it takes One to know One!

Paul appropriately concludes by observing that what we have received from the Spirit is "not the spirit of the world" (man, the creature), "but the Spirit who is from God, that we might know the things that have been freely given to us by God" (verse 12). If you really want to know the things of God, you must connect with a personal God (the Spirit) who alone can discover the "things" of God.

I know that it is hard for me to comprehend what goes on in the minds of many of my students who come from cultural and language backgrounds differing from my own. It has, however, often proven helpful to get insights from persons who have bridged these cultural chasms and can help me know the "mind" of those I long to better understand. Thus it is with the work of the Spirit—He knows the mind of God because He is a personal and divine being capable of communicating to us God's mind.

Ellen White has given us some very straightforward and concise explanatory comments on 1 Corinthians 2:11 and Romans 8:16: "The Holy Spirit has a personality, else He could not bear witness to our spirits and with our spirits that we are the children of God [comment on Romans 8:16]. He must also be a divine person, else He could not search out the secrets which lie hidden in the mind of God [and then cites 1 Corinthians 2:11]" (White, *Evangelism,* p. 617).

When we place these verses alongside Acts 5 and Ephesians 4:30, they form a powerful testimony to both the personality and deity of the Spirit.

John 14-16

These chapters, ushering in John's narration of the final scenes of our Lord's earthly ministry, contain wonderful and comforting words of counsel. One of the great themes of Jesus' counsels to His disciples is that of the Holy Spirit.

Jesus is saying to them that His time of trial and departure approaches, but they should not let their hearts be troubled (John 14:1). And one of the great consolations that would emerge from the trying scenes ahead would be the sending of the Holy Spirit: "And I will pray the Father, and He will give you another Helper ["Comforter" in KJV], that He may abide with you forever—the Spirit of truth, whom the world cannot receive, because it neither sees Him nor knows Him; but you know Him, for He dwells with you and will be in you. I will not leave you orphans; I will come to you" (verses 16-18).

As Jesus continues His wonderful words of counsel, the gift of the Holy Spirit continues to be a theme permeating not only chapter 14, but also chapters 15 and 16. In John 14:26 Jesus declares, "But the Helper [Comforter], the Holy Spirit, whom the Father will send in My name, He [Greek *ekeinos,* literally "that one," or He in the masculine gender] will teach you all things, and bring to your remembrance all things that I said to you." Similar words appear in John 15:26: "But when the Helper comes, whom I shall send to you from the Father, the Spirit of truth who proceeds from the Father, He [again the Greek *ekeinos* in the masculine gender] will testify of Me."

It is, however, in John 16 that this wonderful discourse, so filled with the promises of the coming of the Spirit and His work, reaches its climax. In verses 7 through 17 we find some of the most hopeful and helpful words that Jesus would ever speak:

"Nevertheless I tell you the truth. It is to your advantage that I go away; for if I do not go away, the Helper will not come to you; but if I depart, I will send Him to you. And when He has come, He will convict the world of sin, and of righteousness, and of judgment: of sin, because they do not believe in Me; of righteousness, because I go to My Father and you see Me no more; of judgment, because the ruler of this world is judged.

"I still have many things to say to you, but you cannot bear them now. However, when He [Greek *ekeinos,* masculine gender], the Spirit of truth, has come, He will guide you into all truth; for He will not speak on His own authority, but whatever He hears He will speak; and He will tell you things to come. He [Greek *ekeinos,* again in the masculine gender] will glorify Me, for He will take of what is Mine and declare it to you. All things that the Father has are Mine. Therefore I said that He will take of Mine and declare it to you" (John 16:7-15).

What is truly remarkable about the passage is the many straightforward evidences for the personality of the Spirit.

First of all, we should observe that while the word "Spirit" (Greek *pneuma*) is in the neuter gender in Greek, the personal pronoun *ekeinos* ("that one," or "He," clearly used to refer to the neuter Spirit) is in the masculine gender. It is this grammatical fact that has led the majority of translators to render the other personal pronouns called for in these passages as "He" rather than "it" or "that one" (as the anti-Trinitarian New World Translation of the Jehovah's Witnesses has done).

What follows is a detailed listing of the personal, masculine pronouns used in John 14-16, once more highlighting the masculine pronoun *ekeinos:*

"He may abide" (John 14:16); "whom," "sees Him," "knows Him," "know Him," "He dwells" (verse 17); "whom the Father will send," "He *[ekeinos]* will teach" (verse 26); "the Helper comes, whom I shall send to you," "He *[ekeinos]* will testify" (John 15:26); "I will send Him to you" (John 16:7); "when He has come, He will convict" (verse 8); "when He *[ekeinos]*, the Spirit of truth, has come, He will guide you. . . . He will not speak on His own authority, but whatever He hears He will speak; and He will tell" (verse 13); "He *[ekeinos]* will glorify Me, for He will take" (verse 14).

The neuter Spirit *(pneuma)* can certainly be interpreted to be impersonal, but the fact that the personal pronouns are masculine (especially *ekeinos*) and appear repeatedly, strongly indicates the personhood of the Spirit.

While the fact of the masculine gender of the Greek *ekeinos* offers strong evidence for the personality of the Spirit, it is by no means the only support. We find still other indications for the personality of the Spirit.

"Helper" (also translated as counselor or comforter) "is a term commonly used to speak of a person who helps or gives comfort or counsel to another person or persons, but is used of the Holy Spirit in John's gospel (14:16, 26; 15:26; 16:7)" (Grudem, p. 232).

Scripture ascribes other activities to the Spirit that are highly personal or interpersonal: teaching (John 14:26), bearing witness (John 15:26; cf. Rom. 8:16), convicting of sin, righteousness, and judgment (John 16:8); guiding into truth, speaking, hearing, and telling (verse 13); glorifying God, taking, and telling (verse 14). All of them strongly suggest the personal and interactive nature of a divine person, not a celestial "thing."

Acts of the Apostles

Furthermore, not only does the Gospel of John portray personally interactive actions by the Spirit, but they also appear in the Acts of the Apostles. The Spirit forbids or does not allow certain things (Acts 16:6, 7), speaks (Acts 8:29; 13:2), and evaluates and approves a particular course of action (Acts 15:28).

The Use of the Words "Power" and "Spirit"

Wayne Grudem has raised an interesting point about the manner in which a number of Bible verses employ the impersonal term "power" in association with the Holy Spirit. Carefully follow his argument:

"If the Holy Spirit is understood simply to be the power of God, rather than a distinct person, then a number of passages would simply not make sense, because in them the Holy Spirit and his power or the power of God are both mentioned. For example, Luke 4:14, 'And Jesus returned in the power of the Spirit into Galilee,' would have to mean, 'Jesus returned in the power of the power of God into Galilee.' In Acts 10:38, 'God anointed Jesus of Nazareth with the Holy Spirit and with power,' would mean, 'God anointed Jesus with the power of God and with power' (see also Rom. 15:13; 1 Cor. 2:4)" (*ibid.*, pp. 232, 233).

2 Corinthians 13:14

One final piece of evidence for the Spirit's personality comes from 2 Corinthians 13:14: "The grace of the Lord Jesus Christ, and the love of God, and the communion of the Holy Spirit be with you all. Amen."

The first thing to note about the verse is that it describes the Holy Spirit as the third named being headed up by God the Father and the Son. The vast majority of Bible-believing Christians agree that the Father and the Son are personal divine beings. Most certainly the "grace" that comes from Jesus Christ can have only a personal origin. The "love of God" obviously suggests the personality of the Father, since love is the essence of any interpersonal experience and expresses caring and concern. Second Corinthians 13:14 then mentions the Holy Spirit in a most straightforward way, strongly suggesting that He is a personal, coordinate divine being—the third person of the tripersonal Godhead.

Grudem has expressed it this way:

"When 'the Holy Spirit' is put in the same expression and on the same level as the other two persons, it is hard to avoid the conclusion that the Holy Spirit is also viewed as a person and of equal standing with the Father and the Son" (*ibid.*, p. 230).

The way Paul here depicts the Holy Spirit's relationship to the Father and the Son Grudem refers to as "a coordinate relationship." He goes on to explain that "since the Father and the Son are both persons, the coordinate expression strongly intimates that the Holy Spirit is a person also" (*ibid.*, p. 232).

Second Corinthians 13:14 is not the only verse "where the Holy Spirit is put in a coordinate relationship with the Father and the Son" *(ibid.)*. Matthew 28:19, 1 Corinthians 12:4-6, Ephesians 4:4-6, and 1 Peter 1:2 all reflect this same type of "coordinate relationship with the Father and the Son." These verses present strong evidence that the Spirit is not "just the 'power' or 'force' of God at work in the world" *(ibid.)*, but rather a distinct person of the Godhead.

The second thing to notice about the "coordinate relationship" of the Spirit with the Father and the Son (in 2 Cor. 13:14) is that it associates the Holy Spirit with "communion" (NKJV), or "fellowship" (NIV). This word, directly descriptive of the workings of the Spirit, strongly suggests interpersonal communications between relational beings—that is, personal beings, whether they be human, angelic, or divine.

Not only does the passage support the personality of the Spirit, but it also suggests the profound unity or oneness inherent in the doctrine of the Trinity. Here are three divine beings lined up together in such a way as to point to Their oneness of purpose in imparting grace and love to God's people through Their deep fellowship with one another and the redeemed.

Furthermore, it seems to be an almost unconscious expression of the Spirit's personality for Paul to conclude his second letter to the Corinthians with a farewell greeting that simply links the work of the Father, the Son, and the Spirit together as a fully united personal force for the redemption of lost humanity. The verse is a transitional passage to further biblical evidence for the full deity of the Spirit and the profound unity found within the Godhead.

The Full Deity of the Spirit

In the first chapter we suggested that Acts 5 provides persuasive evidence for the deity of the Spirit. Peter told Ananias that he had lied to the Holy Spirit (Acts 5:3) and then explained, "You have not lied to men but to God" (verse 4), strongly implying that Ananias had directly made falsehoods to God the Holy Spirit, not to God the Father or God the Son.

Furthermore, the passages that speak of a strong coordinate relationship between the Father, the Son, and the Spirit not only suggest the personality of the Spirit, but also the deity of the Spirit (Matt. 28:19; 2 Cor. 13:14; 1 Cor. 12:4-6; Eph. 4:4-6, etc.). In other words, they "assume significance for the doctrine of the Holy Spirit, because they show that the Holy Spirit is classified on an equal level with the Father and the Son" as a divine person (*ibid.,* p. 237). To suggest that the Holy Spirit is a created being or impersonal force would appear entirely inappropriate when Scripture repeatedly places the Holy Spirit in such an equally coordinate position with the Father and the Son. There is, however, further Bible evidence for the full deity of the Spirit.

Psalm 139:7, 8 asks, "Where can I go from Your Spirit? Or where can I flee from Your presence? If I ascend into heaven, You are there; if I make my bed in hell, behold, You are there." Once again, we have a passage addressed to the Lord (YHWH), and the psalmist attributes to God's Spirit the uniquely divine characteristic of omnipresence—something not characteristic of created powers or beings.

Once again, we find Grudem helpful: "It seems that David is equating God's Spirit with God's presence. To go from God's Spirit is to go from his presence, but if there is nowhere that David can flee from God's Spirit, then he knows that wherever he goes he will say, 'You [Lord] are there' " *(ibid.).*

Along the same line, 1 Corinthians 2:10, 11 attributes another unique characteristic of deity to the Holy Spirit—omniscience: "For the Spirit searches all things, yes, the deep things of God. For what man knows the things of a man except the spirit of the man which is in him? Even so no one knows the things of God except the Spirit of God." Does not the ability to explore "the deep things of God" and to know "the things of God" strongly imply omniscience?

Another striking evidence of the Spirit's deity is that Scripture portrays the Spirit as the author of the new birth. Yet the work of giving new spiritual life is an act unique to God. First John 3:9 speaks of being "born of God." Thus the new birth, accomplished by the Spirit, Scripture elsewhere also described as being wrought out by God—strongly implying the work of the new birth is the act of a divine being.

The Oneness or Personal Triunity of the Godhead

In chapter 1 we suggested some important evidence for the profound oneness of the tripersonal Godhead. The use of the inherently plural word *'echad* in Deuteronomy 6:4, the singular "name" employed to describe the Father, Son, and Holy Spirit in Matthew 28:19, and the plural "Let *Us* make man in *Our* image" of Genesis 1:26 all powerfully suggest the deep unity manifest among the divine persons of the Godhead. This language unmistakably has God speaking of Himself with plural references. What is interesting is the way this kind of evidence shows up in other places in the Old Testament.

In addition to the "let Us make man in Our image" terminology of Genesis 1:26, we encounter similar plural God language in the following passages:

1. Referring to the sin of Adam and Eve, "the Lord God said, 'Behold, the man has become like one of *Us,* to know good and evil'" (Gen. 3:22). 2. In the story of the great sin of the people at the Tower of Babel, God said, "Come, let *Us* go down and there confuse their language" (Gen. 11:7). 3. Isaiah 6 records a remarkable vision in which the prophet saw "the Lord sitting on a throne, high and lifted up" (verse 1). During it Isaiah reports hearing "the voice of the Lord saying: 'Whom shall I send, and who will go for *Us?*'" (verse 8). While none of them are coercive, their cumulative force provides interesting evidence from the Old Testament for the plurality of persons within the Godhead.

Summary

We are not finished presenting the Bible evidence. But let me ask you this: Is what we presented in these first four chapters sufficient enough to make even the most noble of the Bereans inclined to some sort of tripersonal understanding of the Godhead?

Maybe you are still not convinced. If so, I beg you to stay with me for at least a couple more chapters. The next chapter will address the Trinitarian evidences found in the book of Revelation, then the final two chapters of this first section will deal with the passages that the anti-Trinitarians have traditionally regarded as evidence for their position. Let's now turn to the great visions of John the revelator.

---

* Unless otherwise noted, biblical citations in this chapter are from the New King James Version.

Chapter 5

TRINITARIAN EVIDENCES IN THE BOOK OF REVELATION

It is the conviction of the authors of this book that no study of the Godhead would be complete for Seventh-day Adventists without giving careful attention to the book of Revelation.[1]

This great visionary book, along with Daniel in the Old Testament, has provided the compelling, prophetic framework for Adventism's mission to the world. We have found special significance in the great scenes portrayed throughout the book, especially chapters 11 through 14, which have always stood out as especially significant.

The question that now confronts us is this: Is there a trinitarian theme undergirding the prophetic panoramas of this climactic Bible book in which "all the books of the Bible meet and end" (White, *The Acts of the Apostles,* p. 585)?

As the Adventist experience with the Revelation has unfolded, it has become more and more apparent that the heart of this fascinating book occurs in chapters 11 through 14. Furthermore, one of the really striking things about these chapters is the way the conflict between the forces of good and evil comes down to a struggle between the divine Godhead (Father, Son, and Holy Spirit) and Their satanic imitations (the dragon, the beast, and the false prophet).

What is becoming more and more clear to the best commentators (both lay and scholarly) on the book of Revelation is that the dragon is a counterfeit parody of the Father; the leopardlike beast seeks to supplant and parody the work of the Son; and the false prophet is Satan's deceptive version of the workings of the Holy Spirit (Paulien, pp. 105-150).

Now if these observations have any truth to them, it just makes sense that the book of Revelation would contain, as one of its key themes, strong indications of the profound unity of the true "heavenly Trio," the full deity of Christ, and the personhood of the Spirit. Is there such credible evidence?

While the book of Revelation does not directly address the issue of the Godhead, it definitely appears to have at least a "trinitarian" backdrop (at bare minimum) that may actually be a major theme permeating the revelator's expression of the Godhead. This chapter will present evidence in support of the three major aspects of the Trinitarian concept of God:

(1) the Godhead manifest as a personal and profoundly united threesome,

(2) the full deity of Christ, and

(3) the personhood of the Holy Spirit.

The most obvious evidence comes from chapters 1-5, 21, and 22.

Evidences From Chapters 1-3

We find the Trinitarian nature of the God of the Apocalypse immediately suggested in the introduction to the book. Revelation 1:4, 5 declares the entire vision to be "from Him who is and who was and who is to come, and from the seven Spirits who are before His throne, and from Jesus Christ."[2] Clearly the passage has the Father, Spirit, and Son in focus. It is straightforward in introducing a heavenly Threesome. While the reference to "Jesus Christ" is undeniable, the expressions "seven Spirits" and "Him who is and who was and who is to come" merit some further comment.

The most obvious reasons the book presents the Holy Spirit as the "seven Spirits" has to do with:

1. The symbolic significance of numbers (technically known as numerology) in the book. Seven, along with 12, 3, 4, and 8, are the most striking. Seven, however, is the most prominent and most likely represents the completeness, or perfecting and creative power of God.[3]

2. The implication that the Spirit speaks and is available to all of the seven churches.

3. The Spirit's involvement in the providences of God working through the numerous series of seven in the book—seven churches (Rev. 2:1–3:22), seals (Rev. 6:1–8:1), trumpets (Rev. 8:6–11:15), thunders (Rev. 10:2-4), signs (Rev. 12:1–14:20), and plagues (Rev. 15:1–16:21).[4]

The title given to the Father, however, is a bit more complex. Revelation 1:8 calls the same being "who is and who was and who is to come" also "the Alpha and the Omega, the Beginning and the End," "the Lord," and "the Almighty." Who is this "Lord" of verse 8? Is He the Father or the Son?

It is important to note that Revelation never applies the expressions "Him who is and who was and who is to come" and "the Almighty"[5] explicitly to Jesus (cf. Rev. 4:8; 11:15, 17; 16:5, 7).[6] This is rather strong, implicit evidence that the one called "Him who is and who was and who is to come" (NJKV) in Revelation 1:4 refers neither to the Son nor the Spirit, but exclusively to God the Father.

As already noted in chapter 1 of this book, it is very instructive that the title "the First and the Last" used in succeeding verses (Rev. 1:10-13, 17, 18) is very similar to the title "Alpha and Omega" and that Revelation applies it to Jesus. Furthermore, we also noted that in Revelation 22:12, 13 Jesus directly appropriates the expression "the Alpha and the Omega, the Beginning and the End" to Himself (in addition to the title "the First and the Last"). This use of these titles, along with the fact that "the First and the Last" terminology derives from a description of Yahweh Lord in Isaiah 44:6, provides strong evidence of the full equality and oneness of the Father and the Son as the coeternal rulers of the universe.

Furthermore, such a seemingly easy equation of the identity of the Old Testament God with the Jesus of the New Testament offers stunning evidence for the almost unconscious and spontaneous reckoning of many of the Father's characteristics to the Son. It is a striking phenomenon in Scripture that presents a constant source of consternation for the Arians.[7]

While the evidence for the divine unity of the Godhead and the full deity of the Son is especially compelling in the Apocalypse, suggestions for the personhood of the Spirit, while not as convincing, are still suggestive.

The initial evidence appears in the letters to the seven churches. Each letter concludes with the same exhortation: "He who has an ear, let him hear what the Spirit says to the churches" (Rev. 2:7, 11, 17, 29 and 3:6, 13, 22). Scripture almost always associates speech in the context of spoken messages with communication taking place between persons. Thus the Spirit's speaking to the churches suggests the personhood of the Spirit.[8]

Evidence From Chapters 4 and 5

These chapters contain the most dramatic (and possibly compelling) evidence for a Trinitarian theme in the book of Revelation (implicit at the very least, if not explicit).

Ranko Stefanovic has persuasively argued that the best way to understand these chapters is to see them as portraying the enthronement of Christ as king at the time of the day of Pentecost in Acts 2 (Stefanovic, pp. 1-8 and 292-301). This striking vision draws on the imagery of the inaugural ceremony of the kings of Israel. It invested the king with covenant authority by virtue of the fact that he held the law of Moses (the covenant book) in his right hand.

The thrust of all this seems to indicate (in Revelation 4 and 5) that the covenant privileges of the people of God are being restored through the rule of the triune God who reigns not only by virtue of the creative power of the Father (Rev. 4:11), but through the redemptive exploits of the "Lion of the tribe of Judah, the Root of David" (Rev. 5:5) who has become a bloodied, sacrificial Lamb (verse 6).

Chapter 4

This stunning and comprehensive vision of the heavenly enthronement scene unfolds in the kind of Trinitarian manifestation so reflective of the early church's growing convictions of the eternity and triune oneness of the God of Israel. Without doubt the central figure of chapter 4, called the "One [who] sat on the throne" (verse 2) and who is worshiped as "Lord God Almighty, who was and is and is to come!" (verse 8), is God the Father.

The titles in Revelation 4:2 and 8 are clearly consistent with the scene given in Revelation 1:4, 8. Once more we should point out that while Jesus shares the title the "First and the Last" with the Father in chapter 1, the book of Revelation never calls Him the "Almighty" or the One "who was and is and is to come!" (Rev. 4:8).

Furthermore, we should note that before the throne (and closely associated with the 24 elders of verse 4 and the four living creatures of verses 6-8) are the "seven lamps of fire [which were] burning before the throne, which are the seven Spirits of God" (verse 5). This scene, which vividly portrays the close association of the seven Spirits with the 24 elders and the "four living creatures," strongly implies that the Holy Spirit is the inspiring catalyst that prompts the hymns of praise found in verses 8 and 11.

This vision of the Spirit is consistent with the later Trinitarian convictions of the church that the Spirit has willingly subjected Himself to the Father (and the Son) to proceed forth from Them and to inspire the intelligent beings of the universe to acknowledge the "worthiness" of the Father as the Almighty Creator-Lord. But the Spirit, however, is not merely content to prompt hymns of adulation to the Father. Scripture also presents Him as profoundly bound up with the Son in His work as the chief agent of redemption—the Lion/Lamb of Revelation 5.

Chapter 5

We can safely conclude that (1) Revelation 5 is a continuation of the vision begun in chapter 4 and that (2) the Son is the key figure in focus as this great covenantal/inaugural scene reaches its climax.[9] Revelation portrays the kingly facet of the Son's person through the imagery of the lion (verse 5), yet the key imagery that leads to the great hymns of worship in this chapter (verses 9, 10, 12, 13) has to do with the scene presenting the Son as the atoning sacrificial lamb (verses 6, 9-12).

A number of Trinitarian features of the vision catch our attention. First of all, we should observe that the "seven Spirits," previously pictured as "seven lamps of fire burning before the throne" (Rev. 4:5), Revelation 5 now envisions as the "seven eyes" of the slain Lamb and calls them the "seven Spirits of God sent out into all the earth" (verse 6).[10]

Such a close identity of the Spirit with the Son is quite consistent with the broader teachings of John regarding the relationship between the Son and the Spirit outlined in the fourth Gospel (especially chapters 14-17). The Spirit reaches out to enlighten the whole world. He is the One who "will glorify Me [the Son], for He will take of what is Mine and declare it to you" (John 16:14).

Thus it seems fair to conclude that the vision of Revelation 5 seeks to teach us that the sacrificially redemptive exploits of the Lion/Lamb enable the Spirit to send with convicting power a laser beam of spiritual and redemptive light "into all the earth" (verse 6).

Second, while heaven finds the Lion/Lamb worthy to open the sealed book held in the hand of the Father because the Son has been slain, He is worthy to be slain only because He is the Son (the passage does not identify Him as such, but we recall Jesus Christ from earlier in the book, and we know He and the Lion/Lamb are one and the same). No mere human being could die as a ransom for many (Matt. 20:28). Only God could pay the price required for breaking His laws. But the Father, who had not become incarnate, could not die this death. Thus the Son took human flesh, indivisibly human and God, so God—the Son—could become the sacrificial Lamb and pay the cost.

Israel had forfeited the covenant privileges of the kingdom through its unfaithfulness, but the slain Lamb, sent as the Father's coruler Lion/Lamb, brings about salvation and covenant restoration.[11]

Third, we see the equality of the "Lord God Almighty" of Revelation 4 and the Lion/Lamb of chapter 5 strongly suggested by the fact that the worship of the Lord God Almighty by the 24 elders and the four living creatures in chapter 4 (verses 8, 9) now (in chapter 5) expands to both "Him who sits on the throne" [the "Lord

God Almighty"—the Father] *and* to the Lamb (verse 13).

The whole matter of worship merits further explanation. Repeatedly the book of Revelation associates acts of worship by creatures ("living creatures" [Rev. 4:9; 5:8], "the twenty-four elders" [4:10; 5:14], and John the revelator [19:10; 22:8, 9]) with "falling down" before the subjects of their adoration. In chapters 4 and 5 not only do worshiping creatures fall down before the "Lord God Almighty" who "sits on the throne" and "created all things" (Rev. 4:8, 9, 11; 5:14), but they also fall down "before the Lamb" (Rev. 5:8).

What should we make of such acts of worship? Are not such scenes clear-cut evidence that Jesus the "Lamb" receives the same sort of worship as the Father? Can we not then conclude that such worship is powerful evidence of Christ's full deity?

Furthermore, such a conclusion becomes even more convincing when we compare the scenes of worship in Revelation 4 and 5 with those in Revelation 19:10 and 22:8, 9. In both of the latter passages John the revelator finds himself so overwhelmed by the visions he receives that he falls down before the feet of an angel "to worship him" (Rev. 19:10; "I fell down to worship before the feet of the angel" [Rev. 22:8]). Now carefully observe that each time that John does this the angel rebukes him and commands him to "worship God" (Rev. 19:10; 22:9). What can we conclude from such scenes?

If the Lamb in Revelation 5 is only an angel or a created god, would it not have been idolatrous for Him to receive worship? Of course it would have been! But we see no such rebuke given to the "four living creatures" and the "twenty-four elders" as made to John. The contrasts between the acts of prostrating worship manifest in Revelation 4 and 5 and the same acts of obeisance in 19:10 and 22:8, 9 strongly suggest the full deity of the Lamb.

Maybe we could sum it up this way—Revelation clearly regards the "Lion/Lamb" Son of God, along with God Almighty (the Father), as legitimate objects of heavenly worship. If Christ is not God, then we have idolatry. If He is some sort of semigod, then we have a case of polytheism. The anti-Trinitarians must decide if Jesus is fully God or simply some sort of semitranscendent demigod. If He is fully God, then the worship is perfectly acceptable. But if He is not, then the only two alternatives are that we have either idolatry or polytheism (both censured in Scripture).

Fourth, not only do the 24 elders and the four living creatures offer praise and adulation, but Revelation 5 now amplifies and expands this transcendent scene of heavenly worship with the praises of "ten thousand times ten thousand, and thousands of thousands" of angels (verse 11) and "every creature" in heaven and earth (verse 13)—all directed both to "Him who sits on the throne, and to the Lamb" (verse 13).

As the implications of the redemptive exploits of the slain Lamb become apparent to all the orders of the created beings of the universe, we observe a seemingly spontaneous manifestation of worship indiscriminately directed to the Father and the Son. Needless to say, it offers powerful evidence of Their profound equality as divine corulers of the restored kingdom. Yet we find still more implications in these scenes of worship.

Fifth, the most compelling evidence for the equality of the Father and the Son appears in the hymns of chapters 4 and 5. As previously pointed out, the hymns contained in Revelation 4:8 and 11 focus on the Father, the "Lord God Almighty." The first two hymns of chapter 5 praise the Son (verses 9, 10, 12) and the final hymn glorifies both the Father and the Son (verse 13). We should carefully note that the hymn of verse 12 addresses the Son, and the final hymn of verse 13 has as its object both the Father and the Son.

What is truly compelling, though, is that both of the last two hymns assign characteristics to the Son that chapter 4 attributed to the Father. Though a bit repetitious, carefully observe how the hymns used the various expressions.

First, verse 12 deems the "Lamb" "worthy" "to receive power and riches and wisdom, and strength and honor and glory and blessing." In verse 13, however, the final hymn attributes to both the Father and the Son many of the same characteristics or privileges addressed to the Son in verse 12—especially "blessing and honor and glory and power," descriptive terms previously associated with the Father in Revelation 4:11.

J. Ramsey Michaels has forcefully expressed the implications of these "paean[s] of praise." Initially commenting on Revelation 5:12, Michaels says: "Again it is the Lamb that is worshiped, but what he 'receives' is now more than the sealed scroll. To him are ascribed the very predicates (glory, honor, and power) which in 4:11 were reserved for God himself. Indeed the list has more than doubled in length. God and the Lamb are the recipients of precisely the same kind of homage from the heavenly court.

"This equality between God and Christ reaches a crescendo in the fourth and last hymn, a paean of praise from 'every creature in heaven and on earth and under the earth and in the sea, even all things that are in them.' . . . Thus, using the vocabulary of worship rather than of speculative thought, the Book of Revelation has succeeded in elevating the familiar Davidic Messiah to the level of deity" (Barker, p. 367).

The compelling evidence just presented for the full equality of the Father and the Son is the most forceful indication in the book of Revelation for the full deity of Jesus Christ. If Jesus has all of the "predicates" (or characteristics) and royal prerogatives of the Father, then the full deity of the Father must be the full deity of the Son.

While the evidence for the full deity of Christ is strongest in these chapters, we also find indications of the personhood of the Spirit, though in less dramatic form. In chapter 5 the "seven Spirits" become the "seven eyes" of the Lamb "sent out into all the earth" (verse 6). Scripture most often associates eyes with personal intelligence, and thus the imagery provides some suggestive evidence for the reality of the Spirit as a personality.

Evidences From Chapters 21 and 22

In Revelation 21:1-6 we witness one of the most touching scenes of the entire book. The "first earth had passed away" and "a new heaven and a new earth" had come forth with their "New Jerusalem" capital. The One "who is and who was and who is to come" (Rev. 1:4 and 4:8) has now literally "come" to the earth with the New Jerusalem and dwells with His people. The verses undoubtedly refer to the Father God, whom Scripture portrays as doing the fatherly thing—wiping "away every tear from their eyes" (Rev. 21:4). His very comforting presence seems to have completely banished death, sorrow, crying, and pain.

Furthermore, we will catch many insights when we compare Revelation 21:1-6 with Revelation 7:9, 17. Revelation 21 depicts the "great multitude" of the redeemed as standing before the throne and "the Lamb who is in the midst of the throne will shepherd them and lead them to living fountains of waters. And God will wipe away every tear from their eyes." Here the vision portrays the close working relationship between the Father and the Son in comforting the redeemed after their pilgrimage through the kingdom of the devil and sin. At the very least it suggests the profound "oneness" in purpose of the first two members of the Godhead.

Then Revelation 21:22, 23 presents a vision of Their profound oneness. As he described the glorious New Jerusalem, John "saw no temple in it, for the Lord God Almighty and the Lamb are its temple." Here we find the oneness of the Godhead portrayed primarily through the imagery of the temple. The Old Testament Temple finds its antitypical significance coming to culmination with the compelling suggestion that all the temple imagery ultimately points to the triumph of redemption through the united efforts of the Father and the Son.

Not only do the united Father and Son displace the temple, but Revelation now envisions Them as bringing to completion Their full triumph over the forces of evil and sin. In the Pentecost coronation scene of Revelation 5 the vision climaxes with the worship of "every creature" directed to "Him who sits on the throne [the Father], and to the Lamb" (verse 13).

However, this theme of the throne reaches its fullest climax in Revelation 22:1-3. For the first time the book calls the throne "the throne of God and of the Lamb." Now it is explicit: the Father and the Son are full corulers, both seated on the throne sharing all of the covenant prerogatives secured through Their common redemptive efforts (achieved through Their vanquishing of the usurping forces of evil and restoring the covenant blessings of the redeemed).[12]

The vision of the corulership of the Father and the Son is the final piece of compelling evidence for Christ's full deity. Clearly the Son shares not only the titles "Alpha and Omega, the Beginning and the End," but also all of the royal prerogatives of the eternal Father on the throne of the universe. Such royal titles and the rights and powers of a shared but equal rulership strongly suggest that the full and eternally divine nature of the Father is also the very same essential nature of the Son. In the climactic scene of the entire book the Father and the Son are one and equal. What Scripture can say about the nature and the authority of the one can be said of the other.

Quite obviously the enthroned Father and Son are the focus in these chapters, but is the Holy Spirit completely absent? Is the Spirit in this scene of glorious triumph? Once again we observe the Spirit doing the two things in this setting typical of the redemptive functions He has exercised all along:

1. He is drawing lost humanity back into covenant relationship with the Godhead, especially as He works through "the bride," the church in its gospel mission. "And the Spirit and the bride say, 'Come!' And let him who hears say, 'Come!'" (Rev. 22:17).

2. The Spirit works, but He does so from the throne of the Father and the Son. Is it going too far to suggest that the "river . . . of life" proceeding from the throne (verse 1) represents the life-giving power of the Spirit who bestows the grace of God on a world in desperate need of restoration? We have both biblical and Jewish literary evidence for identifying the "river of life" with the Holy Spirit.[13]

Biblical Evidence

Just about every commentator has noted that the "river of life" imagery of Revelation 22:1 derives primarily from Ezekiel 47:1-12 and Zechariah 14:8-11. Ezekiel 47:1-12 records a vision of water issuing from the portal of the Temple in Jerusalem.[14] Using the interpretive principle of the analogy of Scripture (comparing scripture with scripture, the clearer shedding light on the more obscure), Keil states the case for a figurative interpretation of the water:

" 'Water,' which renders the unfruitful land fertile, and supplies refreshing drink to the thirsty, is used in Scripture as a figure denoting blessing and salvation, which had been represented even in Paradise in the form of watering (cf. Gen. xiii.10) . . . Where the *blessing* answers to the water, the Spirit is named as the principal form in which the blessing is manifested, 'the foundation of all other salvation for the people of God' " (Keil and Delitzsch, p. 360).

Furthermore, Ezekiel 36:24-27 speaks of the sprinkling of "clean water." The passage closely identifies this cleansing water with the Spirit placed within the stony flesh that creates a "heart of flesh" in full conformity with God's "statutes."

The vision of the "day of the Lord" in Zechariah 14:8-11 echoes Ezekiel 47, with "living waters" flowing from Jerusalem. The waters flow both toward the Dead and the Mediterranean seas and have a restorative effect on the "land" and the city of Jerusalem. The same principle of analogy that applies to Ezekiel 47 would also illuminate this passage.

As for the New Testament evidence for water being emblematic of the Spirit, it is interesting that the most persuasive cross-references appear in the writings of John. He clearly associates water with the workings of the Holy Spirit (see John 7:37-39 and compare with 3:5, 4:10-14, and 1 John 5:8-10). The clearest reference is John 7:37-39: " 'He who believes in Me, as the Scripture has said, out of his heart will flow rivers of living water.' But this He spoke concerning the Spirit" (verses 38, 39).

If one concedes the common authorship of the fourth Gospel and the book of Revelation, the interpretation of the "river of life" as the Holy Spirit proceeding from the throne becomes even more appealing.

While the evidence for understanding the "river . . . of life" pictured in Revelation 22:1, 2 as symbolizing the Holy Spirit is not absolute, we must emphasize that this scene is fully in line with the Trinitarian claims of the church and the thrust of Scripture that the Spirit gladly works redemptively with the Father and the Son.[15]

Summary

The evidence for the oneness and the equality of the Father and the Son and the close association of the Spirit with them is quite compelling and strongly suggests that one of the great permeating themes of the Apocalypse is the triune nature of the Godhead. Certainly the evidence for the divine unity of the Three and the full deity of Christ is more extensive than that given for the personhood and full deity of the Holy Spirit. But the close association of the Spirit with the Father and the Son in these three major settings (chapters 1-3, 4 and 5, and 21 and 22) and the trappings of personhood ascribed to the Spirit (speaking and intelligent, personal eyes) provide credible evidence of the Spirit's full deity and personality.

ENDNOTES

[1] This chapter is a condensed, slightly edited version of an article by Woodrow Whidden entitled "Trinitarian Evidences in the Apocalypse" and published in the *Journal of the Adventist Theological Society* 11, Nos 1, 2 (2000): 248-260.

[2] Unless otherwise noted, biblical citations in this chapter are from the New King James Version.

[3] See the perceptive discussion of numerology in the book of Revelation by G. K. Beale, *The Book of Revelation: A Commentary on the Greek Text,* pp. 58-64.

[4] While many of the older commentaries interpret the "seven spirits" as referring to the Holy Spirit, a difference of opinion appears between the two latest magisterial commentaries on the Revelation. David Aune, *Word Biblical Commentary: Revelation 1-5,* provides an excellent summation of the positions of the major ancient and modern commentaries (vol. 52, pp. 33, 34) and goes on to clearly deny the position of the older commentaries. He suggests that they refer to "the seven principal angels of God" (p. 34). In contrast to Aune, G. K. Beale interprets them as "a figurative designation of the effective working of the Holy Spirit" (Beale, p. 189).

[5] While it is true that Revelation never refers to Jesus as the "Almighty," the following passages strongly suggest that He also bears this divine title: compare Genesis 17:1 and 35:11 with Exodus 6:2, 3 and 3:6, 13-15. When we place these passages with John 8:58, it becomes clear that the Lord God of the Old Testament applies to the Jesus of the New Testament and this "Lord" who is Jesus calls Himself "God Almighty." Furthermore, Revelation 5:6 describes Christ as a Lamb having "seven horns." In the book of Revelation "horns" symbolize ruling power and "seven" denotes fullness, perfection, or completeness. Thus the "seven horns" of the Lamb in Revelation 5:6 strongly suggest fullness of the might and power that inheres in the deity of Christ.

[6] We should carefully note that in Revelation 11:17 the expression "who is and who was and who is to come" (NKJV) should, according to the best manuscript evidence, not have the phrase "who is to come." The NIV reflects this manuscript evidence: "We give thanks to you, Lord God Almighty, the One who is and who was." Stefanovic suggests that

the reason for this is that the scene here depicted is one in which the Father has come—"The kingdom of the world has become the kingdom of our Lord and of his Christ" (verse 15, NIV).

[7] Compare this usage in Revelation 1 with Hebrews 1:10-12, in which the author of the book of Hebrews easily applies to Jesus a psalm (Ps. 102:1, 25-27) originally directed to the Lord (Yahweh). It offers strong evidence that, in the mind of the biblical author, the Christ of the New Covenant is the Yahweh of the Old Testament.

[8] Similar instances of the Spirit speaking occur in Revelation 14:13 and 22:17.

[9] See Aune, pp. 329-338, and Beale, pp. 337, 340-348.

[10] Once again, we find evidence of the Feast of Pentecost setting of chapter 5 as the moment in redemptive history when Christ is enthroned as spiritual Israel's king. One of the powerful effects of this enthronement is that the Spirit of God is "sent out into all the earth" (verse 6); this phrase is absent in Revelation 1:4 and 4:5, strongly implying that the moment of enthronement was not to be portrayed until Revelation 5:6.

[11] On the identity of the scroll, see Beale, pp. 339-342.

[12] Stefanovic suggests that *until* this scene in the book, Christ has subordinated Himself to the Father. Now, however, with the full triumph of the gospel of the true Trinity over the false gospel of the counterfeit one, Christ is no longer subordinated to the Father (suggestions shared in personal conversations, to be published in a forthcoming commentary).

[13] The earliest major modern commentator to take this position was H. B. Swete (pp. 294-300).

[14] Compare the passage with Joel 3:18: "a spring will go out from the house of the Lord" (NASB).

[15] Beale seems to be somewhat attracted to this interpretation and his conclusions are appealing: "If the waters symbolize the Spirit, as in the similar portrayal in John 7:37-39, then Rev. 22:1 is an early picture of the later Christian confession that the Spirit proceeds from the Father and the Son. . . . As in Ezekiel 47, the living water flows from the temple, though now God and the Lamb are the temple (21:22). Though the Holy Spirit may be in mind, the water metaphor primarily represents the life of eternal fellowship with God and Christ, which is borne out by the way 22:3-5 develops 22:1, 2" (Beale, p. 1104).

Chapter 6

BIBLICAL OBJECTIONS TO THE TRINITY

While the evidence presented in the first five chapters seems quite appealing to us, we are well aware of a number of biblical passages that others have traditionally used as evidence against the Trinitarian position. In addition, many have rejected the Trinity doctrine on the grounds that it is logically incoherent. In this chapter, and its supplement, we will address the major texts used by the anti-Trinitarians. The following chapter will deal with the charge that the Trinity doctrine lacks logical coherence.

Of the biblical passages normally cited to disprove the Trinity, Arians and others employ the vast majority to discredit the teaching of the eternal deity of Christ. We must not duck or lightly pass over such passages. Any truth that claims to be biblical should be able to stand in the face of all the inspired evidence, even those passages that appear to contradict the majority view. If the contradictory data is compelling, maybe the alleged "truth" needs to be seriously modified or even given up. And no one should be fearful of making such a move, if indeed any belief—including the Trinity—should turn out to be unbiblical.

In fact, giving up doctrines that finally reveal themselves to be unbiblical can be a highly liberating experience. My own mother had given up on God and the Bible because of the doctrine of the eternal, conscious torment of the lost. It was not until the witness of Bible-believing Adventist Christians showed her what Scripture really teaches that she was able to think more clearly about God as love and the Bible as a love letter from Him. It was only when she realized that the doctrine of conscious, unending torture in hell was neither biblical nor consistent with God's character of love and justice that she was able to consider the possibility that God loved her personally.

The question before us now is this: Is there sufficient evidence in the Bible that might compel us to give up the doctrine of the Trinity as unworthy of the God of the Bible?

The Key Bible Passages Cited by Anti-Trinitarians

When one boils down the Bible evidence, only a relatively few passages appear at first glance in any way damaging to the Trinitarian position. What follows are the most often cited: John 3:16; Colossians 1:15; Hebrews 1:6; 5:5-10; John 17:3; 1 Corinthians 8:6; 1 Timothy 2:5, 6; 1 Corinthians 15:24-28; and Revelation 3:14 from the New Testament and Proverbs 8:22 from the Old Testament.

What follows will be an in-depth treatment of the first five texts. The last four we will examine in the supplement to this chapter. We have supplied the supplement for those who want a more extensive and exhaustive treatment of the contrary evidence.[1]

Some Preliminary Observations

We will give special attention to each of the above passages. Before we begin, however, it might prove helpful to get some basic perspective about Jesus. Always we should keep in mind that the Bible clearly teaches that He is a being with a dual nature. While Scripture calls Him God (John 1:1) and addresses Him as "O God" (Heb. 1:8),[2] the same Bible also declares that "the Word became flesh" (John 1:14) and describes Him as "the Man Christ Jesus" (1 Tim. 2:5).

In other words, when considering any text referring to Jesus it may prove helpful to ask whether the passage has in mind His deity or His incarnate humanity. Max Hatton puts it in a slightly different way. "Does [any particular] verse apply to the *nature* of Christ? Or, does it apply to His *position?*" (Hatton, p. 76). Then he proceeds to make the following sensible observation: "If this rule is applied, a lot of seemingly difficult passages will be seen to provide little cause for concern" *(ibid.)*.

Some passages that seem to point to the position of subordination that Christ takes in relationship to the Father could very well be speaking from the perspective of His incarnate state rather than in His glorified status (either before or after His earthly sojourn in human "flesh").[3]

Another important consideration involves how we interpret the Bible. Here the issue pertains to whether we should interpret some passages literally or whether we may treat them more figuratively. Maybe we could illustrate it this way. While we often refer to Jesus as the Son and frequently call the first person of the Godhead the Father, do we really want to take such expressions in a totally literal way? Or would it be more appropriate to interpret them in a more metaphorical way that draws on selective aspects of sonship and fatherhood?

For instance, if one wants to totally literalize "Father," would this mean that there must be an eternal heavenly "Mother of God" (maybe the Holy Spirit)?

Another illustration or two should clarify the point. One anti-Trinitarian has accused Trinitarians of denying that Jesus is a "true" Son of God (he means literal), since they reject the idea that the Son was literally generated as a divine being (called Son) by God the Father. Of course he uses "generate" to mean to beget a son in the same sense that earthly fathers procreate. But if we employed the same type of literal interpretation, since Jesus in John 15:1 clearly claims that He is the "true vine," must we then literally understand Jesus to be a grapevine? Most obviously, Jesus is here speaking figuratively or illustratively. Could it be the same case with the expressions "Father" and "Son"?

John 3:16

This, the most beloved of all memory verses, contains the well-known phrase "He [God] gave His only begotten Son." As noted above, the gist of the anti-Trinitarian interpretation of this text claims that God the Father has literally generated, or "begat," a divine being (the Son) sometime in the ages of eternity past as some sort of semidivine person. The Arians teach that it was an act of direct creation. The semi-Arians suggest that Jesus sort of split off from the nature of the Father to form a separate divine person. Thus both groups consider Jesus, the Son, to be an inferior "god," not a true and eternally preexisting being such as the Father. What are we to make of such an interpretation?

First of all, the expression "only begotten" is a translation of the Greek word *monogenes*. The word is a combination of two Greek words: *monos,* meaning "only" or "alone," and *genos,* "kind," or in the more extended sense, "sort," "family," "race," or "nation" (the English word "gene" derives from this Greek word). To put it as succinctly as possible, the word signifies "unique" or "one of a kind."

An illustration from my own family experience might prove helpful. My late brother Donald was the oldest son in our family of five siblings. He was truly a brilliant, colorful, even outrageous personality. People either really liked him or were almost totally repulsed by his singular disposition and expression. I recall our father often describing Donald's "uniqueness." "If I could father sons for another 1,000 years, I would never sire another one like Donald!" he would say. Donald was not the "only" son begotten by our father, but in his father's mind he was certainly the most "unique."

Now, what is the biblical meaning of this important term? Are John and the Bible writers using the term in the strict sense of the analogy of normal human relationships, strongly suggesting a preexistent father literally begetting a son? Is this what the term *monogenes* means?

The word's broader use in the Bible suggests otherwise.

The word *genos* derives from the Greek verb *ginomai,* which means to "come" or "come to be," not from the Greek word *gennao,* to "father" or "beget." Thus the word *monogenes* does not refer to God the Father generating Jesus as His literal, semidivine Son. It rather indicates Jesus' uniqueness as the incarnate Son—the God/man who has "come to be" an in-fleshed human while retaining His fully divine nature as one "equal with God" the Father (John 5:18). Could there be any manifestation in the history of the universe more "unique" than the Creator-God becoming "flesh" (John 1:14)?

How Scripture uses *monogenes* to refer to the uniqueness of a son we see well illustrated in Hebrews 11:17, which calls Isaac Abraham's "only begotten *[monogenes]* son." It is apparent that the author of Hebrews is not trying to literally say that Isaac was Abraham's only, solitary son. The patriarch had other sons, including Ishmael. Most obviously the writer is referring to Isaac as the "unique" son of the promise of God through faith.

But what about the biblical expressions "Father" and "Son"? What do the terms mean if they do not specify a "father" begetting a son?

There are three possible answers:

1. Does "son," as employed in the Bible, refer only to generation or fatherly priority in time, having to do with physical or filial derivation? Or can it have a wider, more figurative, illustrative meaning? Please note the following use of the "son" imagery.

In numerous places in the Bible "son" indicates a person's or grouping's distinguishing character. The Bible refers to the "sons of Zion" (Lam. 4:2), "sons of Belial" (1 Sam. 2:12), "sons of God" (Gen. 6:4), "sons of men" (Eccl. 2:8), "sons of light" (John 12:36), "sons of the prophets" (2 Kings 2:3), "sons of the stranger" (Isa. 56:6), "sons of the alien" (Isa. 61:5), "sons of thunder" (Mark 3:17), and the "sons of disobedience" (Eph. 2:2; 5:6).

Probably the most singular and striking use of this characteristic imagery comes from our Lord when He said to the Jews that "you are of your father the devil" (John 8:44). Now certainly no sane Bible interpreter wants to interpret John 8:44 literally! Most obviously what the Bible seeks to primarily communicate with the imagery of "son" is that it refers to the most characteristic trait or distinctive attribute of a person or group of persons called "son(s)."

2. The imagery of Father also denotes the intimacy of the relationship between the first person of the Godhead with the second person. Such an interpretation is very much evident in the later chapters of John's Gospel, especially in chapter 17.

3. Yet there seems to be something even more telling in the imagery of Father and Son employed in the Gospel of John. Once more, note the following from John 5:17, 18: "But Jesus answered them, 'My Father has been working until now, and I have been working.' Therefore the Jews sought all the more to kill Him, because He not only broke the Sabbath, but also said that God was His Father, making Himself equal with God." In these verses John clearly suggests that the people understood Jesus' claim to have God for "His Father" as a claim of equality with God rather than some sort of subordination of a lesser god to a greater God. Jesus "said that God was His Father, making Himself equal with God."

Furthermore, the succeeding verses strongly suggest an intimacy typical of strong father-son relationships. "Most assuredly, I say to you, the Son can do nothing of Himself, but what He sees the Father do; for whatever He does, the Son also does in like manner. For the Father loves the Son, and shows Him all things that He Himself does" (verses 19, 20).

Far from suggesting that the Father generated or begat the Son as some sort of derived or created semigod, the imagery of Father and Son points to the eternal and profound intimacy that has always existed between the first and second persons of the Godhead as divine "equals" through all eternity (past, present, and future).

Colossians 1:15, 18

Closely related to the expression *monogenes* is the Greek term *prōtotokos*. Translators usually render *prōtotokos* as either "firstborn," or "first-begotten." Note its usage in Colossians 1:15, 18: "He [Christ] is the image of the invisible God, the *firstborn* over all creation." "And He is the head of the body, the church, who is the beginning, the *firstborn* from the dead, that in all things He may have the preeminence."

The usual anti-Trinitarian interpretation claims that the term "firstborn" refers to the Father begetting Jesus as the first being which He "created" at some point in time before the origin of the world. Is such an interpretation intended by the biblical writers' use of the Greek word translated "firstborn" *(prōtotokos)?*

Before we present a fuller explanation of the meaning of "firstborn" in Scripture, Max Hatton offers a couple interesting, preliminary observations. "Let it be said, one cannot be born and created at the same time. . . . Had it been Paul's wish to say that Christ was 'first-created,' he had the word *protoktistos* available. But neither Paul nor any other Bible writer uses this word with reference to Christ" (*ibid.,* p. 91).

What then is the biblical definition of "firstborn"?

While the expression "firstborn" does draw upon the actual historical fact of birthright privileges that belonged to the literal firstborn, the Bible applies, or uses it in reference, to Christ in a nonliteral manner. It has no real reference to Christ's being born or begotten as a "god" deemed to be the first created being in time. Rather, Scripture employs it to indicate the position of privileged honor and dignity, or the preeminence of the firstborn son who receives the "birthright" inheritance. The latter meaning is the main way Bible writers use it. Carefully note the following.

Scripture clearly indicates David's special status among his brothers by calling him the "firstborn" (Ps. 89:20-27). Yet he was not the literal "firstborn." In fact, David was the *youngest* son of his father.

Furthermore, not only does the Bible label individuals as firstborn who were not actually the oldest, but both the Old and New Testaments refer to "Israel . . . my son, even my firstborn" (Ex. 4:22, KJV). In the same vein, the New Testament speaks of members of Christ's church as belonging to the church of the "firstborn" (Heb. 12:23).

What are we to make of such a pattern? Is the Bible telling us that only literal "firstborn" offspring can make up both literal and spiritual Israel? Quite obviously the answer is an emphatic no!

The New Testament employs the term "firstborn" eight times. Of the eight instances, at least two indicate that someone was actually born first. Luke 2:7 seems to speak in a literal manner when it says that Mary "brought forth her firstborn Son," and Hebrews 11:28 refers to "firstborn" Egyptians.

The main use in the New Testament, however, seems to be

figurative, drawing upon the privileges and preeminence of the literal firstborn. Thus Scripture designates redeemed human beings as "the general assembly and church of the firstborn who are registered in heaven" (Heb. 12:23). Obviously the church does not consist only of literally firstborn human beings. The expression "firstborn" emphasizes their preeminent status among the "sons of God."

Both Paul and John also employ this figurative or metaphorical usage of "firstborn" to refer to Christ as "the firstborn from the dead" (Col. 1:18), or "the first begotten of the dead" (Rev. 1:5, KJV). Most certainly neither is trying to convince us that Jesus was the first person ever literally brought back from the dead (God raised Moses and Lazarus before Him, to name just two).

Quite obviously the apostles were seeking to communicate that Christ's resurrection grants Him the privileged status of the "firstborn" in the sense that His victory over death enables Him to "have the preeminence" in "all things" having to do with victory over death and the granting of eternal life.

The figurative or metaphorical use of "firstborn" communicates Christ's "preeminent" authority over death so that "He might be the firstborn among many brethren" (Rom. 8:29).[4] And who are "the brethren" among whom He is the "firstborn"? Obviously they are those that trust Him as the life-giver through the power of His resurrection.

We could illustrate the biblical concept of "firstborn" preeminence this way: while Bill Gates was not the first person to engage in the computer software business, he could justly be called the "firstborn of software" in the sense of his universally recognized and dominant preeminence in the software industry. We could say the same of Michael Jordan as the "firstborn" in the world of basketball, and Mother Hale's preeminence could well be characterized as the "firstborn" of self-sacrificing, motherly care for the tragic crack babies of New York.

In a further application, Paul describes Christ as "the firstborn over all creation" (Col. 1:15). What does the apostle have in mind here? In the same way that Christ, as the "firstborn" from the dead, communicates His preeminence over death, so His being the "firstborn over creation" strongly reveals His preeminence over creation as the Creator of "all things." Such language has nothing to do with Him as the first being ever created.

Paul further communicates Christ's preeminence in creation as Creator by declaring that all things were created "through Him and for Him" and "in Him all things consist" (verses 16, 17). Thus just as the "brethren" can be saved from death only through the preeminence of the "firstborn from the dead," so they can have existence only through the preeminence of the One who is the "firstborn over all creation" (verse 15).

That Christ was not the literal "firstborn son" generated by God the Father we see further supported by the context of Paul's theology of Christ's divinity in Colossians. Right after Paul declares the figurative "firstborn" "preeminence" of Christ "over all creation" and "from the dead," in verse 19 he declares that "it pleased the Father that in Him [Christ] all the fullness should dwell."

The question that immediately jumps out at us is Did Paul mean to indicate that the Father allowed only the "fullness" of a qualified deity (some semidivine quality of nature) to dwell in the incarnate Christ? We find the answer in Colossians 2:9, in which the great apostle clearly declares that in Christ "dwells all the fullness of the Godhead bodily." The reader will recall that in chapter 2 we saw that the word translated "Godhead" is the Greek *theotēs,* which literally means the very essence of divinity, not just its trappings or selected characteristics. And this very essence of divine nature dwells "bodily" in the incarnate Christ, the "firstborn"!

Hebrews 1:5, 6 and 5:5-10

Once more we are dealing with a further use of the expression *prōtotokos* ("firstborn"), only now the biblical author employs it in conjunction with his interpretation of Psalm 2:7 and Christ who is "begotten" by the Father as a "Son." "[Christ] having become so much better than the angels, as He has by inheritance obtained a more excellent name than they. For to which of the angels did He ever say: 'You are My Son, today I have begotten You'? [Ps. 2:7]. . . . But when He again brings the *firstborn* into the world, He says: 'Let all the angels of God worship Him'" (Heb. 1:4-6).

What is the writer of Hebrews seeking to teach in these verses? As we pointed out in chapters 1 and 2 earlier, he is here beginning the key theme of the letter by exalting Christ as the one who is "better." His first "better" comparison contrasts Christ with the angels. As good and great as the angels are, the biblical writer exalts the superiority of Christ by arguing that God never called any angel "Son" or "begotten," nor did He command anyone to worship angels. Rather, the good—but inferior angels—are to "worship" Christ. Thus Christ is quite obviously "better" than the angels.

Therefore, in this context, what are we to make of the fact that God calls Christ "My Son," "begotten" by God, and the "firstborn"?

The anti-Trinitarians are quick to give these terms a very literal interpretation in the sense that Christ is a truly "begotten, firstborn Son" generated by the Father. Thus they conclude that Christ is a "god" of lesser deity and dignity than the eternal Father. But is that what the passage teaches?

Obviously, what is in mind here is not Christ being generated by the Father as a divine being, at best a diminished or semideity. Rather, the writer is presenting Christ as being "begotten" as the "firstborn Son" of God in the Incarnation.

In the literary context of Hebrews 1, Christ is a Son of God in the sense that He, who is the eternal, fully divine Son, has become "begotten" as the "firstborn" in the flesh of humanity so that He might have redemptive preeminence over the "angels" who worship Him. Furthermore, Hebrews calls Christ "begotten" and the "firstborn" in the sense that He, the incarnate God/man, became the "firstborn" of all humans, whom He came to save. Without such a divine/human uniqueness and preeminence over all other humans, we would have no salvation from sin.

Most certainly Paul is not seeking to diminish Christ's deity by proclaiming Him the incarnate God/man. His becoming human in the Incarnation as a "begotten" "firstborn" human Son of God in no way diminishes His eternal and full deity. Once more, the very context of Hebrews 1 precludes such a conclusion.

As pointed out in previous chapters, Hebrews 1 strongly argues for the full deity of the incarnate Son. Hebrews 1:2, 3 declares Christ to be not only (1) the maker of "the worlds," but also (2) the one who is "the brightness of [the Father's] glory," (3) the "express image of His person," and (4) the upholder of all things "by the word of His power." Verse 6 evidences His full deity through the command given to the angels to "worship Him" (Christ). In verse 8 God directly addresses Christ as "O God," whose throne is an eternal seat of power. Verses 10-12 apply to Christ Psalm 102:25-27, a hymn of praise clearly addressed to the Lord of the Old Testament, Yahweh—the eternal, self-existent one. Most certainly the book of Hebrews assumes that the Lord Yahweh of Psalm 102 is none other than the incarnate Christ to whom the angels direct worship and subordinate themselves.

"Begotten" manifests a similar usage in Hebrews 5:5-10: "So also Christ did not glorify Himself to become High Priest, but it was He who said to Him: 'You are My Son, today I have begotten You' [Ps. 2:7]. As He also says in another place: 'you are a priest forever according to the order of Melchizedek' [Ps. 110:4]; who, in the days of His flesh, when He had offered up prayers and supplications, with vehement cries and tears to Him who was able to save Him from death, and was heard because of His godly fear, though He was a Son, yet He learned obedience by the things which He suffered. And having been perfected, He became the author of eternal salvation to all who obey Him, called by God as High Priest 'according to the order of Melchizedek' [Ps. 110:4]."

It is obvious that "begotten" in Hebrews 1:5 refers to Christ's appointment by the Father to the office of high priest of the heavenly sanctuary. Once more the context strongly suggests that Scripture is not using "begotten" in any sense of the Father God generating a Son who is a lesser god, but with the connotation of Christ being made the divine/human high priest.

The author of the book of Hebrews goes to great pains to

demonstrate that not only is Christ the eternal God who is "without father, without mother, without genealogy, having neither beginning of days nor end of life" (Heb. 7:3), but is also fully human in His incarnate experience. It is a combination of both of these essential aspects of His unique person that qualifies Him to be "a priest forever according to the order of Melchizedek" (Heb. 5:6).

Once more, it is the literary context of Hebrews 5:5-10 that provides the clue that Christ is "begotten" in the sense of being made man or incarnate in human flesh. Verse 7 speaks of "the days of His flesh, when He had offered up prayers and supplications, with vehement cries and tears to Him who was able to save Him from death." It is in this sense of total, prayerful dependence and intimate relationship to the Father that Scripture can describe Jesus as a "begotten" "Son" of the Father (verses 5, 8). It clearly portrays a dependent subordination of Christ functioning as the human "Son," not some subordination of Christ's divine nature to that of the Father.

In other words, Scripture terms Jesus as "begotten Son" in the sense of His incarnate humanity and His intimate, dependent relationship to His Father during this period of His human vulnerability. In His humanity He was qualified to be an effectual high priestly intercessor, not only by virtue of His eternally existent divine nature, but also through learning faithful "obedience by the things which He suffered" (verse 8) as a dependent, "begotten" human being. Such obedient suffering "perfected" His humanity so that "He became the author of eternal salvation, . . . called by God as High Priest" (verses 9, 10).

L. E. Froom sums up the point of Hebrews' use of Psalm 2:7 and Christ as God's "begotten Son": " 'This day have I begotten thee' indicates Christ's entrance into human form, with its progressive sequence" of His "incarnate Birth, Baptism, Resurrection, and Priesthood. All are involved in and grow out of His momentous birth in human form, for He returns the second time as the Son of man. . . . That is the larger scope of the intent of Psalm 2:7" (Froom, pp. 308, 309).

The imagery of "begotten," as used in the book of Hebrews, has no reference whatsoever to Christ being generated or "begotten" by God the Father as some sort of lesser god, derived from the substance or essence of the Father's divine nature.

John 17:3

Many often employ this well-known passage—an inspirational call to Christians to seek a deeper knowledge of God—to deny the full deity of Christ: "And this is life eternal, that they may know You, the only true God, and Jesus Christ whom You have sent."

Those opposed to the equality of the Father and the Son claim that Jesus' affirmation that the Father is "the only true God" shows that Christ excludes Himself from being identified with the full deity of the Father. Is this what Jesus was suggesting?

In His great high priestly prayer, it is quite apparent that Jesus is not discussing the relationship of His own divine nature with that of the Father; but "the need for people to recognize the only true God as opposed to idols and other false gods" and "the need for recognition of Himself as the means of salvation" (Hatton, p. 78). Erickson expresses it this way:

"In speaking of the Father as the only genuine (*alēthinos,* the Greek 'true') God, Jesus is contrasting the Father not with the Son, but with the other claimants to deity, the false gods. Indeed, Jesus links himself very closely with the Father here. Eternal life is not only knowing the Father, but also knowing the one whom he has sent, Jesus Christ" (Erickson, *Christian Theology,* p. 714).

Furthermore, the context of the Gospel of John presents us with plenty of evidence for the full deity of Christ. If Jesus is here claiming that the Father is exclusively the only manifestation of the "true God" in the universe, it contradicts Jesus' equality with God the Father so plainly evident in John 1:1, 5:18, 8:58, and 10:30-33. Besides, if the Father is the "only true God" in contrast to Jesus, would it not be logical to conclude that any other person designated as "God" (such as Jesus) would be a false god? This does not appear to be what Jesus is driving at in the context.

1 Corinthians 8:6

We will first cite the larger context of Paul's statement here.

"Therefore concerning the eating of things offered to idols, we know that an idol is nothing in the world, and that there is no other God but one. For even if there are so-called gods, whether in heaven or on earth (as there are many gods and many lords), yet for us there is one God, the Father, of whom are all things, and we for Him; and one Lord Jesus Christ, through whom are all things, and through whom we live" (1 Cor. 8:4-6).

In a manner very similar to their treatment of John 17:3, the anti-Trinitarians use this passage as proof that the Father is the "one God" and since the passage does not explicitly call Jesus the "one God," therefore He is only some lesser, divine Lord. Should we follow the logic of the anti-Trinitarian interpretation, Max Hatton has suggested that we would reach the following troubling conclusion: "If this verse precludes Jesus from being God, because it says only the Father is God, it must also preclude the Father from being Lord because it says that Jesus is the only Lord!" (Hatton, p. 80).

Furthermore, in the context Paul is discussing idols and the issue of whether believers should eat food previously offered to them. The key to understanding the entire passage is to see that verses 5 and 6 are an explanation or further interpretive elaboration of the meaning of the expression in verse 4 that states "There is no other God but one." And who is this one God? Paul answers that we can define this "one God" as "the Father . . . and one Lord Jesus Christ" (verse 6). "If Paul did not think of Jesus as being God, why did he mention Him in this context? Was he trying to prove that only one God exists by demonstrating that he had two?" *(ibid.)*.

Most certainly Paul is not seeking to oppose the deity of the Father to the Son, but contrast the deity of both to the false gods and idols of first-century pagan religion. If the apostle is here denying the full deity of Christ, we have him in clear contradiction of his express claims in Colossians 2:9, in which he says that in Christ all the full essence of deity dwells bodily, and Philippians 2:5, in which he clearly suggests that Christ was "equal with God." Wayne Grudem observes that "1 Cor. 8:6 does not deny that God the Son and God the Holy Spirit are also 'God,' but here Paul says that God the Father is identified as this 'one God.' Elsewhere . . . he can speak of God the Son and God the Holy Spirit as also 'God.' Moreover, in this same verse, he goes on to speak of 'one Lord, Jesus Christ, through whom are all things and through whom we exist.' He is here using the word *Lord* in its full Old Testament sense of 'Yahweh' as a name for God, and saying that this is the person through whom all things were created, thus affirming the full deity of Christ as well, but with a different name. Thus this verse affirms both the unity of God and the diversity of persons in God" (Grudem, p. 239).

Conclusion

We have completed our examination of the passages most often used to discredit the full deity of Christ and the doctrine of the Trinity. For those who want a more exhaustive survey of problematic texts, we urge that you read on in the supplement that immediately follows this chapter.

But for now, we would pose the following questions: Can one really say that the passages studied in this chapter (and the supplement) nullify the abundant evidence presented in the previous five chapters? Is it not quite apparent that the problem texts become problems only when one assumes an exclusively literalistic interpretation of such expression as "Father," "Son," "Firstborn," "Only Begotten," "Begotten," and so forth? Does not such literalism go against the mainly figurative or metaphorical meaning that the Bible writers use when referring to the persons of the Godhead? Can one really say that the Bible writers meant such expressions as "the only true God" and "one God, the Father" to exclude the full deity of the Son, Christ Jesus?

We would humbly suggest that the weight of Bible evidence strongly points to the full and eternal deity of Christ as one in nature, character, and purpose with the Father (and the Holy Spirit). Furthermore, what proves to be quite ironic is that some of the most compelling evidence for the equality of the Father and the Son occurs in contexts that employ the very metaphors of "Father" and "Son" (especially John 5:16-23).

Now, what about the logical objections that the doctrine of the Trinity lacks rational coherence? To this issue we now turn our attention in the next chapter.

Supplement to Chapter 6

OTHER TEXTS USED AGAINST THE TRINITY

1 Timothy 2:5, 6

The first six verses of 1 Timothy 2 give one of the greatest testimonies to the universal scope of God's redemptive purposes. Note the following phrases so familiar to grateful Christians: "God our Savior, who desires all men to be saved" (verses 3, 4) and "the Man Christ Jesus, who gave Himself a ransom for all" (verses 5, 6). Some have used verses 5 and 6, however, to deny the full deity of Christ Jesus: "For there is one God and one Mediator between God and men, the Man Christ Jesus, who gave Himself a ransom for all" (1 Tim. 2:5, 6).

Anti-Trinitarians interpret the passage to mean that since there "is one God" and it calls Jesus "the Man Christ Jesus," therefore Jesus is not fully God, only a human mediator. Most certainly, though, Paul is not excluding Christ as a divine "mediator." In this context, however, Paul would naturally emphasize the human component of being an effectual "Mediator between God and men." Please note carefully that in verses 1, 2, and 8 the apostle is spotlighting the necessity of "supplications, prayers, intercessions . . . for all men" (verse 1) so that "all men" can "be saved" (verse 4). Therefore it should not surprise us that in this setting of the theme of human intercessory prayer for "all men," the mediatorial office of Christ in His humanity would receive the emphasis.

Please recall that in the book of Hebrews this theme of Christ as the mediator and intercessor (as our heavenly high priest) stresses the need for Him to be both fully human and divine. Hebrews 2:14-18 accents the human Christ and Hebrews 7:3—in which Christ (like Melchizedek, who is "made like the Son of God") is declared to be "without father, without mother, without genealogy, having neither beginning of days nor end of life . . . remains a priest continually"—now clearly highlights the divine Jesus.

In 1 Timothy 2, however, Paul, without excluding Christ's deity, uplifts His profound identity with those He mediates for before God. Someone has wisely observed that "being God, Jesus can perfectly represent God to men, and being man He can perfectly represent man to God." Hatton comments that "only by being God can Jesus fully comprehend the claims of God and only by being man can Jesus fully comprehend the needs of men" (Hatton, p. 79).

1 Corinthians 15:24-28

Looking forward to the "kingdom" of "God the Father," Paul describes the final triumphant work of Christ: "Then comes the end, when He [Christ] delivers the kingdom to God the Father, when He puts an end to all rule and all authority and power. For He must reign till He has put all enemies under His feet. The last enemy that will be destroyed is death. For 'He has put all things under His feet' [citation from Ps. 8:6]. But when He says 'all things are put under Him,' it is evident that He who put all things under Him is excepted. Now when all things are made subject to Him, then the Son Himself will also be subject to Him who put all things under Him, that God may be all in all."

Those opposed to the Trinitarian teaching of the equality of the divine nature of the Father and the Son cite this passage to prove that Christ possesses an inferior nature to that of the Father. What should we make of this interpretation?

First of all, it is obvious that we have here some sort of "functional" subordination of Christ to the Father at "the end." Christ is clearly "subject to Him . . . that God may be all in all" (verse 28). The key question, however, is whether this passage teaches that Christ's deity is somehow an inferior, or derived deity, when compared to that of the Father. But it simply does not address this question.

Earlier in this chapter we pointed out that it is important to differentiate between Christ's *nature* and His *position,* or *function,* during His incarnation. It could well be that Paul is here teaching an eternal but functional *position* of subordination by the Son to the Father. Such subordination will most likely be based on the fact that Jesus will forever retain His humanity.

As to why Christ does this, we can only guess. The most likely reason, however, is that our incarnate Lord God will maintain solidarity with humans whom He has purchased with His shed blood for all eternity. Thus Christ will always be subject to the Father in ways quite similar to His subordination to the Father during His earthly sojourn. But this in no way implies that the divine *nature* of Christ is inferior to that of the Father.

Furthermore, this is not the only picture we have of the eternal rule of Christ in relationship to the Father's reign. Revelation 22:1, 3 call the throne of God "the throne of God and of the Lamb." Thus while Paul, in speaking of the Resurrection in 1 Corinthians 15, can picture Christ ("the firstborn from the dead" [Col. 1:18]) as in functional subordination to the Father, yet in Revelation 22:1, 3 the Father and the Son appear to share one throne as fully equal corulers over the everlasting kingdom.

The two passages do not inherently contradict each other. It is just that in 1 Corinthians 15 Paul seeks to communicate Christ's solidarity with the resurrected humans redeemed into the kingdom; whereas John the revelator wants to show that the Father and Son are fully triumphant in the New Jerusalem as coregents of the eternal kingdom. Thus while we find a functional subordination in 1 Corinthians 15, Revelation 22 depicts the full sharing of the rulership in the everlasting kingdom.

Revelation 3:14

The key controverted expression in this opening greeting to the Laodiceans refers to Christ as "the Beginning of the creation of

God." Arians have understood the term "Beginning of the creation" to mean that Christ was the first, or beginning, creature created by God the Father. While a number of reliable versions use these words, the Greek word actually means "origin or source" rather than the first or "beginning" creature of God's creative acts. The Greek word in question is *arche,* and a host of modern versions translate it as "ruler" (NIV) or "origin" (NRSV).

Such contemporary translations reflect the advances made in the study of New Testament Greek during the past century, a progress in understanding reflected in the comments of the widely respected A. T. Robertson: "The beginning of the creation of God" *(he arche tes ktiseos tou theou).* Not the first of creatures as the Arians held . . . but the originating source of creation through whom God works" (cited in Hatton, p. 93). To be extremely clear about the matter, this expression proclaims Jesus as the beginning cause of creation, or the one from whom all created things originate. He is not the first product of God's creative efforts.

Proverbs 8:22

Here is what the passage says: "The Lord possessed me at the beginning of His way, before His works of old." The Arians interpret the verse to mean that Jesus, here personified as wisdom, was created. Many Christian commentators have understood the verse to apply to Jesus. Seventh-day Adventists share in this tradition of interpretation. Is this verse, however, saying that Jesus was "created"?

While it is true that the Hebrew word *qana* (translated as "possessed" in the NKJV) can be rendered as "created," the more basic and common meaning is not to "create," but to be "brought forth" or "possessed" for a special mission of blessing to the world. In other words, Jesus Christ as the "wisdom of God" (1 Cor. 1:24), has been "possessed" by the Lord or "brought forth" to our rebellious and foolish world to manifest God's wisdom and knowledge.

Furthermore, it is quite evident that we cannot translate the word *qana,* in the context of Proverbs 8, as "created," or it would "create" an impossible description of the infinite God: "If *wisdom* was literally created then we arrive at the difficult situation of there being a time when God was without wisdom. Obviously, this cannot be what is intended. . . . To suggest that there was a time when God lacked wisdom . . . is absurd" (*ibid.,* pp. 94, 95). Enough said!

ENDNOTES

[1] Max Hatton, in his recently released book *Understanding the Trinity,* presents a more extensive treatment of texts used against the Trinity and the full deity of Christ. His highly readable paperback is now available in North American Adventist Book Centers. See especially Hatton's chapter 9, "Answers to Objections to the Deity of Christ," pp. 75-98. And his chapter 12 presents his "Answers to Objections to the Personality and Deity of the Holy Spirit," pp. 109-120. As the reader will note, we have drawn on a number of Hatton's observations in the balance of this chapter and its supplement.

[2] Unless otherwise noted, biblical citations in this chapter are from the New King James Version.

[3] One such text is John 14:28 and Jesus' declaration that "I am going to the Father, for My Father is greater than I." If Jesus were some sort of human or derived "god," then Jesus "would have sounded foolish for stating the obvious. There is no doubt that Jesus was referring to His position (not nature) here" (Hatton, p. 77).

[4] A similar expression, "begotten," drawn from Psalm 2:7, appears in the book of Acts and refers to Christ's resurrection. Paul proclaims that God "has raised up Jesus. As it is also written in the second Psalm: 'You are My Son, today I have begotten You'" (Acts 13:33). Clearly Paul employs the word "begotten" in this verse to speak of the Father bringing Christ forth from the grave, not generating Him as a god. We will further discuss Psalm 2:7 later when we examine the way the author of Hebrews (Heb. 1:4-6 and 5:5-10) uses it to indicate Christ's incarnation and qualification to be a high priest after the order of Melchizedek.

Chapter 7

LOGICAL OBJECTIONS TO THE TRINITY

The biblical testimony given in chapters 1 to 6 strongly suggests that the God revealed in the Scriptures is one God who has been manifested as three divine persons. To many anti-Trinitarians the concept of one equaling three seems patently illogical. Millard Erickson has cogently suggested that Trinitarians need to give a credible and coherent account of how we can logically conceive three as one.

Erickson then goes on to suggest that the real-life, practical world in which we live would not tolerate such fuzzy, three = one math. If you or I went to the grocery store and took three loaves of bread to the checkout counter and tried to persuade the clerk that they were really one and all that we have to pay for is one, the clerk might be tempted to quickly call for store security (Erickson, *Trinity,* pp. 43, 44).

Thus it is quite acceptable for Trinitarians to give some reasonably coherent account that seeks to explain how one is three and three is one in the life of the Godhead. The question is this: What is it about the nature of the triune Godhead that makes the alleged persons called Father, Son, and Holy Spirit "one"?

The first response to the question of the logic of Trinitarian thought is to admit that we are dealing with an extremely profound mystery. While I readily believe the Bible when it says that Adam and Eve became "one" and were yet two, I have yet, however, to fully fathom the ways of any man with any maiden (Prov. 30:19). Yet in loving relationships, there does appear to develop a profound oneness. Are we then to say that loving relationships are totally illogical and incoherent? I think not. And this seems to be the best way to give a coherent account of the mystery of the Trinity and its plural oneness.

Once more Erickson seems to sensibly point the way to a credible and harmonious solution: "We therefore propose thinking of the Trinity as a society, a complex of persons, who, however, are one being. While this society of persons has dimensions to its interrelationships that we do not find among humans, there are some illuminating parallels. Love is the binding relationship within the Godhead that unites each of the persons with each of the others" (*ibid.,* p. 58).

It should come as no surprise to us that Erickson then appeals directly to 1 John 4:8, 16.

1 John 4:8

"God is love." Do we truly comprehend the depths of this inspired statement that is so disarming in its seeming simplicity? I would suggest that these three words have a profound contribution to make to our understanding of a God who has eternally preexisted in something like Trinitarian "oneness."

Once more the judicious comments of Erickson are suggestively intriguing: "The statement . . . 'God is love,' is not a definition of God, nor is it merely a statement of one attribute among others. It is a very basic characterization of God" *(ibid.).*

In the early stages of my Christian experience I must confess that I was quite indifferent to the issues that have swirled around the subject of the Godhead. It was, however, when I began to more carefully reflect on the evidence presented in the first six chapters of this book that I began to sense that something deep, even wonderfully complex, is unfolding when the Bible defines ultimate reality.

The issue began to focus around the question of a God who shines forth from the pages of Scripture as one who is intensely personal and loving in nature. Then one day it began to penetrate into my rather rationalistic attitude toward religion and biblical theology that the God of heaven is primarily the God of loving grace, not abstract rationality.

The expression "God of loving grace" began to raise amazing thoughts in my mind about love as the essence of both human and divine existence. I clearly remember the day when my brother Phillip shared with me the gist of the following line of thought:*

If God is truly—in His very essence—the God of "love" (John 3:16 and 1 John 4:8), then we need to consider the following implications.

Could one who has existed from all eternity past and who made us in His loving image—could this God truly be called love if He existed only as a solitary being? Is not love, especially divine love, possible only if the one who made our universe was a plural being who was exercising "love" within His divine plurality from all eternity past? Is not real, selfless love possible only if it proceeds from the kind of God who was and is and shall be a God of love eternally? Is the Creator God, who is called love, in any way finally dependent upon His created beings to reveal and demonstrate His love?

Carefully note the articulate ways that Erickson, Bruce Metzger, and Otto H. Christensen make this crucial point:

"There is a sense in which the fact that God is love requires that he be more than one person. Love must have both a subject and an object. Thus, prior to the creation of other persons, humans, God could not have really loved, and thus would not have been truly love. If, however, there have always been multiple persons within the Trinity itself, among whom love could be mutually exercised, expressed, and experienced, then God could always have been actively loving. Genuine love requires that there be someone who can be loved, and this would necessarily be more than mere narcissism. . . . Because God is three persons, rather than two, there is a dimension of openness and extension not necessarily found in a love relationship between two persons, which can sometimes be quite closed in nature" (*ibid.*, pp. 58, 59).

"The Unitarian professes to agree with the statement that 'God is love.' But these words, 'God is love,' have no real meaning unless God is at least two Persons. Love is something that one *person* has for another *person*. If God were a single person, then before the universe was made, he was *not* love. For, if love be of the essence of God, he must always love, and, being eternal, he must have possessed an eternal object of love. Furthermore, perfect love is possible only between equals. Just as a man cannot satisfy or realize his powers of love by loving the lower animals, so God cannot satisfy or realize his love by loving man or any creature. Being infinite, he must have eternally possessed an infinite object of his love, some *alter ego,* or, to use the language of traditional Christian theology, a consubstantial, co-eternal, and co-equal Son" (Metzger, p. 83).

"[God's] self-communion and association within Himself, wholly independent of the created universe, is impossible to an essence destitute of personality. Only the plural unity of the Trinity explains this, for there must be someone to be known. Likewise there must be someone to be loved. There was a time when the universe was not, and if God's blessedness and perfection depended upon the universe, then there would have been a time when God was neither self-conscious [nor] blessed. Inspiration and reason both demand a triune God composed of Father, Son, and Holy Spirit" (Christensen, p. 70).

Have we not discovered that the most profound of human unities are those of selfless love? Could we experience such profound loving unions if there did not exist a deeply united, plural God of infinite love who has defined the very essence of the universe and the existence of those creatures made more especially in His image? The very essence of living in love flows from the great triune Godhead of loving grace!

To put it as plainly as I can: If God is love, then the very basis of the created universe must be personal love. I would suggest that infinite, eternal personal love is the very substance of what makes the universe expansive and logically coherent. Although love cannot be fully explained, without it things would prove hopelessly sterile.

Could it be that a universe created by a loving and expansive Trinity has a logic that transcends that of the physical world? One would certainly hope so!

Furthermore, I would suggest that the implications for reality as defined by an eternally and infinitely loving Trinity have deeply rewarding possibilities when it comes to clarifying the theological issues that flow from the doctrines of creation, sin, redemption, heaven, the problem of evil, and the ultimate meaning of divine and human social existence. "If reality is fundamentally physical, then the primary force binding it together is electromagnetic. If, however, reality is fundamentally social, then the most powerful constituting force is that which binds persons together, namely, love" (Erickson, *Trinity*, p. 58).

Why don't we opt for the logic of a "reality [that] is fundamentally social," a world created and benevolently ruled over by the Trinity of eternal love?

We will return in section 3 for a fuller discussion of the theological and practical implications of Trinitarian belief. But before we do so, we now need to consider the issues of how Trinitarian and anti-Trinitarian thought have developed through the centuries since the time of the apostles. It is to these issues that we now turn our attention.

---

*Though Phillip Whidden was the one who first brought the following concepts to my attention, I have since discovered that Wayne Grudem (p. 247), Otto H. Christensen (p. 70), and Bruce M. Metzger (pp. 81-84) have articulated essentially the same concepts (none of them footnoted their source for these ideas, however).

Bibliography for Section One

Aune, David. *Word Bible Commentary: Revelation 1-5.* Dallas: Word Books, 1997. Vol. 52.

Barker, Glenn W., William L. Lane, and J. Ramsey Michaels. *The New Testament Speaks.* New York: Harper and Row, 1969.

Beale, G. K. *The Book of Revelation: A Commentary on the Greek Text.* Grand Rapids: William B. Eerdmans Pub. Co., 1999.

Christensen, Otto H. *Getting Acquainted With God.* Washington, D.C.: Review and Herald Pub. Assn., 1970.

Erickson, Millard J. *Christian Theology.* 2nd. ed. Grand Rapids: Baker Books, 1998.

———. *God in Three Persons: A Contemporary Interpretation of the Trinity.* Grand Rapids: Baker Books, 1995.

———. *Making Sense of the Trinity: Three Crucial Questions.* Grand Rapids: Baker Books, 2000.

Froom, LeRoy Edwin. *Movement of Destiny.* Washington, D.C.: Review and Herald Pub. Assn., 1971.

Grudem, Wayne. *Systematic Theology.* Grand Rapids: Zondervan Pub. House, 1994.

Hatton, Max. *Understanding the Trinity.* Alma Park Grantham, Lincolnshire, England: Autumn House, 2001.

Johnson, Alan F., and Robert E. Webber. *What Christians Believe: A Biblical and Historical Summary.* Grand Rapids: Zondervan Pub. House, 1993.

Keil, C. F., and Delitzsch, F., *Commentaries on the Old Testament: Ezekiel.* Grand Rapids: William B. Eerdmans Pub. Co., 1952. Vol. II.

Metzger, Bruce M. *The Jehovah's Witnesses and Jesus Christ.* Princeton, N.J.: The Theological Book Agency (reprinted from the April 1953 *Theology Today*).

Morris, Leon. *The Gospel According to John.* The New International Commentary on the New Testament. Grand Rapids: William B. Eerdmans Pub. Co., 1971.

Neufeld, Don. F., ed. *Seventh-day Adventist Bible Dictionary,* rev. ed. Washington, D.C.: Review and Herald Pub. Assn., 1979.

Paulien, Jon. *What the Bible Says About the End-Time.* Hagerstown, Md.: Review and Herald Pub. Assn., 1994.

Seventh-day Adventists Believe . . . A Biblical Exposition of 27 Fundamental Beliefs. Hagerstown, Md.: Review and Herald Pub. Assn., 1988.

Seventh-day Adventist Church Manual. 16th ed. Hagerstown, Md.: Review and Herald Pub. Assn., 2000.

Stefanovic, Ranko. *The Backgrounds and Meaning of the Sealed Book of Revelation 5.* Berrien Springs, Mich.: Andrews University Press, 1996.

Swete, H. B. *The Apocalypse of St. John: The Greek Text With Introduction Notes and Indices.* London: MacMillan and Co., Ltd., 1906.

Thayer, J. H. *The New Thayer's Greek-English Lexicon of the New Testament.* Peabody, Mass.: Hendrickson Publishers, 1981 (orig. 1889).

The Seventh-day Adventist Bible Commentary. Washington, D.C.: Review and Herald Pub. Assn., 1952-1957. 7 vols.

Wallace, Daniel B. *Greek Grammar: Beyond the Basics.* Grand Rapids: Zondervan Pub. House, 1996.

Whidden, Woodrow W. "Trinitarian Evidences in the Apocalypse." *Journal of the Adventist Theological Society* 11, nos. 1, 2 (2000): 248-260.

White, Ellen G. *The Acts of the Apostles.* Mountain View, Calif.: Pacific Press Pub. Assn., 1911.

———. *The Desire of Ages.* Mountain View, Calif.: Pacific Press Pub. Assn., 1898.

———. *Evangelism.* Washington, D.C.: Review and Herald Pub. Assn., 1946.

SECTION TWO

The History of the Trinity Doctrine From A.D. 100 to A.D. 1500

GLOSSARY FOR SECTION TWO

Docetic—from the Greek verb *dokeo,* meaning "to seem" or "to appear as if." A docetic view of Christ is one that assumes that Christ is divine but not human. Christ only "appeared as if" he was human.

Gnostic—from the Greek noun *gnosis,* meaning "knowledge." The Gnostic view of the universe contains many levels of existence from the lowest, or material, to the highest, purely spiritual. The lowest level contains creatures and humans who exist only physically. The highest is the realm of pure light and is inhabited only by God. The intermediate levels are inhabited by emanations from God who variously guide humans toward the realm of God by giving them secret passwords or guard the realms from undeserving humans. Salvation for the Gnostic is to learn the secret passwords, or knowledge, that open the doors to the next higher realms. The more of the passwords you have, the higher your soul can ascend after death.

Heteroousios—literally "of different nature," this term boldly denounced *homoousios* as a wrong representation of the relationship between Father and Son and overtly states instead that the Son was of a different nature than the Father. The Greek term contains the prefix *hetero,* meaning "other" or "another" or "different" attached to the verb of being, used to denote the nature of a thing: *ousios.*

Homoion—literally "like," this is the most ambiguous of the terms suggested in the place of *homoousios.* It skips any reference to the nature, *ousios,* of the Father or Son and simply suggests that They were "similar" without defining in what way They were similar.

Homoiousios—literally "of similar nature," this is one of the terms suggested in the place of *homoousios,* which was used to suggest that the nature of the Son is very much like that of the Father, but not identical. The word employed for the nature of a being is still there, *ousios,* but the prefix *homo,* meaning "the same," has been made into a plural by the addition of an iota, transforming it into *homoi,* thus "similar."

Homoousios—literally "of the same nature," this is the term used at the Council of Nicea to represent the relationship between the Father and Son. It is a transliteration of a compound Greek word containing the prefix *homo,* which means "the same," and the verb *ousios,* which means "to be" or "essence of being." As defined during the fourth century theological debates, it came to represent that the Son is of the same nature as the Father.

Modalism—a severely monotheistic view of God that focuses so intently on God's oneness that it views the Father, Son, and Spirit as three modes, or phases, of the same being. They do not have individuality. Many forms of modalism exist, but the dominant form, as presented by Sabellius, viewed the Father, Son, and Spirit as consecutive, that is, the Father was the chosen mode of God in the Old Testament, the Son during the Incarnation, and the Spirit was the phase of God during the time of the church. The ancient term for this was Sabellianism. It is also known as modalistic Monarchianism.

Pneumatamachoi—literally "fighters against the Spirit," a term coined to describe a group of theologians in the late fourth century who agreed that the Father and Son may be of one nature, *homoousios,* but that this relationship does not extend to the Holy Spirit, which they did not view as having individual identity.

Chapter 8

THE TRINITY IN THE FIRST AND SECOND CENTURIES

The earliest Christian writings available to us—those books we know as the New Testament—clearly present a Father, a Son, and a Holy Spirit. According to Matthew 28:19, the local churches were to initiate new converts to the young Christian religion by baptizing them in the "name of the Father, and of the Son, and of the Holy Ghost." Each of the three Beings was indisputably central to early Christian worship and belief. What was not immediately obvious from the New Testament documents was the relationships between the members of the Godhead. Much of the discussion and disagreement among Christians of the first four centuries consisted of attempts to establish how we should view the relationships between Father, Son, and Spirit. The next two chapters will trace some of the earliest Christian views about God, and will explain how the Trinitarian formula came to be the preferred Christian understanding of the Godhead.

We may see the development of the church's doctrine of God as the story of people coming to terms with Scripture and with what it reveals about God. The early Christians found themselves needing to hammer out their approach to Scripture in two basic areas. First, they had to recognize which writings were to be authoritative, and second they had to work out how to interpret them. Building upon these understandings of Scripture, they then struggled to synthesize the diverse ways in which the Bible spoke about God. What made the task particularly daunting was the fact that no such systematic description had yet been put into human words. Neither language nor philosophy contained the categories they needed to express what Scripture revealed about the Godhead.

The Christian doctrine of God arises from the thought of early Judaism. The first-century Jewish world, out of which Christianity grew, was strongly monotheistic. The Jews stood apart from other religious groups largely because of their strong belief in one—and only one—God. The words of the Shema of Deuteronomy 6:4 came to echo daily in most Jewish homes: "Hear, Oh Israel; the Lord your God, the Lord is One." While it is not absolutely certain that the daily repetition of this prayer goes back to the first century A.D., it is not an accident that it became one of the most universally practiced prayers in Judaism, for the Shema powerfully represents the monotheistic understanding central to the Jewish faith. Although Judaism encompassed a variety of thought groups, including Pharisees, Sadducees, Essenes, and other groups spread throughout the Mediterranean world, on the whole the many different branches held this belief in common. Christianity, which also held the Hebrew Scriptures as authoritative, shared the strong belief in monotheism.

By contrast, the Greco-Roman religious world abounded with many gods. As the Roman Empire expanded, ever more peoples and ever more gods joined the religious mix. The average city in the Roman Empire represented not only a widely diverse ethnic and national population, but also a broad array of pagan deities and temples. However, in the minds of some philosophers there emerged a strong reaction against such a plethora of gods.

Among the Greco-Roman philosophers there grew a strong tide of monotheism that recognized one ultimate God who transcended not only the visible world, but also any pagan gods believed to interact with it. The notion in Greek philosophical thought of a single God above and beyond all others goes as far back as at least the fourth century B.C. At that time, Plato wrote in his *Timaeus* about one transcendent God who made the world through an agent called the "demiurge." Aristotle called this "God above all else" the "Unmoved Mover."

Later, Stoic philosophy knew the transcendent being as the "One." The Stoics tried to maintain the traditional reverence toward the ancient literature about their gods, such as the poems of Hesiod, Homer, and Pindar, while at the same time choosing to believe in the one supreme God. They did so by understanding the humanlike descriptions of their gods with their immoral and ungodly behavior as allegory.

By the second and third centuries of the Christian Era, aspects of all these philosophies, along with several others, had combined together into an eclectic Hellenistic worldview that involved a kind of monotheism, or in some cases a hierarchical polytheism, led by one supreme god. One important feature of this ultimate god of Hellenistic philosophy was his complete transcendence—they believed him to be totally beyond the scope of the world we see and touch. In contrast to the crudeness of the portrayal of the pagan gods in their interactions with humans and the physical world—their jealousies, murders, incestuous acts, gluttonous passions, and adulteries—the philosophers chose to conceive of the one highest God as above the human sphere. Plato, for example, taught that the "real world" was not the physical one, but the world beyond, one of "Ideals"—of pure thought—outside the reach of the human senses.

Judeo-Christian thinkers were able to use the Greco-Roman belief in one completely transcendent god as a point of contact with pagan friends and acquaintances. One way in which Jewish monotheism adapted to the Hellenistic view of god was by introducing agents similar to Plato's demiurge into the story of Creation, protecting God Himself from direct involvement with material substance. For instance, in one of the Aramaic paraphrases of Genesis, known as Targum Neofiti,[1] we find a remarkable number of insertions in which an agent of God does the physical things that Genesis itself attributes to God. Note this quote from Genesis 1 of Targum Neofiti: "From the beginning with wisdom the *Memra* of the Lord created and perfected the heavens and the earth. . . . And the *Memra* of the Lord said: 'Let there be light.'"[2] The *Memra* acts here as God's agent so that God, who is transcendent, need not be portrayed as soiling Himself with material things of Creation. The *Memra* also speaks for God, since God Himself could not be viewed as having such human characteristics as a mouth or a voice.

One prominent Jew who suggested that the agents did the work of God was Philo of Alexandria. Philo was a Jewish intellectual living in the great Egyptian city of Alexandria at the time of Jesus and Paul. A wealthy and educated Greek-speaking Jew, Philo found himself immersed in both the Jewish and the Greco-Roman cultural worlds. As a result, he often sought to harmonize the Jewish and Greco-Roman philosophical concerns for monotheism. He wrote prolifically on various areas of Torah interpretation and used a rich mixture of literal and allegorical interpretations in treatises on the lives of Abraham, Joseph, and Moses. Also he took great care to point out that every physical description of God in the Torah is figurative. In this way he protected the transcendent God from assuming physical attributes. Beyond that, he portrayed God's interactions with the physical, or sense-perceptible, world as being carried out by various agents such as Justice, Sophia (Wisdom), and particularly, the Logos (Word).

In his treatise *On the Making of the World* Philo portrayed the Logos—a well-known Stoic agent of God—in a twofold way, both as the idea of the physical universe and as its maker. That is, Philo suggested that on the first day of Creation God, the great eternal Mind, conceived the idea of the entire world and made the Logos as the image of that idea. One might understand the concept by thinking of an architect planning a building and then making a model to visualize what that building will be like. For Philo, the Logos was that model of the whole created universe, though not a physical model. The Logos, however, was not just a passive model but an active one who actually made what God planned. Thus the Logos was the creative agent, or demiurge, who created the world visualized in the mind of the transcendent God.

The Greco-Roman philosophical concern to see the one God as transcending worldly activity and anthropomorphic—or human-like—characteristics Christian interpreters of Scripture also came to share. As we shall see, it is a major factor in several of the early erroneous attempts at describing Christ and the Godhead, and became an integral part of the Arian views of the Son in the fourth century.

In about A.D. 180 Theophilus, bishop of Syrian Antioch, wrote a series of three short books for the well-read pagan Autolycus, who was attracted to the monotheistic view of God but whom Theophilus felt was not ready to hear the whole truth about Jesus Christ. In chapter 15 of the second book he employed the word "trinity," although not with the same meaning inferred by later Christians. Theophilus' use of the term was not intended to represent a three-person Godhead at all. Rather, he used the term to describe God and two agents, Logos and Sophia, who stood in relationship to God very similar to the agents of God described by Philo of Alexandria. Theophilus called Logos and Sophia "the two hands of God." Further, he portrayed the Logos as the agent of God who represented Him when He needed to appear and act in the physical world, stating, "the God and Father of the universe is unconfined and is not present in a place. . . . But his Logos, through whom he made all things, who is his Power and Wisdom, assuming the role of the Father and Lord of the universe, was present in paradise in the role of God and conversed with Adam. . . . Since the Logos is God and derived his nature from God, whenever the Father of the universe wills to do so he sends him into some place where he is present and is heard and seen" (Theophilus of Antioch *Ad Autolcum* 2. 22).

Note that Theophilus identified both Logos and Wisdom, as well as Power, as a single agent of God, and called this agent the Son of God. Theophilus was not an early representative of Trinitarian theology, but one who overtly presented Christ as an agent of God, a lesser being. Theophilus does not mention Jesus Christ by name in the entire work, but always refers to Him in terms of an agent of God. This highlights the difficulty that second-century Christians had in understanding and communicating their strong belief in only one God, and at the same time their worship of a Father, Son, and Holy Spirit.

Second-century Christians explored several ways of viewing

Christ, some of them already dealt with in the writings of the New Testament. "Docetism"—a word based on the Greek verb *dokeo,* meaning "to seem like" or "to appear as if"—comprised a wide range of beliefs that viewed Christ as only *seeming* to be human. The basic tenets included a belief that Jesus was a human being completely separate from Christ, who was a divine being. This distinction allowed the divinity to be separate from humanity, and to avoid its subjection to human mortality, passions, and changeableness. Paul's warning in 1 Corinthians 12:3 against those who would say "Jesus be cursed" rather than "Jesus is Lord" is a defense against just such a Docetic belief. Similarly, the admonition to test every spirit in 1 John 4:1-3 identifies the spirit of antichrist as a denial that Jesus Christ came in the flesh. First John 1:1-3 portrays Jesus Christ as both eternally *with* God the Father and as perceivable by human senses—that is, as both God and human.

In the Gospels the people surrounding Jesus often view Him as simply human and not as God, largely because He looked and acted like a human. Very shortly after His return to heaven, however, the opposite temptation surfaced, and some Christians began to view Christ as God but to deny that He actually became a human being. The splitting of Jesus from Christ allowed them to have it both ways: Jesus could be human, while Christ was divine. However, the New Testament books repeatedly make it clear that Jesus is the Christ. The logic problem that this entailed became the source of controversy for hundreds of years. The Christological controversies of the second through fifth centuries addressed this problem directly. In the context of our study of Trinitarianism, the focus cannot be on Christology except to show the strong desire on the part of such early theologians to protect divinity from being portrayed in ways that they felt were not proper to God.

We may, for the sake of simplicity, classify the many Docetic understandings of Christ already widespread in the second century into two general groups: the Marcionites and the Gnostics. Marcion was a merchant shipowner born and raised in Pontus, just below the Black Sea. In the middle of the second century he showed up in

Rome as a Christian believer—not an average Christian believer, but an intensely rigorous one. Apparently he had sold his shipping business and donated the proceeds to the church in Rome, following the example of the earliest church portrayed in Acts. Marcion gained great influence with the Roman church in two ways. As a patron he assisted the church through his wealth and influence, and he was a fervent religious leader.

Marcion's beliefs as a Christian were no more average than his behavior. He distinguished between Christ and the God of the Old Testament, portraying the latter as a just but incompetent deity who acted as Creator of the evil physical world. This lawgiver God, the God of crude justice who took "an eye for an eye and a tooth for a tooth," Marcion suggested, was incapable of love or grace or of offering salvation. Christ, on the other hand, was a much higher deity. Marcion portrayed Christ as the God of love and grace, capable of forgiveness and of offering salvation. In short, Marcion believed that the Jewish god was a poor bumbling deity, while Christ was a good and saving God completely independent from, and superior to, the God of the Old Testament.

Obviously, Marcion could not believe in a separation between God the Father and God the Son and still maintain that the Hebrew Scriptures were valid revelations about Christ. Therefore he rejected the Old Testament as inferior to the Scriptures of the newly revealed God. Marcion believed that the Hebrew Scriptures belonged to the inferior God, whereas the new Scriptures, containing much of what we now call the New Testament, were an accurate portrayal of Christ, the God of salvation and love. Because the Gospels portray Christ as intimately connected with the Father, who is the Old Testament God, Marcion also had to reject much of what is in the Gospels. In fact, he accepted as Scripture only parts of the Gospel of Luke and some of the letters of Paul, and purged each of them of any reference to the Father. Although it would have been completely unacceptable to most Christians, Marcion's list is the earliest defined canon—or list of authoritative scriptural books—we now have for the Christian Scriptures. In reaction to Marcion's list, another early Christian leader, Irenaeus, argued for the acceptance of four Gospels—Matthew, Mark, Luke, and John—out of the many then currently circulating.

Marcion's views probably would have had little appeal to many Christians unless an anti-Jewish sentiment was already present. Ancient sources make it clear that such a sentiment was fairly widespread at this time. The *Epistle of Barnabas,* probably written in Alexandria around A.D. 130, and Justin Martyr's *Dialogue With Trypho the Jew,* probably written near Rome about A.D. 150, both portray a desire to distance Christianity from anything Jewish. Just as important for the growth of Marcionism was that believers had not yet widely explored the parameters of Christian teaching. Although the writings of Paul and John were in circulation at this time, warning about the coming wolves and antichrists who would bring false doctrine, nobody expected them to be such moral and generous Christian believers as Marcion. After all, he had given up his means for the good of the community just as the zealous believers in the apostolic church had done. He lived a moral life and taught a rigorous ethic. In short, he did not look like a wolf to his fellow church members.

In the end, most Christians, even in Rome, accepted the four Gospels as revealing authoritative information about Christ and thus rejected Marcion's view of Christ and his limited scriptural canon, and they returned the merchant's money as unacceptable. His challenge actually helped to stimulate the decisions concerning which writings the Christian community should give authority to as Scripture. The teachings of Marcion also stimulated much thought about how to formulate a view of Jesus Christ that would cover everything inspired documents revealed about Him.

Another major challenge to the Christian understanding of Jesus Christ came from the many different Gnostic groups within and around Judaism and Christianity during the second century. We might, for our purposes, define Gnosticism as a religious philosophy that believed in an ultimate God in the highest heaven whose emanations were lesser gods living on lower levels of the heavens. For

Gnostics, spiritual darkness filled the material world, and only those who had special knowledge could ascend into the heavens after the death of the physical body. In some systems of Gnosticism, this knowledge came in the form of passwords that contained the power to defeat the "archons" who guarded each level of the heavens. Many Gnostics used Scripture as a code that held secret knowledge within its words, but not in its literal meaning.

In the first part of his work *Against Heresies,* Irenaeus described some of the myths concerning the emanations of God that Gnostics believed to populate the heavens. Irenaeus defeated the myths using Scripture, but in the opposite way to how he had overcome Marcion with Scripture. In response to Marcion's rejection of Scripture that disagreed with him, Irenaeus restored the four Gospels and the deleted sections of Paul. The Gnostics, by contrast, tended to accept a much larger number of gospels and letters as Scripture than we do today. As a result, Irenaeus argued for only the four Gospels. But even within those four Gospels and the letters of Paul, the Gnostics managed to "discover" words that contained hidden codes portraying their own understanding of the universe and of God. Therefore, Irenaeus argued for only one right reading of the text—that sanctioned by the true apostolic church. In Irenaeus' view all heretics had originally held this one right reading of Scripture, but had rejected it with evil intent in favor of other interpretations. Unfortunately, Christians had not agreed on any single reading up to this point. Though he claimed to be basing his ideas on *the* original right reading, Irenaeus was in actuality giving the reading he understood to be correct. Fortunately, he did it well, especially when he dealt with the understanding of God.

The Gnostics had essentially come up with a new way to protect the one God from any connection with the material world. Instead of using agents of God, such as the Logos, Sophia, and Justice as portrayed by Philo, or the *Memra* of the Lord as portrayed by Targum Neofiti, they portrayed the Logos and Sophia and a host of others as divinities who were emanations from the one God and had independent existence. In many ways it was a return to the polytheism of the pagans with one ultimate God at the top of the hierarchy. These other divinities, especially in the Valentinian form of Gnosticism, sometimes had names derived from the Christian Scriptures, such as Cross, Savior, or Church. The Gnostics then used such words outside their normal meanings as the basis for their Gnostic reading of Scripture. Irenaeus' job was not just to identify the right four Gospels from which to build an understanding of Jesus Christ, but also to define the right interpretation of the Scriptures.

The argument of Irenaeus and some other Christians who opposed the Gnostic systems was that the Scriptures, rightly interpreted, portray Jesus as the Christ, both real God and real human. The Gnostic forms of Docetism, however, taught that Christ was one of the many emanations from God that made up the population of the heavenly realms, and was not on a par with God the Father, the ultimate and transcendent God. The Docetists rejected the idea that God could be changeable or could suffer. Thus Christendom in the second century contained a number of different Docetic tendencies about Jesus Christ that viewed the Christ as a representative of the world of God, but Jesus as only a human taken over by the Christ.

Several other misconceptions about Jesus Christ were a part of the Christian environment during the second century, including the view of Sabellius. Sabellius developed his ideas in reaction to his fight against tri-theism, which viewed the Father, Son, and Spirit as three separate Gods. He argued that since there was only one God—a God portrayed in the Scriptures in three different forms—then these three must be consecutive. In other words, Sabellius suggested that the Father, Son, and Spirit were three different modes of the same God at different times. In his view, God revealed Himself as the Father during the old covenant, as the Son during His life on earth, and as the Holy Spirit in the time of the church, but They were all one person. Theologians have called the concept Sabellianism or modalism, denoting three modes of the one God. Most Christians have rejected modalism on the basis of Scripture. A myriad of texts reveal the independent personhood of each member of the Godhead, and demonstrate that the Father, Son, and Holy

Spirit existed at the same time. In time theologians came to recognize modalism as another failed attempt to maintain a belief in one God while at the same time recognizing that there is a Father, a Son, and a Spirit.

It was clear that the Bible seemed to reveal God as both one and as three, but no one during the second century managed to find a way to express the full complexity revealed in Scripture. Marcion attempted to resolve this dilemma by eliminating the Father God of the Old Testament along with the most troublesome scriptures, while the Gnostics read Scripture as a code having deep and hidden meanings that supported their belief in the emanation of many "gods" from the ultimate One. Sabellius explored a radical monotheism contrasting strongly with the hierarchical polytheism of Gnostics such as the Valentinians. Others viewed Christ as an agent of the transcendent God. While all of these attempts made sense of part of the revealed writings, none was able to pull together all that Scripture revealed about the Godhead and Jesus Christ. The second century closed with many questions unanswered.

ENDNOTES

[1] This Targum is a Jewish document from Palestine early in the Christian Era that we might think of as a "rewritten Bible" designed to make the Torah understandable in the language of the day.

[2] The term *Memra* is a Chaldean loan word that denotes an authoritative officer or overlord. It is a fitting term for suggesting an agent for the Lord Yahweh.

Chapter 9

THE TRINITY IN THE THIRD AND FOURTH CENTURIES

The second century ended without any consensus as how to describe the relationship between the Father, Son, and Holy Spirit. Scholars had identified those who were demonstrably wrong as heretical and as counterproductive to the church. Irenaeus and others had corrected several wrong conceptions of Jesus Christ, but had not found terms to define what was right. No way of explaining the Godhead had yet emerged that could fit everything that Scripture revealed.

One of the consequences of treating the self-denying Marcion, and others like him, as heretics was that Christians began to identify themselves more on the basis of what they believed than on the basis of how they lived and behaved. This shift heightened the intensity of theological discussion, for the ideas that prevailed would become the means for creating a dividing line between those who belonged inside and outside of the "true" church. Such an atmosphere caused the third- and fourth-century debates on the doctrine of God to rage with increasing ferocity.

Origen, whose scriptural commentaries set the stage for these debates, was likely the single most influential interpreter of the Bible in the history of Christianity. Although he was not always original in his understanding, he most impressively achieved his goal of bringing together valuable early interpretations of Scripture. His numerous commentaries gathered a tremendous amount of previous scriptural interpretation and did, as well, include many of his own viewpoints. Later students of Scripture greatly appreciated both his collected commentary and his original work, viewing him as a repository of Christian interpretation. As a result, Christian teachers considered it important to be seen as agreeing with Origen when engaging in any theological debate during the third and fourth centuries.

Origen grew up a Christian in Alexandria in the last decades of the second century. His parents endured martyrdom for the faith while he was still a teenager, and Origen followed their example of serious, committed Christianity. He lived a disciplined lifestyle and took the literal injunctions of Scripture seriously. The story is frequently told—and is quite possibly true—that as a young man faced with sexual temptations he carried out literally Jesus' statement, "If your right eye offends you, pluck it out." Whether true or not, the very fact that people suggested it of him testifies to his level of commitment to personal morality and spirituality. Because one of the highest principles of biblical interpretation in the early church was that the interpreter must be a spiritual and upright person, Origen's deep commitment greatly enhanced the acceptance of his teachings.

Although he likely did not hold an official church office until late in his life, Origen was a talented teacher of biblical interpretation from a young age. Although church historians have often correctly criticized him as being responsible for directing Christian scholarship into allegorical methods, his excellent literal and typological interpretations of Scripture have been equally influential. One of the reasons for the frequent use of Origen's commentaries was that he covered the books of Scripture so thoroughly. We find few passages that he did not treat, and most later commentators used him even when they disagreed with him.

One of the drawbacks of such meticulous scriptural coverage is that Origen's writings do not lend themselves to systematic consistency. Simply because of their sheer volume and diversity, his writings could be—and were—used to support a great many theological conclusions that Origen no doubt never intended. In fact, some of these very problems led to his condemnation as a heretic two centuries after his death when his writings appeared to come down on the wrong side of theological debates of which he could not possibly have been aware.

The truth is that several sides in the theological debates were able to use his writings as a source of ammunition. During Origen's time people raised more questions about the Godhead than scholars could definitively answer, and he himself seems to have investigated a number of possible resolutions. As is the case with any good writer, Origen slanted his writing in the way that would best respond to the concerns of his perceived opponents. For Origen these adversaries ranged from the Christian Gnostics to the pagan philosopher Celsus. Though he had some detractors, most Christians of the early fourth century regarded Origen as an important part of the orthodox tradition of interpretation, and his influence was such that all sides in the debate wanted to have him as ally.

In book 2 of his *Commentary on John* Origen set out to deal with the heart of the perplexity concerning the Godhead revealed in Scripture—that is, the way in which we may compare the relationship between God the Father and the Son with that between the Son and the human race. Various scriptures identify Jesus as one with the Father and with human beings, yet rationally the relationships seem to be exclusive of each other. How can the Son be the same as the Father and yet be the same as humans? Origen's solution was to use literal interpretations of Scripture to place the Son in an intermediate position, resembling the Father in some ways and humans in others.

Irenaeus had already planted the seed for such a solution by suggesting that the Son was related to both the Father and to human beings in an identical way. He insisted that the Scriptures showed Jesus Christ to be both fully God and fully human, but he lacked the tools and terminology necessary for overcoming the illogic of such a statement. The formula describing Jesus Christ as having a dual nature took a long time to build, and it wasn't until the fifth century that anyone clearly articulated it. Origen, near the beginning of the third century, did not have the structural concepts by which to organize the scriptural information. Instead, he suggested that the connection between God the Father and God the Son is one of participation, with God the Father being the only true God and God the Son being God through participation in the Father's divinity. In one Arian-sounding statement, Origen suggests that the Son "would not remain God if he did not continue in unceasing contemplation of the depth of the Father" (Origen, *Commentary on the Gospel According to John 2:18,* commenting on John 1:1; quoted from the translation of Ronald E. Heine, *Origen: Commentary on the Gospel According to John, Books 1- 10,* p. 99). Origen, of course, would argue that such a thing would never happen, for the Word had always been with God and therefore had always been God and would always remain God. However, the fact that he was willing even to speak of this idea as a theoretical possibility demonstrates that Origen did not hold the Son to be God by nature, but only through participation.

In some portions of his writings Origen also portrayed the Son as effectively coeternal with God the Father, although not of the same nature. His understanding of time caused him to read the Greek word for "beginning" *(arché)* in John 1:1 to mean "before there was time." He applied this definition to the phrase "In the beginning was the Word" in order to denote the eternity of the Son and overtly stated that "before all time and eternity 'the Word was in the beginning,' and 'the Word was with God'" (*ibid.,* 2:9, p. 97). This would place the Son in an intermediate position between God the Father, who was divine by nature, and humans, who are creatures by nature but who may participate in some aspects of the divine.

Arius, from whose name the term *Arianism* derives, also positioned the Son in an intermediate position. Like Origen, Arius' concept of monotheism did not allow any but the transcendent Father to be fully God, but unlike Origen, Arius is much more explicit in his comments about the origin of the Son as a created being. Whereas Origen used ambiguous language to describe the beginning, insisting that when we first know of the Son He is with the Father, Arius spoke boldly and plainly about a beginning point at which the Father created the Son and before which the Son did not exist. One could argue that it was a positive improvement in precision, but in the end the church understood that although it apparently fit well with those scriptures suggesting a beginning for Christ, it contradicted other passages that speak of the full divinity and eternity of the Son. The precision of Arius' attempt proved to be a mistake.

Arius was born in Libya in the middle of the third century A.D. Shortly after the end of the last and longest universal Roman persecution of Christians—that of the Emperor Diocletian at the beginning of the fourth century A.D.—Arius acted as a presbyter in a church in Alexandria. As in many other cities of the empire following the Diocletian persecution, the Alexandrian church underwent years of arguments and accusations over who deserved to be in ecclesiastical positions and how they should exercise their authority. During the persecution, many bishops had fled or given up their Scriptures while other bishops had been martyred. In Alexandria, the metropolitan bishop Peter had at first fled but later, following the revocation of an edict of toleration, had been imprisoned and martyred. Alexander, the bishop elected to replace him, had to deal with the contention and division that had grown up under an unappointed bishop who functioned during Peter's absence. Arius accused Alexander of holding a false view of Christ, possibly taking advantage of his apparent political weakness in order to gain support for his own views in opposition to those of his bishop.

Arius had no way of knowing what was to grow from the debate that followed. The opposing views of Alexander and Arius became central at the Council of Nicaea several years later in A.D. 325, along with the ideas of others, including Eusebius, the church historian and bishop of Caesarea. The Council of Nicaea reportedly consisted of a gathering of more than 300 bishops, along with their entourages of presbyters and attendants, at the town of Nicaea near Constantinople in what is now Turkey. The Emperor Constantine, who called the council, had managed to unite the Roman Empire under his own rule despite the fact that his father had divided the empire between his three sons. Constantine's main goal for the council was to encourage a united Christian church to help hold his empire together. It severely disappointed him to find disagreement between the bishops over so fundamental an issue as the relationship between God the Father and Christ the Son. Although Constantine's hopes for the council never materialized, what the council did accomplish in the end was a rejection of the views of Eusebius of Caesarea and of Arius, and the formation of a statement concerning the Trinity that tended to vindicate the views of Alexander of Alexandria. This statement was essentially the same as a creed that had been established by the church in Jerusalem with added statements anathematizing those views that placed the Son in subjugation to the Father. It states:

"We believe in one God, the Father almighty, Maker of all things visible and invisible;

"And in one Lord Jesus Christ, the Son of God, begotten from the Father, only begotten, that is, from the substance of the Father, God from God, light from light, true God from true God, begotten not made, of one substance with the Father, through whom all things came into being, things in heaven and things on earth, who for us men and because of our salvation came down and became incarnate, becoming man, suffered and rose again on the third day, ascended to the heavens, and will come to judge the living and the dead;

"And in the Holy Spirit" (Peter Toon, *Yesterday, Today and Forever: Jesus Christ and the Holy Trinity in the Teaching of the Seven Ecumenical Councils,* p. 20).

Historically, Arius was not nearly as central to the theological debate as one might assume from the fact that his name has been attached to almost everything anti-Trinitarian for more than 1,600 years. None of the three main groups who opposed the Nicene formula of the Trinity during the fourth century recognized Arius as their representative, nor did any of the three completely agree with his Christology. Nevertheless, because the creed of the Council of Nicaea contained a number of anathemas against the ideas originally prompted by Arius and identified by the council as being untrue of Jesus Christ, any time someone asserted a similar idea, the resulting theology came to be called Arian. Arius did not believe all the things anathematized at Nicaea, but his name has usually been used as the label for any "low" view of Christ—that is, any concept that understands Christ to be less than fully God.

Athanasius, Alexander's young secretary and presbyter in the Alexandrian church, attended the Council of Nicaea. Though he had a minor role in the proceedings, the council was a life-shaping event for him. He spent the rest of his life trying to maintain the Nicene view of Christ as the accepted doctrine of the church. For it he endured imprisonment, exile five times, and threats of execution.

Arius had boldly stated to the council that the Son was a creation of the Father. He based his view on texts easily taken out of context, such as Hebrews 3:2, which could be translated, "faithful to Him who *made* him," and Acts 2:36, which might be translated, "God *made* him Christ." The cause of these difficult readings centers in the Greek verb *poieo* (to do or make), that has ambiguities similar to those found in the English word "make." In English "make" can mean anything from "create" to "appoint." For instance, when you make a cake you are in a sense "creating" it. On the other hand when you make someone a judge or a police officer you are not "creating" them, but "appointing" them to a role. In Acts 2:36 the whole phrase reads: "God has made him both Lord and Christ" (RSV). "Christ," the "anointed one," is a role or office that the Father appointed the Son to. In Hebrews 3:2 we find the same dynamic at play. Reading verses 1 and 2 together makes it clear that Jesus is "faithful to him who appointed him" (RSV) to be apostle and high priest. Again, they are roles like those of a judge or a police officer. Athanasius used arguments such as these to refute the misreadings made by Arius and his allies.

Proverbs 8:22 provided an interesting challenge for Athanasius. We have already dealt with the Hebrew text of this passage in a previous chapter of this book, but Arius and Athanasius used the Greek version of the Old Testament called the Septuagint, which has a slightly different reading. In the Septuagint text, as we have it, the verse states: "God created me [Wisdom] at the beginning of His ways for His works," using the verb *ktizo*—to found, build, or create. This verb usually has the connotation of "bringing into being." Athanasius employed several arguments against applying this literally to the Son. His best one suggested that since the text is actually talking about Wisdom, it is only figuratively applied to Christ. However, since Athanasius had political reasons in Alexandria for not being seen in complete disagreement with Origen, and since Origen had spoken of this passage as referring to Christ, Athanasius interpreted Proverbs 8:22 to mean that Christ underwent a change of status at the time He came to earth. Athanasius argued that "the works" were the works of salvation, including becoming a human, doing the will of the Father while on earth, dying on the cross, etc. In other words, he read the text as referring, not to the creation of the Son from nothing, but to the change in roles necessary for the Son to "do the works" of salvation. This stress on the role changes of the Son explained all three of the texts used by Arius to argue the literal creation of the Son by the Father. However, it created another problem, for if the Son changed roles when He became flesh, it meant that the Son was changeable and thus disqualified Him from being fully God in view of the prevailing definition of divinity. Along with transcendence and oneness, most Hellenistic thinkers regarded divinity as including immutability—that is, unchangeableness—as one of its chief characteristics.

Current popular philosophical view held that God was untouched by any kind of passion or feeling, or by experiences such as suffering and death. But according to Scripture Jesus Christ changed, suffered, and even died! Because there did not yet exist a clear definition of the dual nature of Jesus Christ that understood His divine nature as maintaining the attributes of God at the same time His human nature exhibited the attributes of humanity, this insistence that God match the philosophical description of divinity issued a serious challenge to the Nicene description of the Father and the Son as both fully God. To begin with, Athanasius is apparently speaking of two Gods—or, in fact, three when you add the Spirit—while the philosophical definition of God asserts that He is one and indivisible. In addition, "becoming flesh" certainly suggests a change, particularly since Jesus Christ suffered and died. Jesus simply did not meet the notions of what philosophers thought a real God must be.

For many Christians in the early fourth century who believed that the Son was eternal, this set of unmet expectations led them to assume that the Son was essentially different from the Father. They needed to examine the definitions and the categories picked up from popular thought to see what might properly represent the realities of God as revealed in Scripture. This, in fact, was true of the word "Trinity" itself. Three in one simply defied all mathematical categories in use since the time of Aristotle. It was also true of the term *homoousios,* chosen at Nicaea to represent the Father and Son as of the same nature.

Used in the Nicene Creed and commonly translated as "of one substance" (with the Father), the term had two possible meanings in philosophical usage. It had been employed to denote a group sharing a similar set of characteristics (Aristotle's genus), and also to refer to the characteristics of an individual (Aristotle's specie). Thus believers could construe it as picturing the Father and the Son as either two individuals of one type—that is, two Gods—or one individual divided into two parts—God divided into two modes—the form of a belief taught earlier by Sabellius and known as modalism. Neither adequately represents the relationship between Father and Son. However, Christianity maintained the term for two reasons. Pragmatically, Nicaea had already agreed upon it as a fitting term, and its meaning in this new situation simply needed to be more closely defined. But more important, the term *homoousios* emphasized the correct contrast between God and creature.

All created beings share one set of characteristics, while the persons of the Godhead share a different set of characteristics. Father and Son possess the same nature because They are both on the Creator side of the gulf between Creator and creature. It is a biblical separation. For example, God is worshiped, creatures are not. Revelation 22:8, 9 shows John falling down at the feet of the angel to worship him, but the angel does not allow it because he is a "fellow servant" (RSV) with John. Instead, the angel instructs John to "worship God." Describing the Father and Son as *homoousios*—of the same nature—correctly portrays why both the Father and the Son should receive worship: *They* are *the* Creator.

This is a simplified version of the basic argument used by Athanasius in favor of the terms "Trinity" and *homoousios*. By the time of his death in 373, Athanasius had convinced most Christian theologians of the necessity of using the new terminology rather than restricting themselves to terms appearing in the Bible. Increased precision and conciseness were necessary so that everyone involved in the debate could be sure of what the others meant by their words. Because of the language barriers between those speaking and writing in Greek and those using Latin, and the further challenges of those who knew Greek only as a second or third language, it took decades for everyone to understand the new meanings of these terms. Political alignments and realignments also played a major role in the discussion about terms and their meanings.

In many ways these struggles resembled the problems faced today in trying to establish international telecommunications protocol. It is not enough to be able to make a faster communications chip—it is also necessary to get all the parties who will use that chip to agree on how it should function and how to format the data. Thus it takes not only creativity and knowledge, but a willingness by all parties to stick with the dialogue until they understand all the issues and address the disagreements.

The church spent the half century between the Council of Nicaea in 325 and the Council of Constantinople in 381 in hot debate over the best way to describe the relationship between the Father and the Son, and, in the later portion, the Spirit. A number of factions and strong personalities used political and theological means—and even physical force—to promulgate their views. Three major groups stood in theological opposition to the Nicene formulation. Although by this time Arius was dead and had long since ceased to be the focal point of the discussions, three of the main views proposed as correctives to the Nicene formula as championed by Athanasius, Athanasius and Epiphanius now labeled as "Arian" and "Semi-Arian" positions.

"Arian," the first of the labels, referred to a variety of opinions sharing the basic attitude that the whole idea of further describing the relationship between Father and Son was a bad idea. Instead of *homoousios*—of the same nature—from the Nicene formula, this group used the more ambiguous term *homoion* (or "like") to indicate that the Son is *like* the Father. The faction preferred the word because of its simplicity and because it appears in the Bible. The fact that Scripture never employed it to describe the relationship between Father and Son did not seem to bother them. They just wanted a biblical term. But this understanding of the Son as *like* the Father did not further the discussion of the relationship between Father and Son at all. Nor was it meant to. It was an attempt to return to the time before the Council at Nicaea when the church tolerated great diversity on the topic. Unfortunately, such an attempt was somewhat like trying to put the toothpaste back into the tube after someone has squeezed it out.

The second position, often referred to as a "Semi-Arian" one, attempted to temper the Nicene term *homoousios*—of the same nature—to describe the relationship between Father and Son with the idea that the Father and Son were similar rather than the same. This group came to be associated with the term *homo**i**ousios*—of a similar nature—meaning that the Son is similar to the Father in nature. Note that the only difference in the spelling of the two terms was a single letter—an iota—that made the term plural rather than singular. This meant that the sameness has the element of plurality, forcing the meaning away from "sameness" to "similarity."

Church history generally considers Basil of Ancyra to be the spokesperson of the second group. Basil became bishop of Ancyra when the emperor deposed the previous bishop, Marcellus, because of his support of the Nicene formula. Basil of Ancyra's term *homo**i**ousios* sought to eliminate the potential for the radical unity of modalism or for any division of the nature of God. The fear was that if the Father and Son are the same, then identifying Them as Father and Son divides the one essence. Basil's faction further argued that things that are merely alike, rather than the same, can never actually be the same being, therefore there exists no danger of dividing the unity of God. Unfortunately, with this reasoning only the Father was fully God, for the position identified the nature of the Son as only "like" that of God. Even though Basil of Ancyra attached many caveats to the term "creature," he still ended up applying that designation to the Son.* Once again theologians basically portrayed the Son both as subordinate to the Father and as a creature. And once again it happened because they viewed the Son as a mixture of the characteristics of God and of humanity. Portraying the characteristics of the Son as "like" God, in contrast to depicting the Son as sharing the same nature and characteristics with the Father as God, always leaves the Son as less than fully God. Experimentation with this term allowed people to see that no matter how much less than God Christ is pictured, anything less than God is still not God. The alternative to God is creature, and no matter how you define *creature* the question arises: Is it right to worship a creature? Yet Christians had always worshiped Jesus as God.

The third position we can generalize under the term *heteroousios*—of different substance. Theologians used it to stress the dissimilarity of the natures of the Father and the Son. In the fourth century this group became associated with the name of Eunomius, although their founder was Aetius. More recent times have designated them as Neo-Arians. After having been denounced by a number of councils and rejected from numerous local churches, the Neo-Arians ordained their own bishops and established their own church, not an unusual practice for the time.

In many ways this group was more self-consistent than either the *homoion* or *homoiousios* factions. They considered the Father ungenerated, the Son generated by the Father, and that the Father generated the Son from a different *ousios* (nature) than His own. According to Aetius, there was no Trinity, but rather a hierarchy with the true God as the head and the Son and Spirit as subordinates of different natures. The strength of this view is that it maintains monotheism without the need to redefine any terminology or categories. The weakness is that Jesus Christ is not God. It is interesting to note that the *heteroousios* church allegedly had a distinct baptismal formula, baptizing not in the name of the Father, Son, and Holy Spirit, but rather in the death of Christ alone.

The Nicene statement had been extremely brief in its mention of the Holy Spirit. In response to this, yet another group arose who were comfortable with the Nicene formula describing the nature of the Father and Son as *homoousios,* but arguing that the Spirit could not have the same substance with the Father and Son. Their detractors called them the *pneumatamachoi*—fighters against the Spirit.

Several circumstances in the decade or so before the Council of Constantinople in 381 prepared the way for this gathering in which the Trinitarian formula finally became the official orthodox theology of the Christian church. One event with extremely important repercussions for the council was the coronation of Emperor Theodosius, who was committed to the *homoousios* formula. For 50 years each new emperor had made different allegiances with the various theological groups. Sometimes a single emperor would change his mind several times as to which group to support and which to obstruct. One emperor, Julian, for a short time even tried to turn the empire back to paganism and away from Christianity altogether. Emperor Valens, who died in 378, was the last emperor to openly back an Arian theology and support Arian theologians. It is doubtful whether the emperor's support or opposition alone would have determined the outcome of the Council of Constantinople, for only 75 years earlier another emperor—Diocletian—had tried to manipulate and destroy the church through force and had failed. Christianity had expanded for centuries despite imperial censure or approbation. However, the fact that the new emperor, Theodosius, was in favor of the Nicene formula greatly aided its acceptance.

Another factor preparing the way for the council was the theological writings and political leadership of three Cappadocian theologians: Basil of Caesarea; Basil's friend, Gregory of Nazianzus; and Basil's younger brother, Gregory of Nyssa. They became the theological and political will behind Trinitarianism when the aging Athanasius left the scene. Basil and his friend Gregory were both educated in the philosophical schools of Athens and spent years studying Christian theology and scriptural interpretation. In addition, Basil had traveled extensively around the Mediterranean world and had a wide network of Christian theologian friends. Their broad experience uniquely prepared them for carrying on the work of Athanasius, but it was through uncertain and changing times that they struggled.

Basil compared the situation of bishops and emperors changing minds and switching sides to "a naval battle being fought in the midst of a raging tempest, in which the two fleets are so broken up by the storm that banners can no longer be seen, signals are no longer recognized, and one cannot distinguish one's ally from one's foe" (Basil of Caesarea, quoted from the introduction of *St. Basil the Great: On the Holy Spirit,* trans. David Anderson, p. 7). His analogy describes well the middle decades of the fourth century, especially the time leading up to the Council of Constantinople in 381.

All three Cappadocians wrote treatises and letters exploring and solidifying the Trinitarian theology and creating a standard terminology. They spoke of the Father, Son, and Holy Spirit as simultaneously three in regard to *hypostasis*—personhood—but as one in regard to *ousia*—nature. The Cappadocians extended the shared nature of the Father and the Son to include the Holy Spirit, clarifying the vagueness of the Nicene Creed. In his work *On the Holy Spirit* Basil argued for a recognition of the relationship between Father, Son, and Holy Spirit as of one substance and of equal rank, and therefore as worthy of worship.

It was in the context of worship that Basil made his most effective arguments. Other theologians had challenged him on his use of the prepositions *with* and *together with* in the benediction: "Glory to the Father *with* the Son *together with* the Holy Spirit." They had claimed that in the benediction prayer used at the end of the worship service the prepositions must read "Glory *to* the Father *through* the Son *in* the Holy Spirit." Basil argued in response that the Scriptures make no such close differentiation in the use of prepositions with Father, Son, or Holy Spirit. The authors of Scripture used a variety of prepositions for all three persons of the Godhead. Some had also asserted that this specific use of prepositions showed a subordination of the Son and Spirit to the Father. Basil demonstrated from Scripture that such a subordination of the Son involved only His incarnation. In addition, Basil argued that even though such precision in the use of prepositions was common in philosophy it was foreign to Scripture, and he pointed out how the Bible used almost every combination of the common prepositions to describe the Father, the Son, and the Holy Spirit. The theologian went through literally scores of scriptural passages demonstrating the wide use of prepositions with all three persons of the Godhead. Although it made for tedious reading, it enabled him to disarm the urge to make meticulous distinctions between prepositions. In so doing, he also showed that the prepositions *through* and *in* did not necessarily subordinate the Son and Spirit to the Father.

One example of the overlap in the scriptural use of prepositions appears in Romans 11:36: "from him and through him and to him are all things" (RSV). Basil demonstrated from the context that the passage uses all three prepositions of the Son, but even if his enemies insisted on applying them to the Father, it would not change the argument, for all three would then be applied to the Father. With either reading, a distinction that insists on all things coming *from* the Father *through* the Son cannot be justified in light of the passage. With reference to the Spirit, both Matthew 1:20 and Galatians 6:8 use the preposition *from* in this regard. Matthew 1:20 records the angel telling Joseph not to be afraid to take Mary as his wife because the child conceived in her is "from the Holy Spirit" (NIV). Galatians 6:8 portrays eternal life as coming "from the Spirit" (Basil, pp. 7, 8). Basil's scriptural examples go on and on for chapters, thoroughly demonstrating that the Bible portrays unity and equality among the three members of the Godhead.

Intellectually Basil won his argument from Scripture, but pragmatically it was through the practice of Christian worship that he persuaded the Christian bishops to recognize the Holy Spirit as fully God. He showed how in baptism and in prayer Christians had worshiped the Father, Son, and Holy Spirit alike through the centuries despite all the theological arguments of the fourth century. Every group, with the possible exception of the *heteroousios* party of Eunomius, had continued to worship the Son and the Spirit in spite of their theology. Basil brought this home forcefully in the last chapters of *On the Holy Spirit,* and the realizations that he provoked set the stage for the Council of Constantinople's full recognition of the Son and Holy Spirit as persons in the Godhead, alongside the Father.

It is true that the Council of Nicaea and the Council of Constantinople did make declarations that we must now reject because they disagree with Scripture. Even some aspects of Athanasius' understanding of the Son today seem to cause more problems than they solve, including his description of the Son as "eternally begotten." But such things are neither part of, nor necessary to, the Trinitarian formula of God as three in one—that is, three persons sharing one nature as one God. Although as Adventists, we may not recognize the councils as authoritative, we must recognize the value of Basil's arguments from Scripture and from worship. We do not accept the Trinitarian formula based on the authority of church dogma or of church councils, but on the fact that it best represents what Scripture presents about the Father, Son, and Holy Spirit as one God.

---

*See the construction of the fragments of Basil of Ancyra in R. P. Hanson, *The Search for the Christian Doctrine of God,* pp. 352, 353.

Chapter 10

THE TRINITY IN THE MIDDLE AGES

The Council of Constantinople in 381 finally established Trinitarian beliefs in most areas of the church. However, various types of Arian Christians continued to exist in pockets, including those associated with Aetius and Eunomius in Libya, as well as other small groups who did not accept the Trinity as espoused at the Council of Constantinople. Several of the Germanic tribes that converted to Christianity before the decisive Council of Constantinople also carried the label "Arian."

According to popular legend, the Goths learned the gospel through a Christian missionary named Ulfila who descended from a Roman soldier taken captive by a Goth raiding party in Asia Minor in the third century. Ulfila spoke Greek and Latin skillfully, and knew both Greco-Roman culture and the Gothic culture in which he was raised. It is known that he did indeed go as a Christian missionary to the Goths, and Eusebius, bishop of Nicomedia, consecrated him sometime around A.D. 340. Eusebius had studied with Arius under Lucian of Antioch, and was one of only three people who stood up for Arius at the Council of Nicaea in 325. For this reason many have assumed that Eusebius was an Arian sympathizer who must therefore have consecrated Ulfila as an *Arian* missionary, thus making Ulfila's converts Arian in their beliefs. However, it is not clear that Eusebius ever agreed with Arius in his understanding of Christ as a created being, although he certainly disagreed with the idea that Arius should be condemned and also with the Nicene formula of *homoousios*—of the same nature—as a proper explanation of the relationship between the Father and the Son. Most likely the Christianity Ulfila taught the Goths was ambiguous about the Father and the Son rather than espousing an actual Arian doctrine.

After only seven years of direct missionary work, Ulfila found himself thrown out of Gothic territory because of suspected connections with the Roman enemy. If his involvement with the Goths had ended at that point, his work would not have made much impact. After his expulsion, however, he spent years reducing the Gothic language to writing and translating most of the Scriptures into Gothic. His work had a profound impact on the spread of Christianity among the Goths. During this time, Ulfila still opposed the Nicene formula and favored the ambiguous term *homoios*—similar—rather than *homoousios*—of the same nature—as the description of the relationship between Father and Son. His bias crept into his translation of the Gothic Bible, giving it a subtle slant against Trinitarianism.

Whatever the beliefs of the Goths about the Godhead, when these Christian tribes began to invade the Christian Roman Empire during the fifth century, their "orthodox" enemies labeled them as Arians. Whether or not they had actual significant theological differences, the two sides did use different terminology to describe the Godhead. Given the political reasons for each side to see the other as heretical so they could feel justified in their animosity toward each other, they had no real motivation for mutual understanding. Over the next few centuries, the Gothic and Roman Christians alternately attempted to destroy each other and to coexist side by side, and each consistently attempted to maintain its own identity through the use of the labels "Arian" and "Trinitarian." Eventually, the mainstream church with its Trinitarian description of the Godhead absorbed the Gothic tribes, possibly through the influence of some of their Germanic relatives to the west who accepted a later stage of Christianity with its securely Trinitarian belief system.

The main focus of Christian theology after the Council of Constantinople centered upon the further description of Jesus

Christ, in what church history now remembers as the Christological controversies of the fifth and sixth centuries. Trinitarianism as a whole also began to develop in new directions, advancing along spiritual as well as theological lines. Augustine, the bishop of Hippo in North Africa during the early fifth century and probably the most influential theological philosopher in the history of the Western world, was the focal point of this shift in the development of Trinitarian theology after Constantinople.

Augustine accepted the Trinitarian formula basically as stated at the Council of Constantinople, including the council's full and official acceptance of a single set of Greek terms and definitions. He agreed that we should identify the oneness of God in terms of a single nature shared by the Father, Son, and Holy Spirit and expressed by the Greek term *homoousios*—the same term used at the Council of Nicaea more than 50 years earlier. Theologians had defined and refined the term during the past 50 years so that it was finally acceptable to all those attending the council. The Latin-speaking theologians used a corresponding Latin term—*substancia* or substance—with essentially the same meaning as the Greek term. In addition, Augustine accepted the council's usage of the Greek term *hypostasis,* which had become almost universally adopted as the term for expressing the individuality and personhood of the Father, the Son, and the Holy Spirit within the unity of the Godhead, along with its counterpart, the Latin term *persona.* Thus by the early fifth century Christianity had a set formula of terms in Greek and a corresponding set of terms in Latin that meant essentially the same thing and had been well accepted by the majority of the church.

A recognition of the mystery contained within the concept of the three in one, and the desire to know God within this mystery, became the next major thrust in the development of Trinitarian doctrine through Augustine's influential work, *On the Trinity.* In his book Augustine described his own search for a more intimate understanding of God. He read through the entire Bible, contemplating each text about God, and, in so doing, came to understand God as Father, Son, and Holy Spirit—three persons but one God sharing the same nature. He recognized also that this was not a complete description of God—that knowing God was not simply a matter of presenting the mathematical formula of "three in one" or of trying to understand the mystery of God in the characteristics of His shared nature, His omniscience, or His eternity. Augustine instead suggested that knowing God also involved experiencing His loving character, a character that remains a mystery even after we have presented every description and interpreted every revelation in Scripture. In addition, Augustine developed and expressed a profound insight—that when we have produced our fullest description of God, we still do not truly have even a cursory knowledge of Him. Yet enough knowledge is available so that the Christian can understand the basic dynamics of salvation and how to relate to Him and to each other in His sight. At the end of his work, when he had done all he could in his search for God, Augustine announced in exaltation that he had experienced a glorious failure in his search for God, for although he had discovered much, learned much, and knew much, still he did not yet apprehend God Himself. This understanding, according to Augustine, must wait until heaven.

Others even before Augustine had attempted to contemplate God. As early as Philo of Alexandria's *Life of Moses,* theologians had attempted on an internal rather than an external level to understand God through Moses and his experiences. Gregory of Nyssa also wrote a life of Moses, focusing on his interaction with God at Horeb, the holy mountain, where he spoke personally with God for extended periods of time. Here, Gregory tried to understand a personal, not just a theoretical, God through Scripture. However, it was Augustine's writings, above all, that set the stage for the medieval attempts to understand the mystery of God from the inside—to contemplate and apprehend God, not just to classify and cognitively understand Him.

Having acknowledged that Augustine's book *On the Trinity* is primarily a spiritual quest, we should state that it was also the most meticulously argued and intricately defined philosophical treatise on the Trinity up to his time. Augustine's major goal was a spiritual connection with God, as far as humanly possible, but his method included careful interpretation of Scripture and detailed logical steps from each question to each conclusion. Much in the book eventually became part of the Trinitarian dogma of the medieval Catholic Church, but the church organized it on the basic Trinitarian formula expressed at the Council of Constantinople. He gives a great deal of attention in book 5, for instance, to the "begetting" of the Son by the Father, carefully defining it in a way that maintained the coeternity and equality of the two. The same applies to the Holy Spirit "proceeding" from the Father and the Son. Neither concept, though, is part of the central Trinitarian formula of three in one.

These are further clarifications of the relationships within the Godhead that the councils of Nicaea and Constantinople alluded to but did not closely define. Like the "eternal generation" of the Son suggested by Athanasius nearly a century earlier, Augustine accepted them as if they were an integral part of the Trinitarian doctrine, although we do not logically need to view them as such. Instead they are attempts to more closely work out the relationships between the three persons in the one God by depicting the Father as the timeless source for the Son and the Spirit. However, this closer definition forces us to either distort the scriptural understanding of time or to subjugate the Son and the Spirit to the Father.

Augustine, in his quest for understanding God, not only used information arising from Scripture and philosophy, but also suggested that because God created humans in His image, we can also gain insights into the Trinity from observing ourselves. His basic argument, given in book 10.4, and clarified in book 14.2, was that the human soul is a trinity of memory, understanding, and will just as the Father, Son, and Holy Spirit are a trinity. The memory, understanding, and will are each dependent on the others, each contain the others, and each by themselves may be called "mind" or "life" or "being." For instance, when distinguishing "memory" from "understanding" one has to use the two terms, but when referring only to "understanding" it can be designated simply as "mind." So the Father is called "Father" in reference to the Son or the Spirit, but may simply be called "God" relative to Himself when not being distinguished from the Son or the Spirit. Also, since the three—memory, understanding, and will—make up a single mind, it is hard to define where one stops and the other begins. Where, for example, does the function of memory begin to be the function of understanding? It is impossible to say at which point memory turns into understanding, for they are both one mind. In the same way, Augustine argues, it is impossible to distinguish completely between the members of the Godhead, inasmuch as they are one God. Augustine's use of the human soul as an illustration of the Trinity depends on a philosophical view of the human person as having a soul separate from the body, but what he was trying to illustrate shows that he is elaborating upon the basic Trinitarian formula, three interacting within one.

This focus on the understanding and contemplation of God continued through the twelfth century, when the Latin-speaking world rediscovered the writings of Aristotle, and Europe turned to a more cognitive and empirical study of theology and the world. Two of the scholastic theologians who followed the Platonic philosophical theology of Augustine but also incorporated the new empirical theology under the influence of Aristotle were Bonaventure and Thomas Aquinas.

Bonaventure was born in 1217 and spent much of his life connected with the University of Paris, the primary theological institution of scholasticism of the time. While in residence at the university he lectured on the Bible and wrote a commentary on the *Sentences* of Peter the Lombard, the standard way of receiving the degree of Doctor of Theology. Bonaventure joined the Franciscans, and in 1257 became the seventh minister of the order after Francis of Assisi. Augustine and Francis heavily influenced Bonaventure's theology, and it, therefore, was deeply spiritual.

While at Paris Bonaventure wrote a book entitled *Disputed Questions on the Mystery of the Trinity* and so was very much up on the issues involved with the Trinity when he wrote a later book known as *Itinerarium,* or *The Journey of the Mind to God*. In this book he gives six steps for knowing God and coming into union with Him. After beginning with the contemplation of the beauty and order of what God has made, the final steps focused upon a contemplation of the goodness of pure being—a meditation that involved thoughtful consideration of the characteristics of God's nature. For Bonaventure, the highest level the human mind can reach is to become absorbed in the communication between the three persons of the one God. His spiritual goal, in the final steps, he thus crafts around the triune reality of the Father, Son, and Holy Spirit.

It is in the middle steps, however, that his development of Augustinian thought becomes most evident. The third and fourth steps of Bonaventure's journey of the mind to God focus on the human soul. He follows the lead of Augustine in *On the Trinity* by suggesting that one way for humans to know God is through examining the image of God within ourselves. Bonaventure, as did Augustine, saw this image as a triune image. The human soul, he argued, has three components—memory, intellect, and will—within the one soul. The three aspects correspond to the Father, Son, and Holy Spirit in the one God. Thus far Bonaventure has parroted Augustine, but he adds a component that Augustine did not overtly state. The thirteenth-century theologian uses the way in which the intellect and will arise from the memory as an illustration of the procession of the Son and the Holy Spirit from the Father. As one's intellect proceeds from memory as wisdom is gained through remembered events, so the Son, who is the Logos, or Word, proceeds from the Father as His Wisdom. Next, Bonaventure makes a similar, though even more complex, parallel between the will arising from both the memory and intellect and the Spirit proceeding from the Father and the Son. Again, as with Augustine, Bonaventure saw the procession of the Son and Spirit as integral to the doctrine of the Trinity, but it need not be so.

He took much of his understanding of contemplation from Francis of Assisi, the founder of the Franciscans. In particular, Bonaventure tells us in the prologue to his work *The Journey of the Mind to God* that he found the inspiration for the work and for its six-step structure in the vision of Francis in which he saw the six-winged seraph from Isaiah in the form of the Crucified One. Each wing of the seraph represented one step toward contemplation of God, and each pair of wings represented one person of the Trinity. He structured the whole work in threes, using triplets and triplets of triplets. The author gives nearly every piece of information in three parts, and nearly every description has three adjectives. In this way the very words of the work illustrate the three in one of the Trinity. But there is another aspect of the work that Bonaventure derived from Francis. Chapter 1 starts off with: "Here begins the reflection of the poor man in the desert." The "poor man" is obviously Francis, who gave up his wealthy life as a merchant's son to embrace the poverty of Jesus. Yet the "poor man" is obviously more than just a reference to Francis. We must also see it as the condition of all humans "bent" away from God by sin, not able to see God except through grace, and living in this desert of a fallen world. Thus all humans are poor in relation to the riches of God, even those who have chosen the virtuous path of poverty. The only way back from this spiritual poverty is through the ascent of the heart. "But," Bonaventure states, "we cannot rise above ourselves unless a superior power raise us." Thus Bonaventure begins his journey toward contemplating God as Trinity, and toward handing the affections entirely over to God, with a recognition of the human need for being lifted by God. This attitude of poverty Bonaventure received from Francis.

Thomas Aquinas, although he was possibly the most empirical of the thirteenth-century scholastic theologians, also understood something of the impossibility of truly "knowing" God that Augustine expressed at the end of his own spiritual search. Aquinas based both his theological approach and his understanding of the Trinity on Augustine. In his *Summa Theologica* he attempted to show, by entirely empirical means, how human reason can develop a natural theology that parallels what we find revealed in Scripture. During his attempt to understand God rationally, Aquinas pursued questions about the characteristics of God from many different angles. Concerning God's eternity, for example, his questions led him to conclude that God alone is truly eternal. Concerning the omniscience of God, Aquinas decided that only God is all-knowing, because God is eternal and only something eternal can be all-knowing. Unfortunately, such intricate logical questioning can often tangle questioners in thickets of their own making, for the next question would logically be, "If God is both eternal and all-knowing, then can He know Himself completely?" Aquinas came, once again, to the reality that when we are done discussing what we can know about God there still remains much that we cannot know about Him. His true being remains a mystery to us.

That God remains a mystery is easily illustrated by an experience I had with my own son. As I described God to him, I mentioned that He is omnipotent and all-powerful. "You mean He can do anything?" my son responded. Then, without waiting for a response, he promptly asked, "If He can do anything, can He make a rock too big for Himself to move?" It was a question I could not answer. However, it was not one that placed any limits upon God. It had only shown our own lack of ability to apprehend and understand God, demonstrating in a concrete way His ultimate mystery.

Despite all human understanding, description, and agreement concerning how to portray God as a unity of three divine persons worshiped as fully God, we still have not come close to defining or understanding or *knowing* God. Everything that we have accomplished is still simply knowing *about* God. The history of contemplation concerning the mystery of the Trinity is one of constantly learning more about God without ever knowing all about God—and all too often it is a history of having to backtrack. Although humanity has penetrated some levels of the divine mystery and has even codified them, the larger mystery still remains. So Augustine's happy failure in trying to know God and to understand the Trinity can, in many ways, be our happy failure as well. Having a correct view of God and being able to understand His salvation, His forgiveness, and His love better does not take away the mystery of the Trinity—the mystery of who God is.

Bibliography for Section Two

Augustine of Hippo. *The Trinity*. Trans. Edmund Hill. Brooklyn, N.Y.: New City Press, 1991.

Barnes, Michael R., and Daniel H. Williams, *Arianism After Arius*. Edinburg: Clark, 1993.

Basil of Caesarea. In *St. Basil the Great: On the Holy Spirit*. Trans. David Anderson. Crestwood, N.Y.: St. Vladimir's Seminary Press, 1997.

Bonaventure. *The Journey of the Mind to God*. Ed. Stephen F. Brown. Trans. Philotheus Boehner. Indianapolis, Ind.: Hackett, 1993.

Dawson, David. *Allegorical Readers and Cultural Revision in Ancient Alexandria*. Berkeley, Calif.: University of California Press, 1992.

Donovan, Mary Ann. *One Right Reading: A Guide to Irenaeus*. Collegeville, Minn.: Liturgical Press, 1997.

Hanson, R. P. *The Search for the Christian Doctrine of God*. Edinburg: Clark, 1988.

Meijering, E. P. *Orthodoxy and Platonism in Athanasius: Synthesis or Antithesis?* Leiden, Netherlands: Brill, 1974.

Norris, R. A. *God and the World in Early Christian Theology*. London: Adam and Charles Black, 1966.

Pettersen, Alvyn. *Athanasius*. Harrisburg, Pa.: Morehouse, 1995.

Stead, Christopher. *Philosophy in Christian Antiquity*. Cambridge: Cambridge University Press, 1994.

Toon, Peter. *Yesterday, Today and Forever: Jesus Christ and the Holy Trinity in the Teaching of the Seven Ecumenical Councils*. Swedesboro, N. J.: Preservation Press, 1996.

Wiles, Maurice. *Archetypal Heresy: Arianism Through the Centuries*. Oxford: Clarendon Press, 1996.

SECTION THREE

Trinity and Anti-Trinitarianism
From the Reformation
to the Advent Movement

Glossary for Section Three

Anabaptists—group of Christians who, first in 1525, baptized adults on profession of faith. The nickname, coined by their enemies, meant "re-baptizer(s)." Believers' baptism led to a church of "baptized believers only," a concept seen as treason against the state churches that included the whole population, based on infant baptism. See also Restorationists.

Anti-Trinitarian—antagonistic toward or rejecting belief in a Trinity.

Christian Connexion—also spelled Connection. American Restorationist denomination, organized about 1810, merged with Congregationalists in 1931. Christians, as they called themselves, were evangelical Protestants, similar to Freewill Baptists, except that many of them (not all) were anti-Trinitarian.

Deism—a system of natural religion that developed in England and spread to the U.S.A. in the 1700s. While considerable variety existed among deists, some beliefs were shared widely, including supreme faith in human reason; doubt or outright rejection of divine revelation and Scripture; and the belief that while God created the world, He takes no continuing interest in it. Some deists believed that Providence sustained the physical world, but was uninterested in individuals. They had little certainty about life after death.

Doctrine—a teaching of religious belief. As used in this book, doctrine is a more general term than dogma. See also Dogma.

Dogma—in Roman Catholic theology, a religious teaching defined by the church, and which every faithful member is obligated to believe.

Dualism—a philosophical belief that soul (or mind) and matter (or material) are "distinct, equally real" *(Oxford Dictionary of the Christian Church [ODCC]),* and radically contrasting states of existence. Three aspects of Greek dualism that underlie the traditional dogma of the Trinity are (1) distinction of soul and body; (2) radical separation of God and humanity; and (3) contrast between time and timelessness.

Fundamentalism—in Protestant Christianity, a movement that arose c. 1895-1914 in reaction to Modernism, evolution, and higher criticism of the Bible. Fundamentalists believed in (1) the verbal inspiration and inerrancy of Scripture; (2) the deity of Christ; (3) the virgin birth of Christ; (4) substitutionary atonement; and (5) the physical resurrection and literal second coming of Christ. See also Modernism.

Generation—the process of generating or being generated. Some Trinitarian theologians held that only the Father existed from eternity; that both Christ and the Holy Spirit were "generated," i.e., brought into existence, by the Father.

Impassible—free of all passions (feelings and emotions), including compassion. Greek philosophical theology considered impassibility to be an attribute of God.

Limbo—in Roman Catholic theology, the place for souls who are neither eligible for full salvation nor worthy of eternal torment.

Magisterial Reformers—the dominant Reformers, the giants of the sixteenth-century Reformation. Church historians generally consider them to include Luther, Zwingli, and Calvin, of whom Luther and Calvin, through their voluminous writings, have exercised the greatest influence.

Modalist—see Monarchianism.

Modernism—during the late 1800s and early 1900s, a theological movement characterized by embracing evolution and higher critical theories of Scripture, and denying supernatural miracles such as Christ's virgin birth, physical resurrection, and literal second coming. See also Fundamentalism.

Monarchianism—a theological movement of the second and third centuries that tried to safeguard the unity of God by denying the plurality of God. One of two subgroups was that of the **Modalist Monarchians** who "held that in the Godhead the only differentiation was a mere succession of modes or operations." They taught that Father, Son, and Holy Spirit are not separate personalities *(ODCC)*. Sabellius was one of its third-century proponents, and his teaching has been called Sabellianism.

Nontrinitarian—nonbelieving in a Trinity.

Orthodox—(1) right belief as contrasted with heresy. (2) [capitalized]: the branch of Christianity that included the Eastern Roman Empire with its capital Constantinople. Also called Eastern Orthodox or Greek Orthodox, and including national churches such as Russian Orthodox, Serbian Orthodox, and Romanian Orthodox. The Roman church excommunicated the Orthodox churches in 1054.

Rationalists—persons who accepted reason as the supreme authority in matters of belief. Some Christian Rationalists asserted the sole authority of Scripture, but while they rejected the philosophical foundations of medieval theology, their tendency was to elevate human reason above the authority of Scripture. See also Unitarians.

Restorationists—also called **Restitutionists.** Christians who did not wish to merely reform (improve) the church, but who wished to fully restore it to its New Testament condition. Anabaptists were sixteenth-century Restorationists impatient with Luther because he seemed to stop far short of the doctrine and organization of the New Testament church. An American example from the nineteenth century was the Christian Connexion. Seventh-day Adventists regard themselves as Restorationists in the sense that they cherish the goal of "completing the Reformation."

Sabellianism—a theological movement named after Sabellius. See Monarchianism.

Scholasticism, Protestant—a theological method built on the same philosophical foundations used by the medieval scholastics before the Reformation. The Protestant Scholastics held that not only Scripture but also Aristotle was a gift of God, and essential for theology.

Socinians—spiritual descendants of Unitarian leader Faustus Socinus (1539-1604). They denied the preexistence of the Son, believed that Christ was "simply a man," and defined the Holy Spirit as a "virtue or energy" from God. Socinians were the forerunners of present-day Unitarians (Berkhof, p. 96).

Sola scriptura—Latin for "Scripture alone." Popularized by Luther, this slogan stood for the subordination of all human authorities—such as tradition, popes, councils, and emperors—to the supreme authority of Scripture.

Timelessness—the unbiblical notion of Greek dualism that God's eternity is "timeless," that is, an "eternal present," in contrast to human life in time with its past, present, and future.

Trinitarian—related to or favoring belief in a Trinity. Used here as a general term for all who hold some form of belief in one God in three persons.

Tritheism—the belief that the Father, Son, and Holy Spirit constitute three Gods. This view affirms the three-ness of God, but denies His oneness.

Unitarianism—historically characterized by nonbelief in the Trinity and the deity of Christ, teaching the oneness, but not the three-ness, of God. Lacking official doctrines, present-day Unitarians hold reason and conscience to be the ultimate standards of belief and life.

Chapter 11

THE TRINITY IN THE REFORMATION ERA: FOUR VIEWPOINTS

Sola scriptura, Latin for "Scripture alone," furnishes a major clue to understanding the variety of approaches to the Trinity doctrine that developed during the Reformation period. As the battle cry for the popular assault on the authority of the medieval church, practically all shades of religious dissenters used *sola scriptura*—but not all in the same way. The variety of Reformation views on the Trinity closely mirrors the range of attitudes toward, and uses of, *sola scriptura.*

The four groups that we will particularly examine in this chapter represent a continuum of viewpoints on the Trinity, from the traditional to the revolutionary. 1. Because Roman Catholics rejected the sole authority of Scripture, they retained the traditional dogma of the Trinity as developed by Athanasius, Augustine, Aquinas, and others. 2. The mainline Reformers—Luther, Calvin, and their followers—shifted their primary proofs for the Trinity from tradition and philosophy to Scripture, but maintained the Trinitarian formulas of the early Christian creeds. 3. The Restorationist Anabaptists made a more radical break with tradition, seeking to fully restore the doctrine, and even the organizational pattern of the New Testament church. Consequently, while they retained belief in the Trinity, their explanation of it was simpler and closer to the actual words of Scripture. 4. The anti-Trinitarian Rationalists also asserted the sole authority of Scripture, but with reference to the Trinity their conclusions took a sharply different direction. While they repudiated the philosophical foundations of medieval theology (Servetus, p. 67), their own reverence for human reason became another way of compromising the sole authority of Scripture.

It is apparent that "Scripture alone" did not mean the total rejection of all other sources of authority. But it did stand for the subordination of all human authorities—such as tradition, popes, councils, and emperors—to the supreme authority of Scripture. However, even Luther, who initially popularized the slogan, did not always follow it completely. Thus it appears that the Reformers compromised "Scripture alone"—almost fatally—right from the start because its champions could not themselves perceive the extent to which presuppositions contrary to Scripture had already shaped their worldview. Living in a pervasively religious society, few considered that foundational assumptions drawn from Greek philosophy largely predetermined how they interpreted Scripture. Several examples will emerge as we look more closely at the four leading approaches to the Trinity doctrine in the Reformation Era.

The Roman Catholic Dogma of the Trinity

The Roman Catholic view was for all the Reformers the point of departure. As sketched in previous chapters, the Roman Catholic Church had come during the Middle Ages to the conviction that the Trinity was its most "central" and "fundamental teaching" (Pelikan, vol. 3, p. 279). The philosophical formulation of the Trinity was both central and fundamental, because more than any other doctrine it directly depended on Greek philosophical presuppositions. Therefore its definition as a dogma (something required to be believed by all the faithful) placed the stamp of legitimacy on the presuppositions of Aristotle and Plato that it used to interpret Scripture. This was foundational, because the church's theologians employed the same presuppositions for other teachings such as the natural immortality of the soul, which was in turn the necessary prerequisite for belief in eternal torment, purgatory, limbo, and the mediation of the saints, to mention a few examples. Thus the acceptance of the Trinity dogma validated the whole dogmatic structure of the medieval church (see Pelikan, p. 279).

At this point we need to unpack some of the key elements of the Greek philosophy that so powerfully influenced the development of Christian theology. The most important concepts for the present discussion involve the notion of radical dualism. Greek philosophy perceived the whole universe as divided into two categories of existence: soul (or spirit), defined as inherently immortal and good, and material things that were transitory and essentially evil. Such dualism was "radical" in the sense that it involved not merely conflict between good and evil, but drastically contrasting states of existence. This will become clearer as we consider three aspects of radical dualism that underlie the traditional dogma of the Trinity: (1) soul and body; (2) God and man; and (3) time and timelessness. What I offer here is a gross oversimplification, but I have based it in part on the scholarly work of Fernando Canale ("Doctrine of God").

To many people, the most familiar aspect of Greek dualism is the concept that human beings consist of an immortal soul that is naturally good and a mortal body that is basically evil and must eventually die in order to free the soul.

A second aspect of Greek dualism is a particular way of defining God in relation to humanity. Greek philosophy was not atheistic—far from it. Greek *mythology* imagined a pantheon of all-too-human male and female gods, from Zeus to Aphrodite. The Greek *philosophy* of Aristotle and Plato, however, taught one supreme deity absolutely unlike humans. The Greek philosophers understood God as absolute perfection. They called Him the "unmoved mover," because Aristotle believed that if God so much as thought about flawed, mortal, material beings, it would spoil His absolute perfection. He was "impassible," that is, free of all passions (feelings and emotions)—the exact opposite of the God portrayed in Isaiah 53:4-6 and Hebrews 4:15. One historian summarizes the situation:

"Augustine's God, though trinitarian, is made captive to the Greek philosophical theology of divine simplicity, immutability, and impassibility, and turns out to be more like a great cosmic emperor than a loving, compassionate heavenly Father. Anselm denied that God experiences feelings of compassion at all. . . . Those who rightly criticize Deism for subverting biblical teachings by overwhelming them with Enlightenment philosophical and natural religion, ought to consider the extent to which classical Christian doctrines of God have been unduly influenced by Greek philosophical categories of metaphysical perfection" (Olson, *Story of Christian Theology,* p. 530).

For such a God to enter history and interact with human beings in space and time was, by definition, impossible. The only exception to this radical separation of God from humanity was the human soul, understood to be a spark from the divine soul and intrinsically immortal. Because of its imprisonment in a material body, the soul afforded the one point of contact through which the God outside of history could influence humans trapped in time and space.

A third aspect of radical dualism that undergirds the previous two and further asserts the fundamental isolation of God from humanity is the dualism of time and timelessness. The philosophers conceived God's eternity as "timeless," that is, an "eternal present" without past or future—in sharp contrast to human life in time with its past, present, and future. We could diagram these aspects of dualism as follows:

1. God = pure Soul	2. God is impassable; cannot enter history . . .	3. God exists in timelessness, "eternal now."
Radical separation between God's timelessness and human history		
1. Humans = material, evil body + spark of immortal soul	2. . . . except via the human soul.	3. Humans live in time and space.

In every one of these aspects, Scripture provided a much different picture than that offered by dualism. First, instead of a naturally immortal soul in an evil body, Scripture asserted that the body was God's creation and "very good" (Gen. 1:31). Furthermore, the soul was not something that could experience a conscious existence apart from the body (Eccl. 9:5, 6). Rather, the scriptural terminology for a "living soul" refers to the whole person, including the body (Gen.

2:7). Far from being naturally immortal, "the soul that sins will die" (Eze. 18:4, 20). To substantiate this fully is beyond the scope of the present topic, but the sharp contrast between Scripture and Greek philosophy in this area has received increasing recognition from well-known theologians in recent years (Cullmann, Fudge, Pinnock, Stott).

Second, Scripture contradicted the dualistic theory that God cannot intervene in human history. Dualism claimed that as pure soul, He dwelt outside of time and space, and that, furthermore, since He was "impassible"—without compassion, or feelings—He had no interest in human affairs anyway. To the contrary, Scripture portrays God as entering human history, time, and space at will. In Genesis the Lord God walks and talks with the couple in Eden (Gen. 3:8, 9); confronts Cain (Gen. 4:6); intervenes at the tower of Babel (Gen. 11:5), and negotiates with Abraham about Sodom (Gen. 18:16-33). And in Exodus God appears, speaks, and names Himself to Moses at the burning bush (Ex. 3:4–4:17); reveals Himself visibly to 70 elders of Israel (Ex. 24:9-11); and grants Moses a direct view of His person (Ex. 33:19-23).

But Greek philosophy considers such things as simply impossible, unthinkable, and therefore to be interpreted as figurative speech. Whatever the common people understood by such Bible stories (and regardless of how the Bible writers may have regarded their own writings), philosophers "knew" that for deity to enter history was an absurdity, a contradiction in terms that obviously could not be taken as a statement of ultimate truth.

A third area in which Scripture challenged a fundamental premise of Greek philosophy concerns time and timelessness (Gonzalez, *Christian Thought Revisited,* p. 103). Scripture portrays God as greater than time and experiencing time differently than we do (Ps. 90:4; 2 Peter 3:8), but that fact does not exclude Him from life in time. Because He "gives life to the dead and calls those things which do not exist as though they did" (Rom. 4:17, NKJV), He can foresee persons who are presently dead as they will be when He resurrects them (Matt. 22:32). Thus He knows (foreknows) the future, which we cannot. But that is not the same as the concept of timelessness that views God as existing in an "eternal now." The eternity that God lives in (Isa. 57:15) and the everlasting life that He promises to faithful believers (John 3:16) are not the absence of time, but unending time (Ps. 102:27; Isa. 66:22, 23).

Because of these basic conflicts with Scripture, the Greek philosophers and their followers regarded Scripture—and especially the Hebrew Scriptures—as written for the "simple-minded" and greatly inferior to philosophy (*ibid.,* p. 119). Consequently, they evaluated everything in Scripture from the perspective of Greek philosophy. Whatever agreed with philosophy they accepted as true, and whatever did not, they considered as figurative or as a moralizing story for the simple masses.

Notice now what happens to the biblical teaching about God when viewed through the lens of "timelessness." When God says in Malachi 3:6, "I am the Lord, I do not change" (NKJV) He means that His character is unchanging, stable, hence dependable. Utterly trustworthy, He keeps His promises. Hebrews 13:8 makes the same claim for God the Son—that He is "the same yesterday, today, and forever" (NKJV). But "timelessness" says He has no "yesterday," no past or future, but is static, immobile, in an "eternal present."

When Jesus said, "I proceeded forth and came from God" (John 8:42, NKJV), the plain meaning of His speech to those who heard Him say it was a claim: "My witness of the Father is trustworthy because I know Him intimately; it is He who sent Me into the world, and I speak as His appointed representative" (loose paraphrase of John 8:14-17, 28, 29, 38, 42).

But a Greek philosopher would notice immediately that if Jesus came from outside the world, He also came from outside of time, hence He must have preexisted in timelessness. Since timelessness was thought to be an eternal present, if Christ "proceeded" from the Father in timelessness, then His "procession" from the Father is eternal. It had no beginning (past), no ending (future), but is eternally "proceeding." Thus dualism interprets the simple statement of Jesus about His coming into the world as one about His ultimate origins.

We can draw two implications from this. One result of reading the "procession" statements philosophically is that "the Father was the only one of the three persons who did not come from another" (Bonaventure, quoted in Pelikan, vol. 3, p. 278). The Eastern Orthodox concept differs in details, but also holds that only the Father "is ungenerated, the Son is generated by the Father, and the Holy Spirit proceeds from the Father through the Son" (or as some say, "from the Father only" *[ODCC])*.

A second implication is that if eternity is a timeless "eternal present," then whatever happened to God, ever, is still happening and will continue to happen forever. From this comes the theory of the "eternal generation of the Son." Some include the Holy Spirit in this "eternal generation," since He too is said to "proceed" from the Father [John 15:26] *(ODCC)*. This theory has not gone uncriticized. John Calvin, for instance, exclaimed that "it is foolish to imagine a continuous act of generating when it is evident that three persons have existed in one God from eternity" (*Institutes* I. xiii. 29). Yet, despite brilliant, famous, and learned opponents (Gonzalez, *History of Christian Thought,* vol. 3, pp. 91, 92), the theory of the "eternal generation of the Son" remains a part of the Roman Catholic Trinity dogma to this day (Hogan and LeVoir, pp. 12-14). But the concept and its implications have their basis only in the Aristotelian concept of timelessness.

The reason such dogma remains virtually unchanged to the present is that the church has made its logical basis an official part of church law. The Council of Trent, which opened the year before Luther died and closed the year before Calvin died (1545-1563), represented the summation of the Roman Catholic response to the Reformation. After lengthy debate, the council voted that the church cannot base doctrine solely on Scripture as the Protestants argued, but on two sources of authority, Scripture and tradition, of which tradition is the more fundamental. Further, Trent redefined tradition not as the heritage of antiquity, but as the continual inspiration of the church. If the continuing inspiration of the church is a more fundamental authority than Scripture, then the official pronouncements of the church are their own supreme authority. It is the polar opposite of *sola scriptura,* and the reason we have seen no significant change in the Catholic dogma of the Trinity.

The Magisterial Reformers and the Trinity

The major figures who dominated the Protestant Reformation both in the sixteenth century and to the present are Martin Luther (1483-1546) and John Calvin (1509-1564). Luther and Calvin set Scripture above popes, church councils, and tradition; but in theological areas in which they did not see obvious problems, they assumed the church had developed under God's guidance and thus they tended to interpret Scripture in ways that affirmed traditional views. Through all their theological conflicts with the Catholics, they continued to assume that their views of the Trinity constituted common ground (Pelikan, vol. 4, pp. 157, 158). Thus Justo Gonzalez writes that "Luther is perfectly orthodox" and Calvin is "entirely orthodox and traditional" on the Trinity (Gonzalez, *History of Christian Thought,* vol. 3, pp. 41, 126). At a few points, though, they glimpsed the inconsistency between the biblical witness to the Trinity and the speculations of the philosophers. Both Luther and Calvin wished for a Trinity doctrine expressed in strictly biblical terms (Bainton, pp. 58-60; Pelikan, vol. 4, pp. 187, 188, 322). Yet while Calvin criticized the theory of "eternal generation" (*Institutes* I. xiii. 29), and insisted on the sole authority of Scripture, he was also "willing to interpret that Scripture in the light of the early ecumenical councils." He quotes the early Church Fathers "often and usually with approval" (Gonzalez, *History of Christian Thought,* vol. 3, p. 126).

In one sense it is grossly unfair of us to fault the Reformers for failing to achieve in one generation their ideal of a church ruled by Scripture alone. We are painfully aware of what slow progress we make in our own lives. Nevertheless, in hindsight, it is obvious that, being a product of the Middle Ages, they were steeped in a worldview derived from Greek philosophy. While in the strength of God they made major strides toward reshaping church and society in biblical ways, their philosophical education and their immersion in the common worldview made it virtually impossible for them to recognize that they were still to some extent interpreting Scripture through Greek philosophical lenses. Because they did not clearly see the foundational conflict between *sola scriptura* and Greek dualism, the movements they started largely returned in the next generation to medieval assumptions. The result was Protestant Scholasticism, a theological method built on the same philosophical foundations used by the medieval scholastics before the Reformation. The Protestant Scholastics, despite their boasting in the sole authority of Scripture, held that the teaching of Aristotle "was also 'a gift coming down from the Father of lights' [James 1:17]" (Pelikan, vol. 4, pp. 348, 349; Gonzalez, *History of Christian Thought,* vol. 3, p. 241). In this way, the medieval merger of Aristotle and Scripture survived the Reformation and gained a new lease on life a century after Luther.

Such Protestant embracing of Greek philosophy prompted a Roman Catholic rejoinder that if Protestants wanted to retain belief in the Trinity, they might have to "abandon their fundamental principle" of *sola scriptura* (Pelikan, vol. 5, p. 194). This raises one of the fundamental questions of the post-Reformation debate over the Trinity: If one discards the authority of tradition, does the evidence of Scripture still compel one to understand God in a trinitarian way? Some Roman Catholics answered no, but believed it anyway based on tradition. Luther and Calvin said yes, but their descendants seemed less certain about it. A third group would give a biblical yes to the question, but in the process, would simplify the terms of the doctrine.

Anabaptists and the Trinity

The Anabaptists went further than Luther and Calvin in rejecting the authority of tradition. They retained belief in the Trinity, but in a considerably simpler form than that of the traditionalists and scholastics. Church historians describe the Anabaptists as Restorationists (or Restitutionists), because their purpose was not merely to reform, i.e., improve the church, but to actually restore it to its New Testament form—to whatever extent that was possible 15 centuries later (Liechty, pp. 3-7). Specifically, they rejected infant baptism, the basis of the state church, arguing that the church in the New Testament did not include all the persons in a given political territory, but only those who made a personal choice to follow Christ. Therefore the church should reserve baptism for persons mature enough to make a deliberate commitment.

Since all Europeans of that era had already been baptized as babies, society viewed adult baptism as a second baptism. The name Anabaptist, coined by their enemies, meant "rebaptizer." Imperial Roman law had punished such rebaptism by death, and European nations revived the ancient law to deal with the Anabaptists. The Anabaptist conviction that the New Testament church was a church of "believers only" was a judgment that infant baptism was not real baptism and that persons baptized as infants were not really Christians. Hence contemporary society saw Anabaptists as threatening simultaneously the unity of the church and the security of the state. For this reason, their opponents often burned them at the stake or drowned them in a "third baptism" (Snyder, pp. 112, 118, 193).

Anabaptists wrote little on the Trinity because they did not specialize in systematic theology. They believed that one found the primary marks of true Christianity in purity of life and the fruit of the Spirit more than in absolutely precise correctness of belief. While they did not despise correct belief—in fact, they were willing to die for it—for them, true faith would always bear *"visible fruit* in repentance, conversion, regeneration, obedience, and a new life dedicated to the love of God and neighbor, by the power of the Holy Spirit," including the willingness to be martyred if necessary (*ibid.*, pp. 151, 152; italics his).

The first Anabaptist theologian was Balthasar Hubmaier, university educated in theology before he left the Roman Catholic Church. He affirmed the Apostles' Creed, and used the term "Trinity," but did not elaborate on it (Pipkin and Yoder, pp. 348, 349, 361, 430). The chief Anabaptist writer on the Trinity was Menno Simons, from whom the Mennonites take their name. Because of "his intense desire to use only scriptural language," Menno "avoided using the term 'Trinity,'" but he defended from

Scripture the basic concept of one God in three persons (Gonzalez, *History of Christian Thought,* p. 87).

"Restorationist" later expanded to include other Protestant groups who also held the ideal of recovering the doctrine and, as far as possible, the organization of the New Testament church. From points of origin in Switzerland, Germany, and the Netherlands, Anabaptists carried the Restorationist impulse east as far as Russia, north and west to England, and across the Atlantic to North America. In England, Restorationist ideals played a significant part in the development of Baptists, Puritans, and other Separatists, most of whom eventually sent representatives to North America. The Anabaptist emphasis on practice over theory also influenced the Pietist Moravians, who in turn helped shape the thinking of John Wesley and the Methodists. Thus the Anabaptists' more complete rejection of medieval tradition in favor of the authority of Scripture contributed to distinctive ways of reading and thinking about the Bible that would exert a profound influence on the course of American religion, including Adventists, 300 years later.

Anti-Trinitarian Rationalists

The fourth and last group we will consider in this chapter is that of the anti-Trinitarian rationalists. Like Luther and Calvin, they held to the sole authority of Scripture. And like the Anabaptists, church history considers them "radical reformers" for their thoroughgoing repudiation of traditional authority. Unlike the Anabaptists, however, the Rationalists were inclined to criticize even Scripture when it did not seem to meet the criteria of rational logic. Thus they tended to place human reason above the authority of Scripture.

What scholars have termed the "war against the Trinity" began with Michael Servetus (1511-1553) (Pelikan, vol. 4, p. 323). Servetus, a Spaniard, found himself shocked and grieved by the brutal treatment—confiscation of property and banishment or death by burning—meted out to his Jewish and Islamic countrymen for rejecting the Trinity. They were not pagans. But they viewed the Trinity doctrine as belief in three Gods and thus a denial of their faith in one God (Bainton, pp. 14-16).

The reform trajectory that would eventually bring Servetus to the burning-stake in Geneva began when he searched the Scriptures for the word "Trinity" and couldn't find it. Neither could he discover any reference to the "one substance" or the "three persons." He did see the Father, Son, and Holy Spirit, but he never found Them called "three in one," and he was scandalized that Jews and Moors should be burned or exiled for a dogma not even found in Scripture (*ibid.*, pp. 15, 16, 106).

Obviously, Inquisitorial Spain would not tolerate his kind of thinking, so by age 19 Servetus emigrated to Basel, Switzerland, and from there to Strasbourg, France, where he published his first major work, *On the Errors of the Trinity,* in 1531. When both Catholics and Protestants denounced the book, Servetus fled to Lyons, where he worked as a book editor, completed an M.D. at the University of Paris, and became a practicing physician (*ibid.*, pp. 32, 58-74, 82, 97, 123).

In 1552 he published his second major work, *Christianismi Restitutio,* "the Restitution of Christianity." As his book neared completion, Servetus initiated a long and eventually acrimonious correspondence with Calvin in Geneva. When the book came off the press, a fanatical Protestant in Geneva purchased a copy. Learning from Calvin the identity of the author, he reported Servetus to the Inquisition in France. It arrested, interrogated, and imprisoned Servetus. Held temporarily in a small local jail, he managed to escape and began a roundabout journey toward Italy. Unfortunately, he stopped for one night in Geneva, was recognized, arrested, tried, and on October 27, 1553, burned at the stake by Protestants for attacking the doctrines of the Trinity and infant baptism (*ibid.*, pp. 130, 150, 151, 207, 219).

Calvin's role in the condemnation of Servetus "posed the question of religious liberty for the evangelical churches in an unprecedented manner" (*ibid.*, p. 214). Thus the death of Servetus and the backlash it provoked influenced Christian history probably more profoundly than his writings against the Trinity. An eminent Servetus scholar has noted that while Servetus "disliked the traditional terminology of the doctrine, he too was a Trinitarian of a sort, if not an Athanasian." That is, while Servetus opposed the dogmatism, enforcement, and philosophical terminology of the Trinity doctrine, he still personally believed in a Father, Son, and Holy Spirit. Nevertheless, his writings influenced others who developed further the line of reasoning he had started (Wilbur, vol. 1, p. 209).

The most influential recipient of Servetus' writings was Faustus Socinus (1539-1604), an Italian living in Raków, Poland. Socinus lumped together the Trinity and the theory of the eternal generation of the Son and rejected them both as "irrational and unscriptural" (Gonzalez, *History of Christian Thought,* vol. 3, pp. 91, 92). He was active in the Polish Minor Church, but many refer to his followers simply as Socinians. They denied the preexistence of the Son, believing that Christ was "simply a man," though filled with the Spirit, and that He "had special knowledge of God, and at His ascension received dominion over all things. They defined the Holy Spirit as 'a virtue or energy flowing from God to men.'" Present-day Unitarians are doctrinal descendants of the Socinians (Berkhof, p. 96).

Another Unitarian church sprang up in Transylvania, part of present-day Hungary. Francis David (1510-1579) was born a Catholic, but eventually became Lutheran and then leader of the Calvinists (Wilbur, vol. 2, pp. 24-27). Through a colleague exposed to the writings of Servetus, David encountered anti-Trinitarian views, and in a series of debates (1566-1569) convinced the king, the Diet, and much of the populace that the Trinity was a false doctrine that they should abandon. Further, he secured an edict of toleration, guaranteeing to every preacher the right to present the gospel as he believed it, and to every community the right to choose their own clergy (Wilbur, vol. 2, pp. 32-38). Thus Transylvania recognized four legal religions: Roman Catholic, Lutheran, Reformed (Calvinist), and Unitarian (Liechty, pp. 46-50).

Francis David eventually developed a monotheism similar to that of Jews and Muslims, teaching that only the Father should receive prayers and worship. For teaching the "non-adoration of Christ," his opponents labeled him a Judaizer and condemned him for heresy. His death from illness during his trial made him a martyr in the eyes of many and enhanced the credibility of his teachings (Liechty, p. 52; Wilbur, vol. 2, p. 77).

Following the death of David, the Unitarians split into two groups, Sundaykeepers and Sabbathkeepers. In the first generation, the Sabbatarians saw themselves as Christians with significant commonalities with Judaism. They believed (1) in the same God as the Jews; (2) that salvation has come through the Jews; (3) that Christians should observe the Sabbath as do the Jews; (4) that Trinitarianism is an invention of the Papacy; and (5) that believers should not eat pork and should observe the feast days of Leviticus 23 (Liechty, pp. 55-63).

Social ostracism turned into real persecution in 1618, and as a survival tactic, many Sabbathkeeping Unitarians covered their nonconformity by professing membership in the legal Christian churches. Despite this outward profession of Christianity (or perhaps because of an inner revulsion against it), the second-generation Sabbatarians became primarily Jewish in theology, with only secondary elements of Christianity (*ibid.*, pp. 66-73).

By 1638 Transylvania had between 15,000 and 20,000 Sabbatarians. In that year a "great persecution" broke out that threatened Sabbatarians with death unless they renounced the Sabbath and joined one of the four recognized Christian churches. This led to two centuries of secret Sabbathkeeping. For 230 years (1638-1867) the Sabbatarian religion consisted mostly of dietary laws and teaching the children (*ibid.*, pp. 73-79).

When Hungary and Transylvania came under Austrian rule in the early 1700s, Protestant churches lost their legal standing, and the secret Sabbatarians for the first time joined the Roman Catholic Church as a cover. Five years later, the authorities discovered 71 "Roman Catholic" Sabbatarian women because they used the more expensive goose fat instead of pork fat in cooking (*ibid.*, p. 79).

Finally, in 1867, the Hungarian Parliament declared the emancipation of Jews. About 180 people from 40 families came out of Christian churches, announced their conversion to Judaism, and formed a synagogue in Böszödujfalu, part of present-day Romania (*ibid.,* p. 81). Evidently some remained in the Christian churches as well, because L. R. Conradi, who visited Böszödujfalu in 1890, reported that "five families of indigenous Christian Sabbathkeepers in the area" still "nominally belonged to Reformed or Catholic churches" (*Seventh-day Adventist Encyclopedia,* vol. 11, p. 468).

From 1868 to 1941 the Sabbatarians were at peace, but their numbers declined. The end of the Sabbatarian Unitarians came in 1941 with a Nazi ultimatum: reenter the Christian church or be deported as Jews. Many chose deportation and perished in Nazi death camps. Those who professed Christianity had to demonstrate their sincerity by burning their own synagogue, an act that was a psychological blow that completed the destruction of their faith (Liechty, p. 81).

Postscript: Transylvania is part of present-day Romania, which has more Seventh-day Adventists than any other Eastern European country, at least partly because its heritage of indigenous Sabbathkeeping prepared the way for Adventist missionaries. M. B. Czechowski pioneered the Adventist message in Pitesti in the winter of 1868-1869 and L. R. Conradi followed in 1890 (*Seventh-day Adventist Encyclopedia,* vol. 11, p. 468). Of course, in 1868 and even in 1890, Seventh-day Adventists were still more or less anti-Trinitarian, which would have provided additional common ground with the Sabbathkeeping Unitarians.

The anti-Trinitarians of the Reformation period are significant to our topic for several reasons:

1. They held to the sole authority of Scripture, rejecting tradition and speculative philosophy. 2. In their zeal to reject everything derived merely from tradition, they discarded some concepts that, though traditional, did reflect a more or less correct understanding of Scripture. 3. Their doctrinal arguments reveal to us the main antecedents of American and early Adventist anti-Trinitarianism. We do not find much in the biblical anti-Trinitarian reasoning of later centuries that Servetus, Socinus, Francis David, and others did not present in some form.

Summary

During the Reformation, the varieties of belief on the Trinity reflected the range of attitudes toward the authority of Scripture. Roman Catholics, who consciously and deliberately based their dogma on both Scripture and philosophical tradition, had logical grounds for retaining unchanged the medieval view of the Trinity. The leading Reformers made a major effort to ground their beliefs in Scripture alone, but they didn't always realize how much their philosophical assumptions shaped their biblical interpretation. The Anabaptists were sweeping in their rejection of tradition, but they were also radical in their belief that through the power of the Holy Spirit it is possible for ordinary believers to live the commands of Scripture (1 John 5:3, 4). The anti-Trinitarians were right in rejecting tradition, and professing the sole authority of Scripture, but their rationalistic approach led them to spurn tradition so vehemently that they threw out everything handed down by the early and medieval church as being equally a product of apostasy.

In their overall approach to Scripture, Adventists are much closer to the Restorationists than to the Rationalists. Both, however, advocated a radical renunciation of tradition as having any authority in matters of doctrine. Chapter 12 will argue that this renunciation of tradition was in one sense a necessary step toward the recovery of a biblical doctrine of the Trinity. Only by completely setting aside the authority of tradition and relying on Scripture alone could Bible students distinguish concepts found in Scripture from those based only on tradition. Because even if one concludes that some traditional concepts do reflect scriptural truth, it is only by continually testing tradition by Scripture that we can actually preserve the sole authority of Scripture.

The next chapter will follow the trails of mainline Protestantism, Restorationism, and rational Unitarianism through the American scene of the early 1800s.

Chapter 12

TRINITY AND ANTI-TRINITARIANISM IN EARLY AMERICA

The uniqueness of religion in America largely resulted from the fact that within a few years after the American Revolution, the authorities disestablished all churches—that is, deprived them of tax support. Churches that European governments had categorized as either "established" (tax-supported), "heretical" (outlawed), or rarely, "sectarian" (tolerated), all became known in North America as "denominations"—equal before the law and dependent on their own initiative for finance and evangelism. Such a climate allowed people to legally propagate beliefs for which others had died as martyrs in the Old World. Once-persecuted churches now flourished.

The previous chapter distinguished four main groupings of the Reformation period relative to their belief in a Trinity: Roman Catholics, Reformers, Restorationists (Anabaptists), and Rationalists (Unitarians). All of these views appeared in North America before 1800. Early American churches included Roman Catholics, Anglicans (called Episcopalians after the revolt against England), Congregationalists (Puritans), Baptists, Friends, Lutherans, Reformed, French Huguenots, Moravians, Presbyterians, Methodists, Mennonites, Christians (Christian Connexion), Unitarians, and ethnic, linguistic, or theological variations of several of these (Olmstead, pp. vii-ix, 296, 310). Other American churches such as Seventh-day Adventists, Jehovah's Witnesses, Mormons, and Christian Scientists were all yet future in 1800. This chapter will focus on the immediate contributors to the Adventist doctrine of the Trinity—Methodists, Baptists, Christian Connexion, and Millerites—with some brief observations on Deists and Unitarians.

Methodists and Baptists: Democratizing Protestants

The Methodists and Baptists were significant for the development of Adventism in several ways. First, they shared a broad basis of doctrinal and even organizational common ground with the emerging Adventist church (Mustard, pp. 26-32, 249-263). Both had roots going back to the English Reformation. Each had also come under the sway of the sixteenth-century Anabaptists—the Methodists through the Moravians, and the Baptists through English Baptists. And both Methodists and Baptists relied heavily on lay leadership based on their belief in the priesthood of all believers.

By 1855 the Methodists were the largest and the Baptists the second-largest denomination in America. How this came about reveals much about their uniqueness. Many of the other churches placed a high premium on an educated ministry. Their practice of sending ministers back to European universities raised the level of their theological training, but the time and expense involved placed serious limits on their ability to capitalize on the opportunities offered by the westward expansion of the United States.

The Methodists and Baptists, however, were able to rapidly enlarge their ministry and thus keep up with the westward movement of the frontier. Methodists had "circuits," large groups of churches cared for by a single pastor. The pastors, known as circuit riders, made their rounds on horseback. In each town or village they would preach, organize classes, marry the engaged, memorialize the dead, baptize the infants, and then ride on to the next town. When a new settlement sprouted on the frontier, the nearest circuit rider could simply add the new community to his circuit. While the circuit riders were full-time pastors, the large number of churches they each served left plenty of room for lay participation in ministry. Methodists made extensive use of lay preachers, class leaders, and other local church officers to sustain the congregation between visits from the circuit rider (Olmstead, p. 252). Methodists who were active in Millerite Adventism included Josiah Litch, Levi Stockman, and Ellen G. Harmon-White. Ellen Harmon's father, Robert Harmon, was a Methodist class leader and "exhorter" (one who followed the sermon with an extemporaneous appeal) (*Life Sketches,* p. 50; Arthur White, *Ellen G. White,* vol. 1, p. 32).

The Baptists had a different approach, also well adapted to the advancing frontier. Baptist preachers supported themselves, typically by farming. The expected qualifications for such self-supporting pastors were personal spirituality and innate leadership abilities, supplemented by Bible study. Since the system required no formal theological education, pastors could be recruited as fast as the needs arose (Olmstead, p. 251). One of those Baptist farmer-preachers was William Miller, who became the most prominent leader of the Second Advent (Millerite) movement in North America.

Both approaches fostered rapid growth and empowered laypeople to exercise major leadership responsibilities, resulting in the "democratization of American Christianity" (Hatch). One consequence of a reliance on lay leadership was that the presuppositions of traditional theology perpetuated through formal theological education did not have so strong an impact on the local congregations. Given the dominant mood of fierce independence from any overweening authority, civil or religious, such conditions—lay leadership and lack of formal training—favored the growth of churches based on a plain or commonsense reading of Scripture. For all these reasons, Methodists and Baptists became by 1855 the largest and second-largest Protestant denominations in North America, with 1.5 and 1.1 million members, respectively (*ibid.,* pp. 251, 254).

Deists and Unitarians: American Rationalists

In contrast to the relatively orthodox Protesant denominations were two other groups—Deists and Unitarians—that we can include under the general heading of rationalists. Deism represented an application to Christianity of the basic principles of the seventeenth-century Enlightenment, namely, that "nothing should be accepted as true . . . unless it is grounded in the nature of things and is in harmony with right reason." The leading Protestant Reformers based their claims to the authority of Scripture on the agency of the Holy Spirit both in the initial "inspiration of the authors and words" of Scripture and in the subsequent illumination of the readers and preachers of Scripture. In place of this linkage of inspired word with self-authenticating Holy Spirit (1 John 2:20, 27), deists elevated "human reason and natural religion over faith and special revelation." To most deists, the doctrines of the deity of Jesus and of the Trinity were "clearly . . . incompatible with natural religion" (Olson, pp. 520, 521, 530, 531).

Prominent American deists included Thomas Jefferson, Benjamin Franklin, and Joseph Priestley who had immigrated from England. William Miller was an avowed deist for some 12 years, but attended a Baptist church because of family connections (Miller, pp. 2-5), a pattern typical of many deists. Where they were few, they attended whatever churches were available, but where they were numerous enough to form congregations to their liking, the churches they formed were Unitarian. In the 1790s many Congregational churches "became Unitarian with a theology strongly influenced by Deism." The American Unitarian Association organized in 1825 "without creed," "doctrine," or authority beyond the congregation. With Harvard Divinity School as its "official seminary," the denomination has wielded an influence far out of proportion to its numbers, claiming among its members several U.S. presidents and many members of Congress (Olson, pp. 531, 532).

Regarding the Trinity, Unitarians are the spiritual descendants of Faustus Socinus. Representative Unitarians have taken the position that God the Father is the one God, that Jesus was only human, and that the Holy Spirit is only an aspect or power of God, not a divine person. Such a view appeals to reason because of its simplicity. Unfortunately, it achieves its simplicity by ignoring the passages of Scripture that speak of Christ's deity and preexistence, and those that ascribe to the Holy Spirit the attributes of personality. James White once made a reference to the Unitarian concept of God, which he rejected for making "Christ inferior to the Father" (J. White, *Review and Herald,* Nov. 29, 1877). We will look at that statement and its context in the next chapter.

Christian Connexion: American Restorationists

The previous chapter divided Protestants into three groups—traditional Reformers, Rationalists, and Restorationists. A notable example of Restorationism in early American religion was the Christian Connexion. This denomination began with congregations that seceded from Methodist, Presbyterian, and Baptist associations and united under the leadership of Alexander Stone about 1810. Joshua V. Himes, a leading Connexionist minister, who would later become the second-most-influential Millerite leader, wrote in 1833 that the primary purpose of the Connexionists was "to follow more strictly the simplicity of the apostles and primitive Christians," a viewpoint that clearly marked them as true Restorationists. Alexander Stone was a non-Trinitarian, although he never urged the belief as a "condition of membership." In fact, "several" of his ministerial associates did not agree with him on the topic. The evidence suggests that Stone did not make his views prominent. Otherwise, the Christian Connexion was thoroughly evangelical and differed little from Freewill Baptists, with whom, a century later, they considered merging (Conkin, pp. 13, 32).

In 1832, however, Alexander Campbell, founder of the Disciples of Christ, courted the Connexionists. Because Campbell was adamantly hostile to the non-Trinitarians, his merger proposal split the Christian Connexion precisely along the fault line of the doctrine of God. Most of the Trinitarians became Disciples and the non-Trinitarians remained in the Connexion, so that the non-Trinitarian view became dominant in the Christian Connexion after 1832. Writing a year later, Himes noted of the Connexionists that "at first, they were generally Trinitarians," but that since then most had "rejected the Trinitarian doctrine as unscriptural" (Himes, p. 363). The Connexion survived for another century, merging in 1931 with the Congregationalists to form the Congregational

Christian Church (Conkin, pp. 29, 32, 33).

Perhaps the major explanation for the number of Millerites that came from the Connexion occurs in the Connexion's "distinctive principle" that every member "has the right to be his own expositor" of Scripture, and that "diversity of sentiment is not a bar to church fellowship" (Himes, p. 362). Of the three leading founders of Seventh-day Adventism, two (Joseph Bates and James White) had been Connexionists. Not surprisingly, most early Adventists would have agreed with Himes's statement of Connexionist belief "that there is one living and true God, the Father almighty, . . . that Christ is the Son of God . . . [and] the Holy Spirit is the *power* and *energy* of God, that holy *influence* of God by whose agency, . . . the wicked are regenerated, converted, and recovered to a virtuous and holy life" (*ibid.,* p. 363; italics supplied).

The Millerite Adventist Movement

The common cause that brought many Methodists, Baptists, and Connexionists together was the Second Advent (Millerite) movement of the 1830s and 1840s. As noted earlier, William Miller was one of those Baptist lay preachers who also happened to be a very successful farmer. His private research of some 15 years became a movement in 1831 when he—with great reluctance—held his first series of public lectures on the Second Advent. In both its timing and its theological roots, Millerism appeared as the climax of the Second Great Awakening—an evangelical revival that swept the U.S.A. during the 1820s and 1830s. Miller himself held a traditional view of the Trinity, but not without a healthy skepticism of philosophical speculation. "I believe in one living and true God," he declared, "and that there are three persons in the Godhead—as there is in man, the body, soul, and spirit. And if anyone will tell me how these exist, I will tell him how the three persons of the triune God are connected" (James White, *Life of Miller,* p. 59). Obviously the non-Trinitarian tendency in early Adventism did not come from Miller.

Everett N. Dick compiled a list of 174 Millerite lecturers whose denominational affiliations are known. If his list constitutes a representative sample, then approximately 44.3 percent of the Millerite leaders were Methodists; 27 percent were Baptists; 9 percent were Congregationalists; 8 percent Christians (Christian Connexion); 7 percent Presbyterians; 2 percent Episcopalians; 1.5 percent Dutch Reformed; .6 percent Lutherans; and .6 percent Friends (Dick, pp. 166, 167).

While members of the Christian Connexion were thus only one influence among many in the Millerite movement, among the Sabbatarian Adventists in the formative years 1845-1850, two of the three founders (James White and Joseph Bates) had been active in the Christian Connexion. Bates chose the Christian Connexion in preference to the Congregational Church of his parents specifically because he agreed with the Connexionist teachings in favor of baptism by immersion and against the doctrine of the Trinity (Bates, *Autobiography,* p. 205).

The third founder of the Seventh-day Adventist Church, Ellen G. Harmon-White, was the daughter of a Methodist lay leader. Her whole family endured expulsion from the Methodist Church for their belief in a near Second Advent. Since it is well known that she differed with the church of her childhood regarding such cardinal teachings as the fate of the wicked and later the Sabbath, we cannot simply conclude that her views at that time were "Methodist." Chapter 13 will examine the evidence regarding her early beliefs about the Godhead.

In summary, though Adventists acknowledge their indebtedness to Luther, Calvin, and a host of other Christians of the past, Conkin's observation is correct, that in their acceptance of Old Testament "laws, history, and heroes," and in advocating "a version of Christianity least affected by Gentile religions and philosophies," Adventists are "in this sense" "extreme restorationists" (Conkin, p. 115). This accords with the common Adventist conviction that their corporate mission is to bring to completion the Reformation so nobly begun and advanced by Christian giants of the past five centuries. Adventists advocate a Christianity built on the sole authority of Scripture—the whole Scripture, and nothing above or contrary to Scripture. The next chapter will consider how such a view of Scripture has affected the development of the Adventist doctrine of the Trinity.

Chapter 13

TRINITY AND ANTI-TRINITARIANISM IN SEVENTH-DAY ADVENTIST HISTORY

Respecting the trinity, I concluded that it was impossible for me to believe that the Lord Jesus Christ, the Son of the Father, was also the Almighty God, the Father, one and the same being," wrote Joseph Bates regarding his conversion in 1827. Because of his belief, he chose to join the Christian Connexion rather than the Congregational Church of his parents (Bates, p. 205). One might be tempted to dismiss Bates's assessment as simple ignorance of the meaning of trinity, but there were then and remain today a variety of views claiming the term "trinity." Roswell F. Cottrell observed in 1869 that there existed "a multitude of views" on the Trinity, "all of them orthodox, I suppose, as long as they nominally assent to the doctrine" (Cottrell).

That most of the leading SDA pioneers were non-Trinitarian in their theology has become accepted Adventist history, surprising as it sounded to most Adventists 40 years ago when Erwin R. Gane wrote an M.A. thesis on the topic. More recently, a further question has arisen with increasing urgency: was the pioneers' belief about the Godhead right or wrong? As one line of reasoning goes, either the pioneers were wrong and the present church is right, or the pioneers were right and the present Seventh-day Adventist Church has apostatized from biblical truth.

The goal of this chapter is to examine the views of the pioneers and later Adventists and see how they have altered over time in order to evaluate whether the changes represent the result of a growing biblical understanding, or a departure from Scripture to embrace views based on tradition. We will seek substantial answers to the following questions: Could the pioneers have been partly but not wholly right? Is there a biblical doctrine of the Trinity that gradually unfolded to the Adventist Church in God's own time? Does the acceptance of a form of Trinitarianism by Adventists represent the result of a growing understanding of Scripture, an example of why the pioneers rejected the formation of a creed? Or is it a heretical error, a vestige of medieval Christianity without solid basis in Scripture, so that its acceptance in the present-day church represents a departure from the scriptural faithfulness of the pioneers?

We may divide the history of the doctrine of the Godhead in Seventh-day Adventism into five periods: Anti-Trinitarian Dominance, 1846-1888; Dissatisfaction With Anti-Trinitarianism, 1888-1898; Paradigm Shift, 1898-1915; Decline of Anti-Trinitarianism, 1915-1946; Trinitarian Dominance, 1946 to the present. Erwin R. Gane, Russell Holt, and others have treated the first three periods; and Merlin Burt the 1888-1957 period, but none of them have dealt with the Kellogg crisis or the period since 1980.

1. Anti-Trinitarian Dominance, 1846-1888

From about 1846 to 1888 the majority of Adventists rejected the concept of the Trinity—at least as they understood it. All the leading writers were anti-Trinitarian, although we find scattered references to members who held Trinitarian views. Ambrose C. Spicer, the father of General Conference president William Ambrose Spicer, had been a Seventh Day Baptist minister before his conversion to Adventism in 1874 (Anderson, pp. 11-13). He evidently remained Trinitarian, because W. A. Spicer recounted to A. W. Spalding that his father "grew so offended at the anti-trinitarian atmosphere in Battle Creek that he ceased preaching" (Burt, p. 3). S. B. Whitney had been Trinitarian, but in the course of his indoctrination as an Adventist, evidently in 1861 he became a convinced anti-Trinitarian. His experience gives evidence that at least some ministers taught anti-Trinitarianism as an essential element in the instruction of new converts (Whitney). R. F. Cottrell, on the other hand, wrote in the *Review* that while he disbelieved in the Trinity, he had never "preached against it" or previously written about it (Cottrell). A third bit of evidence that not all were agreed on anti-Trinitarianism was the remark of Daniel T. Bourdeau in 1890: "Although we claim to be believers in, and worshipers of, only one God, I have thought that there are as many gods among us as there are conceptions of the Deity" (Bourdeau).

Those who rejected the traditional Trinity doctrine of the Christian creeds had no question about the biblical testimony regarding the eternity of God the Father, the deity of Jesus Christ "as Creator, Redeemer, and Mediator," and the "importance of the Holy Spirit" (Gane, p. 109). They believed that Jesus had preexisted from "so far back in the days of eternity that to finite comprehension [He] is practically without beginning" (E. J. Waggoner, pp. 21, 22). However, they weren't initially convinced that Jesus was without beginning, or that the Holy Spirit is an individual divine person and not merely an expression for the divine presence or power.

The early Adventists set forth at least six reasons for their rejection of the term "trinity." The first was that they did not see biblical evidence for three persons in one Godhead. Earlier chapters have set forth biblical evidences for the concept that God is one (Deut. 6:4), but consists of three persons—Father, Son, and Holy Spirit (Matt. 28:19; 2 Cor. 13:14, etc.) (*Seventh-day Adventists Believe,* pp. 22-25). "Person" as applied to God indicates a being with personality, intellect, and will. Unlike the multiple gods of polytheism, the three persons of the biblical Godhead are profoundly united in purpose, mind, and character, so that despite Their individuality, They are never divided, never in conflict, and thus constitute not three gods, but one God (*ibid.,* p. 23).

How we can explain this has been the subject of much thought and speculation during the centuries. Earlier chapters have noted the heavy influence of Greek philosophy on the doctrinal developments of early and medieval Christian history, leading to such dogmas as the immortality of the soul and Sunday sacredness. It is essential that we reject unbiblical concepts. The use, however, of extrabiblical words to describe biblical concepts is not inherently wrong. The word "millennium," for example, is an extrabiblical Latin term for a thoroughly biblical concept—the 1,000 years of Revelation 20. So also "trinity" is a Latin term meaning "triad" or "trio"—three components that make up one whole. Just as "incarnation"—deity becoming flesh (John 1:14)—is a word not found in the Bible and represents a concept that defies human ability to explain, yet is nonetheless a truth that the Bible teaches and Christians accept, so also with the Trinity.

A second reason the early Adventists gave for rejecting the Trinity was the misconception that the Trinity made the Father and the Son identical. We have already noted Bates's testimony: "Respecting the trinity, I concluded that it was impossible for me to believe that the Lord Jesus Christ, the Son of the Father, was also the Almighty God, the Father, one and the same being." If by not "one and the same being" Bates meant to deny that Christ and the Father are one *in nature,* then he was contradicting Philippians 2:6 and Colossians 2:9. But if, however, he meant that they are not "one and the same *person,*" he was right. D. W. Hull, J. N. Loughborough, S. B. Whitney, and D. M. Canright shared the same view (Gane, p. 104). Adventists today agree with them in rejecting the concept that the Father and Son are the same identical person. As we have seen already, it is an ancient heresy called Modalistic Monarchianism, or Sabellianism after Sabellius, one of its third-century proponents. Modalists "held that in the Godhead the only differentiation was a mere succession of modes or operations." Thus they denied the three-ness of God and asserted that Father, Son, and Holy Spirit are not separate personalities *(ODCC).*

A third and opposite objection to the Trinity doctrine stemmed from the misconception that it teaches the existence of three Gods. "If Father, Son, and Holy Ghost are each God, it would be three Gods," wrote Loughborough in 1861. He correctly rejected tri-theism.

A fourth view was that belief in the Trinity would diminish the value of the atonement (Gane, p. 105). Since the "everliving, self-existent God" cannot die, then if Christ had self-existence as God, He couldn't have died on Calvary, they reasoned. If only His humanity died, then His sacrifice was only a human one, inadequate for redemption (J. H. Waggoner, pp. 173-175). Thus, in order to protect the reality of His death on the cross, the pioneers felt they had to deny that Christ had preexistent divine immortality. Ellen White eventually answered that objection. In 1897 she rejected the earlier reasoning, explaining that when Jesus died on the cross, "Deity did not die. Humanity died" (manuscript 131, 1897). Again she wrote: "Humanity died: divinity did not die" (*Youth's Instructor,* Aug. 4, 1898).

Fifth, Adventists thought that the fact that Scripture calls Christ Son of God and "the beginning of the creation of God" (Rev. 3:14) proved that He must be of more recent origin than God the Father (Smith, *Daniel and Revelation,* p. 487; *Looking Unto Jesus,* p. 10).

Sixth, they argued that "there are various expressions concerning the Holy Spirit which would indicate that it [sic] couldn't properly be considered as a person, such as its being 'shed abroad' in the heart [Rom. 5:5], and 'poured out upon all flesh' [Joel 2:28]" (Uriah Smith, in *Review and Herald,* Mar. 23, 1897).

All of the Adventist objections to the Trinity either rejected extrabiblical speculative forms of Trinity belief or misunderstandings of the biblical witness. None of them is a valid objection to the true biblical teaching of one God in three persons. Yet all of these objections had biblical texts at their core. The views of the church eventually changed because Adventists came to a different understanding of the biblical evidence.

2. Beginnings of Dissatisfaction With Anti-Trinitarianism, 1888-1898

Those who accepted it found that the focus of the 1888 General Conference session on the priority of "Christ our righteousness" sent ripples of renewal through every area of their life, thought, and practice. The exaltation of the cross of Christ called into serious question whether a subordinate, derived divinity could adequately represent the nature and character of Christ. E. J. Waggoner urged the necessity of "[setting] forth Christ's rightful position of equality with the Father, in order that His power to redeem may be the better appreciated" (E. J. Waggoner, p. 19). While by 1890 Waggoner had not yet fully grasped Christ's infinitely eternal preexistence, he argued convincingly that Christ was not created, that "He has 'life in Himself' [John 10:17]; He possesses immortality in His own right." Waggoner insisted on "the Divine unity of the Father and the Son" and averred that Christ is "by nature of the very substance of God, and having life in Himself, He is properly called Jehovah, the self-existent One" (Jer. 23:6), who is on "an equality with God" (Phil. 2:6, ARV), "having all the attributes of God" (*ibid.,* pp. 21-25).

Waggoner was not yet fully Trinitarian, but he saw clearly that a more exalted conception of Christ's work of redemption demanded a higher view of His being as deity. "The fact that Christ is a part of the Godhead, possessing all the attributes of Divinity, being the equal of the Father in all respects, as Creator and Lawgiver, is the only force there is in the atonement. . . . Christ died 'that he might bring us to God' (1 Peter 3:18); but if He lacked one iota of being equal to God, He could not bring us to Him" (*ibid.,* p. 44). The force of such logic leads inevitably to the recognition of Christ's full equality in preexistence as well.

Thus the dynamic of righteousness by faith and its consequences for the doctrine of God provide the historical context for the provocative comment of D. T. Bourdeau in 1890 that "although we claim to be believers in, and worshipers of, only one God, I have thought that there are as many gods among us as there are conceptions of the Deity." Such a comment from a highly respected evangelist and missionary seems to indicate that the collective confidence in the anti-Trinitarian paradigm was showing some cracks. Further evidence that it was the case appeared two years later, in 1892, when Pacific Press published a pamphlet titled "The Bible Doctrine of the Trinity," by Samuel T. Spear. The pamphlet corrected two prevailing misconceptions of the Trinity doctrine, showing that it "is not a system of tri-theism, or the doctrine of three Gods, but it is the doctrine of one God subsisting and acting in three persons, with the qualification that the term 'person' . . . is not, when used in this relation, to be understood in any sense that would make it inconsistent with the unity of the Godhead."

Uriah Smith's *Looking Unto Jesus* was the most comprehensive and carefully nuanced exposition of the non-Trinitarian view among Adventists. Smith emphatically repudiated his earlier view that Christ had been created, but still held that "God [the Father] alone is without beginning. At the earliest epoch when a beginning could be,—a period so remote that to finite minds it is essentially eternity,—appeared the Word." Through some means not clearly revealed in Scripture, Christ had been "brought forth" or "begotten." "By some divine impulse or process, not creation," the Father had given Christ existence. In one paragraph Smith comes surprisingly close to a Trinitarian statement: "This union between the Father and the Son does not detract from either, but strengthens both. Through it, in connection with the Holy Spirit, we have all of Deity" (Smith, *Looking Unto Jesus,* pp. 3, 10, 13, 17). But this slow struggle toward a fuller understanding was completely eclipsed by the emphatic declarations of *The Desire of Ages,* published in same year.

3. Paradigm Shift, 1898-1915

The period from 1898 to 1915 saw an almost complete reversal of Adventist thinking about the Trinity. I say almost, because the paradigm shift did not lead to unanimity on the topic. As Merlin Burt has documented, thought leaders who tended toward the "old view" remained both vocal and influential for many years (Burt).

Nevertheless, the publication of Ellen White's *The Desire of Ages* in 1898 became the continental divide for the Adventist understanding of the Trinity. In *The Desire of Ages* she differed sharply with most of the pioneers regarding the preexistence of Christ, beginning with the first paragraph of the book. Her third sentence in chapter 1 declared: *"From the days of eternity the Lord Jesus Christ was one with the Father"* (p. 19; italics supplied). Yet even this was not sufficiently unequivocal to clarify her position regarding the deity of

Jesus for, as we have seen, others had used similar language without believing in Christ's infinitely eternal preexistence. Later in the book, writing on the resurrection of Lazarus, she quoted the words of Christ, "I am the resurrection and the life," and followed them with a seven-word comment that would turn the tide of anti-Trinitarian theology among Adventists: *"In Christ is life, original, unborrowed, underived"* (*ibid.,* p. 530; italics supplied). Christ didn't ultimately derive His divine life from the Father. As a man on earth, He subordinated His will to that of the Father (John 5:19, 30), but as self-existent God, He had power to lay down His life and take it up again. Thus in commenting on Christ's resurrection, Ellen White again asserted His full deity and equality with the Father, declaring: "The Saviour came forth from the grave by the life that was in Himself" (*ibid.,* p. 785). This, of course, refutes not only the semi-Arian views of early Adventists, but traditional orthodoxy as well. As noted in chapter 11, traditional Trinitarian dogma held that Christ was derived from the Father, hence in His very essence, subordinate to the Father.

Ellen White's assertions of Christ's eternal self-existence came as a shock to the theological leadership of the church. M. L. Andreasen, who had become an Adventist just four years earlier at the age of 18, and who would eventually teach at the church's North American seminary, said the new concept was so different from the previous understanding that some prominent leaders doubted whether Ellen White had really written it. After Andreasen entered the ministry in 1902, he made a special trip to Ellen White's California home to investigate the issue for himself. She welcomed him and "gave him access to her manuscripts." He had brought with him "a number of quotations" that he "wanted to see if they were in the original in her own handwriting." "I was sure Sister White had never written, 'In Christ is life, original, unborrowed, underived.' But now I found it in her own handwriting just as it had been published. It was so with other statements. As I checked up, I found that they were Sister White's own expressions" (Andreasen, "Spirit of Prophecy," p. 20).

The Desire of Ages contained equally uncompromising statements regarding the deity of the Holy Spirit. On pages 669-671, Ellen White repeatedly uses the personal pronoun "He" in referring to the Holy Spirit, climaxing with the impressive statement: "The Spirit was to be given as a regenerating agent, and without this the sacrifice of Christ would have been of no avail. . . . Sin could be resisted and overcome only through the mighty agency of the *Third Person of the Godhead,* who would come with no modified energy, but in the fullness of divine power" (p. 671; italics supplied).

Some received these and similar statements as inspired doctrinal correction for the church. Others, disbelieving that they could have been wrong for so many years, continued to repeat the old arguments. Ellen White's testimony, however, by calling attention to scriptures whose significance the church had overlooked, created an irreversible paradigm shift. (Bible texts that Ellen White cited as supporting various aspects of a Trinitarian view included John 10:30; Col. 2:9; and Heb. 1:3 [all in *Evangelism,* pp. 613, 614]; Matt. 28:19, 20; Prov. 8:30; and John 1:1 [*ibid.,* p. 615]; John 8:57, 58; 11:25; 16:8; Rom. 8:16; 1 Cor. 2:11, 12 [*ibid.,* pp. 616, 617]; and John 14:16-18, 26; 16:8, 12-14 [*The Desire of Ages,* pp. 669-671]). As Adventists, like the Bereans of Acts 17:11, returned to the Scriptures to see "whether those things were so," they eventually came to a growing consensus that the basic concept of the Trinity was a biblical truth to accept and embrace.

While *The Desire of Ages* set in motion a shift in the Adventist understanding of the Godhead, it was not her last word on the subject. Later, during the Kellogg crisis of 1902-1907, Ellen White repeatedly used expressions such as "three living persons of the heavenly trio," while continuing to maintain the essential unity of the Godhead. Thus she affirmed the plurality and the unity—the three-ness and the one-ness—the foundational elements of a simple, biblical understanding of the Trinity. We will treat these statements and their context in the Kellogg crisis in more detail in the next chapter.

Evidence that some recognized *The Desire of Ages* statements as removing the objections to a biblical doctrine of the Trinity is a summary of Adventist beliefs published by F. M. Wilcox in the *Review and Herald* in 1913. Wilcox, editor of the denomination's most influential periodical, wrote that "Seventh-day Adventists believe,—1. In the divine Trinity. This Trinity consists of the eternal Father, . . . the Lord Jesus Christ, . . . [and] the Holy Spirit, the third person of the Godhead" (Wilcox).

4. Decline of Anti-Trinitarianism, 1915-1946

Despite Wilcox's declaration in the *Review* (or perhaps because of it), the debate over the Trinity intensified in the early decades of the twentieth century. At the 1919 Bible Conference the eternity of Christ and His relation to the Father were a major and unresolved subject of debate. Curiously, in view of Ellen White's *The Desire of Ages* statement that Christ's life was "underived," even W. W. Prescott, the foremost proponent of a Trinitarian view at the conference, held that Christ's existence was in some way "derived" from the Father (Burt, pp. 26, 27, 31). At least it shows that the leadership sought a clear biblical understanding, that they were not content to simply accept White's pronouncement without seeing it for themselves in Scripture.

The polarization of American Christianity between modernism and fundamentalism during the first two decades of the twentieth century tended to push Adventists closer to a Trinitarian position, since in so many other areas—evolution, belief in the supernatural, Christ's virgin birth, miracles, literal resurrection, etc.—Adventists opposed the modernists and were in sympathy with fundamentalists (*ibid.,* p. 33).

In 1930, responding to a request from the African Division for "a statement of what Adventists believe" that would "help government officials and others to a better understanding of our work," the General Conference Committee appointed a subcommittee (M. E. Kern, associate secretary of the GC; F. M. Wilcox, editor of the *Review;* E. R. Palmer, manager of the Review and Herald; and C. H. Watson, GC president) to prepare a statement of Adventist beliefs. Wilcox, as the leading writer among them, drafted a 22-point statement subsequently published in the *SDA Yearbook* of 1931 (Froom, *MOD,* pp. 410-414). The second point spoke of the "Godhead, or Trinity," and the third affirmed "that Jesus Christ is very God," an echo of the Nicene Creed. Lest anyone think that Seventh-day Adventists intended to make a creed, the drafters of the statement sought "no formal or official approval" for it. Fifteen years later, when the statement had gained general acceptance, the General Conference session of 1946 made it official, voting that "no revision of this Statement of Fundamental Beliefs, as it now appears in the *[Church] Manual,* shall be made at any time except at a General Conference session" ("Fifteenth Meeting," *Review and Herald,* June 14, 1946, p. 197). This marked the first official endorsement of a Trinitarian view by the church, although one "well known" anti-Trinitarian continued to "uphold the 'old' view" until his death in 1968 (Burt, p. 54).

5. Trinitarian Dominance, 1946 to the Present

From the 1950s to the publication of *Movement of Destiny* in 1971, L. E. Froom was the best-known champion of Trinitarianism among Seventh-day Adventists. His book *The Coming of the Comforter,* when first published in 1928, was unprecedented among Adventists (except for a few passages in Ellen White) in its systematic exposition of the personality of the Holy Spirit and the Trinitarian nature of the Godhead (*Comforter,* pp. 37-57). Froom's leading role in the preparation of the 1957 work *Questions on Doctrine* has been amply documented elsewhere (Unruh, Moon). The book evoked a storm of controversy for certain statements on Christology and the atonement, but its clear affirmation of "the heavenly Trinity" (*QOD,* pp. 36, 37, 645, 646) went virtually unchallenged—perhaps because M. L. Andreasen, its chief critic in other areas, was a convinced Trinitarian (Andreasen, "Christ, the Express Image of God"; Burt, p. 43). Froom's final word was his 700-page *Movement of Destiny,* published in 1971. Despite "instances of special pleading" and problems of historical bias that "diminish the work as dependable history" (Maxwell), it thoroughly documents the progression of Adventist theology toward a biblical Trinitarian consensus.

The climax of this phase of doctrinal development was a new statement of Adventist teachings voted by the 1980 General Conference session in Dallas. The new 27 fundamental beliefs affirmed the doctrine of the Trinity more concisely, but in very similar terms to the 1931 statement officially voted in 1946.*

A major development since 1972 has been the quest to articulate biblical presuppositions grounding a biblical doctrine of the Trinity, clearly differentiated from the dualistic presuppositions that undergird the traditional creedal statements. In a 1972 path-breaking article, Raoul Dederen set forth a brief exposition of the Godhead from the Old and New Testaments. He rejected the "Trinity of speculative thought" that used philosophical terms to describe "distinctions within the Deity for which there is no definable basis within the revealed knowledge of God" (Dederen, p. 13), and advocated rather the example of the apostles: "Rejecting the terms of Greek mythology or metaphysics, they expressed their convictions in an unpretending trinitarian confession of faith, the doctrine of one God subsisting and acting in three persons" (*ibid.*, p. 21).

In 1983 Fernando Canale set forth an analysis and radical critique of the Greek philosophical presuppositions underlying what Dederen had referred to as "speculative thought." Canale's dissertation, *A Criticism of Theological Reason,* showed that classical Catholic and Protestant theology took its most basic presuppositions about the nature of God, time, and existence, from a "framework" provided by Aristotelian philosophy. He argued that for Christian theology to become truly biblical, it must derive its "primordial presupposition" from Scripture, not from Greek philosophy (Canale, *Criticism,* p. 359; p. 402, n. 1).

In the more recent *Handbook of Seventh-day Adventist Theology,* edited by Dederen, Canale authored a seminal article summarizing the conclusions that he has drawn so far from his continued work on the doctrine of God. At various points in the article, Canale clearly differentiates between a doctrine of God reflecting Greek philosophical presuppositions, and one based on biblical evidence.

"In a very real sense, Adventist emphasis on Scriptures as the sole source of data for executing theology has given theological reflection on God a new and revolutionary start. Systematically distrustful and critical of traditional theological positions, Adventists were determined to build doctrines on the basis of Scripture alone. The difficulties implicit in this fresh approach may account for the scant number of Adventist statements on the doctrine of God" (Canale, "Doctrine of God," p. 148).

Canale makes a strong case for the view that because Adventists "departed from the philosophical conception of God as timeless" and "embraced the historical conception of God as presented in the Bible," they have been able to develop a biblical view of the Trinity (*ibid.,* p. 150).

Conclusion

This chapter has sketched the long process from Adventists' initial rejection of creedal Trinitarianism to their eventual acceptance of a biblical doctrine of the Trinity. From a perspective of belief that God was leading the Adventist movement, it appears that a major reason for the long process was that He was not calling the pioneers to a simple choice between Trinitarianism and anti-Trinitarianism. Rather, He was summoning them to develop a new understanding not dependent on Greek philosophy. The only way for the pioneers in their context to effectively separate Scripture from tradition was to abandon every doctrine not clearly supported from the Bible alone. Thus they initially rejected the traditional doctrine of the Trinity, which clearly contained elements not evident in Scripture. As they continued to work on the basis of Scripture, periodically challenged and stretched by the Holy Spirit through the visions of Ellen White, they gradually became convinced that the basic concept of *one God in three persons* did indeed appear in Scripture.

The next chapter will consider in more detail the role of Ellen White in this process.

*The first SDA statement of fundamental beliefs (1872) was the work of Uriah Smith. Its explicitly nontrinitarian stance represented a consensus at the time, but because of strong opposition to any creedal statement, it never received the status of official approval. The second statement (1889), also by Uriah Smith, was capable of being interpreted favorably by either semi-Arians or Trinitarians. The third statement (1931), authorized by a committee but actually written by F. M. Wilcox, editor of the *Review and Herald,* was the first to gain official status. The 1946 General Conference session voted that the 1931 statement should not undergo any change except by vote of the General Conference in session. Thus the Dallas statement of 1980 was the fourth comprehensive fundamental beliefs statement of Seventh-day Adventists and the second to be formally voted by a General Conference session.

Chapter 14

ELLEN WHITE'S ROLE IN THE TRINITY DEBATE

The previous chapter traced the historical change in Adventist theology from an anti-Trinitarian stance to an acceptance of the basic concept of one God comprised in three divine persons. That such a shift occurred no one disputes. What is hotly debated in some quarters is whether that shift represents the step-by-step discovery of a biblical point of view, or an apostasy from a previously held biblical position.

At the core of the debate is the question regarding Ellen White's position and her role in the process of change. Many among both Trinitarians and anti-Trinitarians seem to share a common assumption: that Ellen White did not change—that she was either never Trinitarian or always Trinitarian. Anti-Trinitarians argue (1) that she never corrected the nontrinitarian beliefs of her associates (we will examine that view below); (2) that on the basis of interpreting obscure passages by clearer passages, we should view purported evidences of Trinitarianism in her later writings through the lens of her earlier nontrinitarian statements; and (3) that some of her most explicit statements about God in "three persons" should be attributed to the unfortunate influence of certain of her associates. Of course, to say that her colleagues successfully led her to write false doctrine is a flat rejection of her claim to direct divine guidance and protection from such influence.

We find ample evidence, however, that Ellen White's personal views did alter on a number of subjects, so it is possible that she also experienced a transformation in her understanding of the Godhead as well. When she declared in 1849, "We know we have the truth," she was referring to a specific set of beliefs that defined Sabbatarian Adventism in distinction from other Christian groups. The points included the three angels' messages of Revelation 14 (including the "everlasting gospel," the "commandments of God," and the "faith of Jesus"), Christ's second advent, His priestly ministry in the heavenly sanctuary, the Sabbath, immortality received only through Christ, and the "nonimmortality of the wicked" (White, *Counsels to Writers and Editors,* pp. 30, 31). She did not believe that we had no more truth to discover (letter 5, 1849, in *Manuscript Releases,* vol. 5, p. 200).

When I argue that some of her personal beliefs did change, I'm making a distinction between her past "personal beliefs" and what she received through her visions. At every stage of her life after her first vision, her knowledge of God and His will combined what she had learned through ordinary means such as parental training, church attendance, Bible study, and personal experience, and what she received through visions. Consequently, her personal understanding, especially in the earlier years, contained significant elements not in harmony with her later beliefs, because God had not yet called her attention to them.

For instance, after her first vision affirmed that prophecy had indeed been fulfilled on October 22, 1844, she concluded that a corollary belief of the Millerites was also true—that probation had closed and the "door was shut." It took several years and several more visions before she and her fellow Adventists clearly distinguished between the two concepts and gave up the "shut door."

A second example of a changed view is that after her first vision in December 1844, she continued to observe Sunday as the Sabbath for several more more years. She had not yet learned about the seventh-day Sabbath.

A third example was the discovery of the "time to commence the Sabbath" in 1855. For nine years most of the Sabbatarian Adventists, including the Whites, had observed the Sabbath from

6:00 p.m. Friday to 6:00 p.m. Saturday. Not until 1855, when J. N. Andrews advanced the scriptural concept that Sabbath begins at sunset, did Adventists begin keeping the Sabbath from sundown to sundown. Ellen White herself actually remained unconvinced until she received a vision confirming Andrews' interpretation (A. L. White, *Ellen G. White,* vol. 1, pp. 322-324).

A fourth example is what Adventists have historically called health reform. Until 1863 most Adventists, including James and Ellen White, were heavy meat eaters, even slaughtering their own hogs. Not until after the church had achieved basic organization did God call the attention of the movement to the broader platform of health reform, including complete proscription of pork products and the strong recommendation of vegetarianism (Robinson, pp. 65-85).

In view of these and other areas of doctrinal development, it is not particularly surprising that Ellen White should show both advancement and change in her view of the Godhead. Her reporting of her visions shows a clear progression of increasingly more explicit revelations about the topic.

Before considering that advancement, I would like to make it very clear that I have not found her later statements to contradict what she wrote earlier. Rather, her later statements are increasingly precise and explicit, whereas her earlier statements were more ambiguous. Some of the early statements are capable of being read from either a Trinitarian or non-Trinitarian perspective. But I have not found any statement from her pen that criticizes a biblical view of the Trinity.

The Development of Ellen White's Understanding of the Godhead

One aspect of the *creedal Trinitarianism* rejected by the pioneers was the somewhat curious statement that "there is but one living and true God, everlasting, without body or parts" (*Doctrines and Discipline of the Methodist Episcopal Church* [1856], p. 15). The pioneers vigorously refuted this, citing several biblical passages that portrayed God as having both "body" and "parts" (Ex. 24:9-11;

33:20-23; John 1:18; Heb. 1:1-3; cf. Smith, *State of the Dead,* pp. 27-30).

This question was evidently on the mind of Ellen White as well (not surprisingly, since the creed in question was a Methodist one, and she had been raised Methodist. Furthermore, she was closely associated with those who cited the concept as one of the errors of Trinitarianism). Twice in early visions of Jesus, she asked Him questions related to the "form" and "person" of God. In one early vision, she "saw a throne, and on it sat the Father and the Son. I gazed on Jesus' countenance," she said, "and admired His lovely person. The Father's person I could not behold, for a cloud of glorious light covered Him. I asked Jesus if His Father had a form like Himself. He said He had, but I could not behold it, for said He, 'If you should once behold the glory of His person, you would cease to exist'" (E. G. White, *Early Writings,* p. 54).

About 1850 she reported, "I have often seen the lovely Jesus, that He is a *person.* I asked Him if His Father was a person and had a form like Himself. Said Jesus, 'I am in the express *image* of My Father's *person'* " (*ibid.,* p. 77). Thus she gained visionary confirmation of what her husband had written in a Millerite journal a few years earlier. Expounding on Jude 4, about those who "deny the only Lord God and our Lord Jesus Christ," James White had declared that "this class can be no other than those who spiritualize away the existence of the Father and the Son, as two distinct, literal, tangible persons. . . . The way spiritualizers . . . have disposed of or denied the only Lord God and our Lord Jesus Christ is first using the old *unscriptural trinitarian creed"* (James White, in *Day-Star,* Jan. 24, 1846). Ellen White evidently agreed with her husband that Christ and the Father were "two distinct, literal, tangible persons," but we have no record (before the Kellogg crisis of 1905) of her explicitly criticizing any Trinitarian view as did her husband.

Other hints of her early views came in 1858 with the publication of the first volume of *Spiritual Gifts.* (The title was an assertion of her claim to have received the gift of prophecy.) Her belief in the Holy Spirit is not in question since she links the Father, the Son, and the Holy Spirit in Christ's baptismal narrative (*Spiritual Gifts,* vol. 1, p. 28). But she does not mention the Holy Spirit in connection with the divine councils about Creation and the plan of salvation (*ibid.,* pp. 17, 18, 22-27; see also vol. 3, pp. 33, 34 [1864]).

By 1869 her growing understanding, based on her visions, had clearly forged ahead of her colleagues as she asserted that Christ is equal with God (E. G. White, *Testimonies,* vol. 2, p. 200; cf. Smith, *Revelation,* p. 59). It is also evident that if no one else was listening, at least her husband was. James White's statements on the Trinity are relatively few and far between, but in his next mention of it he follows her lead. In a *Review* article in 1877 he also maintained that "Christ is equal with God." While it did not make him a Trinitarian, another remark in the same article suggests that he was beginning to reexamine the larger picture. "The inexplicable trinity that makes the godhead three in one and one in three is bad enough," he wrote, "but that ultra Unitarianism that makes Christ inferior to the Father is worse" (J. White, "Christ Equal With God," *Review and Herald,* Nov. 29, 1877).

In 1872 she contrasted the angels who "were created beings" with Christ who "had power to lay down His life, and to take it again," showing that Christ was not created (*Review and Herald,* Dec. 17, 1872). Again, she was leading her colleagues. Uriah Smith, who had published his belief that Christ was the first created being, eventually gave up that view (cf. Smith, *Revelation,* p. 59, and *Looking Unto Jesus,* pp. 12, 17).

The progression of Ellen White's unfolding understanding appears to be as follows:

1850 — Christ and the Father are personal beings with tangible form (*Early Writings,* pp. 54, 77).

1869 — Christ is equal with God (*Testimonies,* vol. 2, p. 200).

1872 — Christ was not created (*Review and Herald,* Dec. 17, 1872).

1878 — Christ was the "eternal Son" (*Review and Herald,* Aug. 8, 1878; letter 37, 1887, in *Manuscript Releases,* vol. 15, p. 26; *Youth's Instructor,* Aug. 31, 1887; *1888*

Materials, vol. 1, p. 29; *Review and Herald,* Feb. 8, 1898; *Review and Herald,* Apr. 5, 1906).

A clue to the meaning of Christ being an "eternal Son" may be found in a related statement that in His eternal preexistence, He was not a Son *in the same sense* that He was after being born as a human: "In His incarnation He gained *in a new sense* the title of the Son of God. Said the angel to Mary, 'The power of the Highest shall overshadow thee: therefore also that holy thing which shall be born of thee shall be called the Son of God.' While the Son of a human being, He became the Son of God *in a new sense.* Thus He stood in our world—the Son of God, yet allied by birth to the human race.

"From all eternity Christ was united with the Father" (*Signs of the Times,* Aug. 2, 1905; quoted in *The Seventh-day Adventist Bible Commentary,* vol. 5, pp. 1114, 1115; italics supplied).

One implication of Christ becoming the Son of God "in a new sense" may be that with His human birth He for the first time became a Son in the sense of having a beginning. Sonship in His preexistence denoted that He was of the same nature as the Father, in unity and close relationship, but it did not imply a beginning, derivation from the Father, or the dependent relationship that a small child has with a parent. The relationship of a dependent son to a father was apparently part of what Jesus experienced for the first time, when as a human He became Son of God "in a new sense." One further aspect of this is that His conception and birth as a human was *when* He "proceeded" forth and came from God.

1887 Christ preexisted with the Father from all eternity (*Review and Herald,* July 5, 1887; *The Desire of Ages* [1898], p. 19).

1888 A broader conception of righteousness by faith demands the full deity of Christ.

"If men reject the testimony of the inspired Scriptures concerning the deity of Christ, it is in vain to argue the point with them; for no argument, however conclusive, could convince them. [1 Cor. 2:14 quoted.] *None who hold this error can have a true conception of the character or the mission of Christ, or of the great plan of God for man's redemp-*

tion" (*The Great Controversy* [1888], p. 524; italics supplied).

1888 Christ is "one with the eternal Father,—one in nature, in character, and in purpose" (*ibid.,* p. 493), "one in power and authority" (*ibid.,* p. 495), yet in person, Christ was "distinct" from the Father. "The Lord Jesus Christ . . . existed from eternity, *a distinct person,* yet one with the Father" (*Review and Herald,* Apr. 5, 1906; italics supplied).

1888 Christ was "the only being in all the universe that could enter into all the counsels and purposes of God" (*The Great Controversy* [1888], p. 493; *Patriarchs and Prophets* [1890], p. 34). The context shows that "the only being" is in contrast to the angels. Nevertheless it precedes the fuller exposition of the role of the Holy Spirit.

1890 Christ is self-existent; His deity is not derived from the Father (*Patriarchs and Prophets,* p. 36).

1897 The Holy Spirit is the third person of the Godhead (*Special Testimonies,* Series A, No. 10, p. 37).

1898 Publication of *The Desire of Ages* recapitulates the previous two points: "In Christ is life, original, unborrowed, underived" (*The Desire of Ages,* p. 530) and the Holy Spirit is the "Third Person of the Godhead" (*ibid.,* p. 671).

1901, 1905 Three "eternal heavenly dignitaries," "three highest powers in heaven," "three living persons of the heavenly trio"—the Father, Son, and Holy Spirit are one in nature, character, and purpose, but not in person (manuscript 145, 1901; *Special Testimonies,* Series B, No. 7 [1905], pp. 51, 62, 63; *The Ministry of Healing* [1905], p. 422; all quoted in *Evangelism,* pp. 614-617).

First, this sequence of concepts shows a clear progression from the simple to the complex, revealing that Ellen White's understanding did grow and change as she received additional light. Fernando

Canale has pointed out that the development is similar to the one we find in the New Testament (Canale, "Doctrine of God," pp. 128-130). In the Gospels, the first challenge was to convince the disciples that Christ was one with the Father. Once the disciples' concept of monotheism had expanded to accept "one God" in two divine persons, it was comparatively easy to lead them to recognize the Holy Spirit as a third divine person.

Second, it is clear that Ellen White's concept of the Godhead was essentially complete with the publication of *The Desire of Ages* in 1898. Still 17 years before her death, she was mentally and physically vigorous, at the peak of her literary productivity. The book is not the product of her old age, but the matured work of her very best years. The disposition to dismiss *The Desire of Ages* as not representative of her thought betrays a willingness to set aside the plainest facts because they conflict with preconceived ideas or a cherished goal.

Did she move from a semi-Arian view to a Trinitarian view, or did she privately hold a Trinitarian opinion all along? It may not be possible to give a certain answer to that. The evident progression in the reports of her visions could be the result of her making a careful distinction between her personal opinions and the messages of her visions. For instance, she once declared, "In these letters which I write, in the testimonies I bear, I am presenting to you that which the Lord has presented to me. I do not write one article in the paper, expressing merely my own ideas. They are what God has opened before me in vision" (*Selected Messages,* book 1, p. 27).

It is possible that when her earliest visions contradicted some aspects of her Methodist upbringing (the creed that said God had neither body nor parts), she might have put the rest of her Methodist Trinity views "on the shelf," so to speak, simply to wait and see whether future visions and Bible study would confirm or deny them. So she might have been tentatively Trinitarian in her own opinion, but careful in her writings to express only what God had shown her in vision—the progressive revelation we have observed above.

In any case, her later writings relating to the Trinity never required her to repudiate earlier statements. She simply wrote as specifically as her visions permitted her to do, and as further revelations made the subject clearer, her writings became more explicit. Thus God led the church gently and gradually without, on the one hand, bypassing individual Bible study, or, on the other hand, leading its members to throw up their hands and embrace all the Trinitarian traditions. Why God did not lead them to uncritically embrace traditional Trinitarianism will become clear as we consider two varieties of Trinitarianism in Ellen White's later writings.

Two Varieties of Trinitarianism

As we follow her unfolding understanding, it becomes apparent that she describes at least two distinct varieties of Trinitarian belief. One of them she consistently opposed throughout her adult ministry, and the other she gradually came to agree with. While the earliest hints of it go back to 1846 and 1850, this differentiation became more explicit during the Kellogg crisis of 1902-1907. Because some in recent years have seriously misunderstood certain of the writings of both John Harvey Kellogg and Ellen White from this period, it is necessary to consider this controversy in some detail.

Dr. J. H. Kellogg, medical superintendent of the Battle Creek Sanitarium, was the leading person with scientific credentials among Seventh-day Adventists at the beginning of the twentieth century. Possibly coming under the influence of some intellectual companions from outside of Adventism (Froom, *Movement of Destiny,* p. 351), he eventually became convinced that the life of every living thing was the very presence of God in it, whether it be a tree, flower, animal, or human being. Traces of the view appear in his public presentations and writings, as well as those of some of his Adventist associates, in the 1890s. However, the crisis over it did not erupt until 1902.

Following the Battle Creek Sanitarium fire of February 18, 1902, Kellogg proposed a fund-raising plan to finance the rebuilding. He would donate to the Review and Herald the manuscript for a new book on health. If the Review and Herald would underwrite the costs of publishing, and if the 73,000 members that composed the Seventh-day Adventist Church in 1902 would undertake to sell 500,000 copies at $1 each, the proceeds would both pay off long-standing debts and rebuild the sanitarium. The church accepted his plan. *The Living Temple* was primarily a handbook on basic physiology, nutrition, preventive medicine, and home treatments for common ailments. But the title page quoted 1 Corinthians 6:19 about the body being the "temple of the Holy Ghost," and here and there Kellogg incorporated his theological views.

Space does not permit us to tell the full story here. Suffice it to say that despite heavy criticism from some preliminary readers of the manuscript, Kellogg pressed ahead. On December 30, 1902, however, while the Review and Herald was in the midst of printing the first edition, the publishing house burned to the ground. Among other losses were the printing plates and unfinished copies of *The Living Temple.* Kellogg promptly took the manuscript to another printer and contracted for 3,000 copies at his own expense.

When the book finally reached its eager readers, the most glaring departures from established Adventist theology appeared in the opening chapter, "The Mystery of Life" (Kellogg, *The Living Temple,* pp. 28-30 [original edition]).*

"God is the explanation of nature," Kellogg declared, "—not a God outside of nature, but *in* nature, manifesting himself through and in all the objects, movements, and varied phenomena of the universe." A few pages later Kellogg hinted that the concept of a personal God was essentially a conceptual construct for the benefit of ordinary minds who needed such an ultimately nonfactual accommodation to their intellectual limitations. The implication was that real intellectuals like himself could perceive the spiritual reality beyond the anthropomorphic accommodation (*ibid.,* pp. 30-32).

Evidently reacting to some of his prepublication critics, Kellogg sought to blunt or circumvent their objections by specific reference to the Holy Spirit. He reasoned that if the Holy Spirit could be everywhere at once, and if the Holy Spirit were also a person, then no one could say that the God Kellogg set forth as dwelling in all things was an impersonal deity.

Kellogg's argument in *The Living Temple* continues: "Says one, 'God may be present by his Spirit, or by his power, but certainly God himself cannot be present everywhere at once.'" (The distinction between "his Spirit, or . . . power" and "God himself" marks this objection as coming from one of Kellogg's non-Trinitarian acquaintances [see G. I. Butler to J. H. Kellogg, Apr. 5, 1904, quoted below]). Kellogg answers: "How can power be separated from the source of power? Where God's Spirit is at work, where God's power is manifested, God himself is actually and truly present" (Kellogg, p. 28). Here Kellogg is not thinking clearly, as a brief illustration will show. If the president of my country issues an order to mobilize the armed forces, the president's *power* would reach right down to the home of my neighbor in the army reserves, but that's clearly different than the president visiting my neighbor's house in *person.*

The church hotly debated Kellogg's view for several years. Since leading Adventist writers had already pointed out its weaknesses, Ellen White at first hoped that it would not be necessary for her to get involved. By September 1903, however, Kellogg's views had gained adherents. When he claimed publicly that the teachings of *The Living Temple* "regarding the personality of God" were in accord with the writings of Ellen White, she could remain silent no longer. "God forbid that this opinion should prevail. We need not the mysticism that is in this book," she declared. "[T]he writer of this book is on a false track. He has lost sight of the distinguishing truths for this time. He knows not whither his steps are tending. The track of truth lies close beside the track of error, and both may seem to be one to minds which are not worked by the Holy Spirit, and which, therefore, are not quick to discern the difference between truth and error" (letter 211, Sept. 22, 1903, in Spalding-Magan, pp. 320, 321).

In a follow-up letter, she zeroed in on the core issue: "The Lord Jesus . . . did not represent God as an *essence pervading nature,* but as a *personal being.* Christians should bear in mind that God has a personality as verily as has Christ" (*ibid.,* Sept. 23, 1903, p. 324; italics supplied).

A few weeks later Kellogg defended his view to George I. Butler, former president of the General Conference and now the president of the Southern Union. "As far as I can fathom the difficulty which is found in the Living Temple," Kellogg began, "the whole thing may be simmered down to this question: Is the Holy Ghost a person? You say No." (Butler was of the old school who held that the Holy Spirit was an aspect or power of God, but not a person.) Kellogg continued: "I had supposed the Bible said this for the reason that the personal pronoun 'he' is used in speaking of the Holy Ghost. Sister White uses the pronoun 'he' and has said in so many words that the Holy Ghost is the third person of the Godhead. How the Holy Ghost can be the third person and not be a person at all is difficult for me to see" (J. H. Kellogg to G. I. Butler, Oct. 28, 1903a, Adventist Heritage Center, Andrews University).

Here is a fascinating example of Kellogg as a debater. Essentially he is saying, "I have been misunderstood. I didn't claim that the Father is in everything; it is the Holy Spirit who is in everything. And if the Holy Spirit is a person, then Ellen White is wrong in saying my view undermines the personality of God." Thus he sought to outmaneuver Ellen White's reproof and maintain the legitimacy of his own opinion. It's a truism that statistics can lie. Kellogg shows here that logic can also lie. He was attempting to convince Butler that the pantheism of *The Living Temple* was simply a scientific version of the same doctrine of God that Ellen White had set forth in *The Desire of Ages*.

Butler, however, was not fooled. "So far as Sister White and you being in perfect agreement is concerned, I shall have to leave that entirely between you and Sister White. Sister White says there is *not* perfect agreement. You claim there *is*. . . . I must give her the credit . . . of saying there is a difference" (G. I. Butler to J. H. Kellogg, Apr. 5, 1904; italics supplied).

As the conflict dragged on into 1905, Ellen White wrote another document that exposed the matter to the church in such stark lines that no one could misunderstand. The manuscript offers perhaps the most radical, foundational indictment she ever wrote against a false view of the Trinity, followed by one of her most explicit descriptions of what she considered to be the true understanding. In this document, published in 1905, she labels the first view "spiritualistic," "nothingness," "imperfect, untrue," "the depths of Satan" [Rev. 2:24], and "the trail of the serpent." She said those who received it were "giving heed to seducing spirits and doctrines of devils, departing from the faith which they have held sacred for the past fifty years" (*Special Testimonies,* Series B, No. 7, pp. 61-63).

In contrast to the view that she unsparingly denounced, she set forth another concept that she regarded as "the right platform," in harmony with "the simplicity of true godliness," and "the old, old times . . . when, under the Holy Spirit's guidance, thousands were converted in a day" (*ibid.,* pp. 63, 64). The antagonism between two opposing perspectives could scarcely be drawn in more stringent terms in a theological context than a disagreement between doctrines of "seducing spirits" and the doctrine of "the old, old times" of the original Pentecost. What she is talking about is two contrasting teachings about the Trinity. Here is the first, attributed explicitly to "Dr. Kellogg" and his associates in "our leading medical fraternity":

"I am instructed to say, The sentiments of those who are searching for advanced scientific ideas are not to be trusted. Such representations as the following are made:

" 'The Father is as the light invisible; the Son is as the light embodied; the Spirit is the light shed abroad.' 'The Father is like the dew, invisible vapor; the Son is like the dew gathered in beauteous form; the Spirit is like the dew fallen to the seat of life.' Another representation: 'The Father is like the invisible vapor; the Son is like the leaden cloud; the Spirit is rain fallen and working in refreshing power.'

"All these spiritualistic representations are simply nothingness. They are imperfect, untrue. They weaken and diminish the Majesty which no earthly likeness can be compared to. *God can not be compared with the things His hands have made.* These are mere earthly things, suffering under the curse of God because of the sins of man. The Father can not be described by the things of earth" (*ibid.,* p. 62; italics supplied).

Then, in the very next sentence, she defines what she understands to be the truth about the Godhead. "The Father is all the fulness of the Godhead bodily, and is invisible to mortal sight.

"The Son is all the fulness of the Godhead manifested. The Word of God declares Him to be 'the express image of his person.' 'God so loved the world, that he gave his only begotten Son, that whosoever believeth in him should not perish, but have everlasting life.' Here is shown the personality of the Father.

"The Comforter that Christ promised to send after He ascended to heaven, is the Spirit in all the fulness of the Godhead, making manifest the power of divine grace to all who receive and believe in Christ as a personal Saviour. There are three living persons of the *heavenly trio;* in the name of these *three great powers*—the Father, the Son, and the Holy Spirit—those who receive Christ by living faith are baptized, and *these powers* will co-operate with the obedient subjects of heaven in their efforts to live the new life in Christ" (*ibid.*, pp. 62, 63; italics supplied).

In charging that Kellogg with his "spiritualistic" Trinity doctrine was "departing from the faith" that Adventists had "held sacred for the past fifty years," she clearly refutes the assumption that all doctrines of the Trinity are the same and that the pioneers' objection to one of them demands the rejection of all. She saw at least two varieties of Trinitarianism—one that portrayed a personal, tangible God, and the other that spiritualized Him as impersonal, philosophical, but ultimately unreal.

Significantly, Ellen White condemns Kellogg's view of the Trinity in almost identical terms to those her husband James used in 1846 when he rejected the "old *unscriptural trinitarian creed*" for "spiritualiz[ing] away the existence of the Father and the Son, as two distinct, literal, tangible persons." This is consistent with the interpretation that she saw similarities between the creeds that claimed God was "invisible, without body or parts" and Kellogg's "spiritualistic representations" of God under metaphors of light and water.

Further, Ellen White claimed that in Kellogg's heresy she "recognized the very sentiments" she had opposed among spiritualizing ex-Millerites in 1845 and 1846 (*Selected Messages,* book 1, p. 203). It implies that she associated the spiritualizing of the post-disappointment fanatics, the creedal teaching that God is formless and intangible, and Kellogg's impersonal concepts of God all under the general heading of "spiritualistic theories" (*ibid.,* p. 204).

This insight is directly related to the current debate within Adventism, because some have concluded that Kellogg's view, which Ellen White condemned, is the same view of the Trinity later accepted by the church—a premise obviously not supported by the evidence. She teaches that a false concept of the Trinity makes God seem distant, untouchable, impersonal, unreal; and that a true biblical view of the Trinity shows God to include three individual divine personalities who are united in nature, character, purpose, and love (*The Ministry of Healing,* p. 422).

Her support for a biblical view of the Trinity became so explicit during the years between 1902 and 1907 that by 1913, F. M. Wilcox, editor of the denomination's most influential periodical and one of the original five trustees appointed by Ellen White to superintend her estate, could write in the *Review and Herald* without fear of contradiction by her, that "Seventh-day Adventists believe,—1. In the divine Trinity. This Trinity consists of the eternal Father, . . . the Lord Jesus Christ, . . . [and] the Holy Spirit, the third person of the Godhead" (Wilcox, "The Message for Today," *Review and Herald,* Oct. 9, 1913). The statement, in an article summarizing the fundamental beliefs of Seventh-day Adventists, follows directly after an article by Ellen White, so it is virtually certain that in examining her published article, as she habitually did, she would also have seen the Wilcox piece.

Conclusion

Regarding the paradigm shift in the Adventist view of the Trinity, this chapter has addressed two questions: Did the change constitute a progressive discovery of a biblical view, or an apostasy from a biblical view? and, What was Ellen White's role in the process? The evidence has shown that the visions received by Ellen White led the denomination through clearly discernible stages toward full acceptance of a biblical concept of the Trinity. That concept was essentially complete in 1898 when she published *The Desire of Ages,* and her statements of 1901-1906 were sufficiently explicit that by 1913 the editor of the *Review and Herald* could affirm—without fear of her contradiction—that "the divine Trinity" is a fundamental Adventist belief.

However, the evidence is also clear that Ellen White recognized at least two major types of Trinitarian belief, one that she consistently opposed all her life, and another that her visions progressively led her to agree with. The view she eventually came to agree with portrays the three members of the Godhead as tangible, personal individuals, living from eternity in union of nature, character, purpose, and love, yet each having an individual identity. This is a simple, biblical view of the Trinity, as contrasted with traditional views based on the presuppositions of Greek philosophy.

If one holds that among all the human elements of Adventist history, we also find evidence of a divine hand at work, then one can also suggest an explanation of why the process proceeded so slowly, even tortuously, from initial rejection of the "old unscriptural trinitarian creed" to eventual acceptance of the biblical elements of Trinitarianism. The explanation that to me is most compelling is that God was leading the movement toward a biblical theology, free from the controlling influence of Greek philosophy. The traditional dogma of the Trinity, based on dualistic presuppositions, was incompatible with the biblical data.

The only way the pioneers could separate the biblical elements of Trinitarianism from the traditional elements was to disallow completely tradition as a basis for doctrine, and struggle through the long process of reconstructing their belief on Scripture alone. In doing so, they retraced many of the steps of the ancient church in accepting first the equality of Christ with the Father, and then Their equality and unity with the Holy Spirit as well. In the course of this journey, the pioneers' theology showed temporary similarities to some of the historical heresies. Their repudiation of tradition as doctrinal authority was costly in terms of the ostracism they endured as perceived "heretics" and in terms of the time it would take them to discover from Scripture a comprehensive doctrine of God, but the results justify the conclusion that God was leading them all along that path.

---

*The criticism of the book was so fierce that for the second printing Kellogg rewrote certain pages. The publisher even inserted the new pages in unsold copies of the first edition by cutting the original pages out and pasting the substitute pages in their place. Examples of the original edition, the altered edition, and a later edition are available at the Center for Adventist Research, Andrews University, Berrien Springs, Michigan.

Supplement to Chapter 14

ELLEN WHITE ON THE TRINITY:

The Basic Primary Documents

The Mystery of the Godhead and the Incarnation

This truth [that "Christ was one with the Father before the foundation of the world was laid"], infinitely mysterious in itself, explains other mysterious and otherwise unexplainable truths, while it is enshrined in light, unapproachable and incomprehensible" (*Review and Herald,* Apr. 5, 1906).

"In contemplating the incarnation of Christ in humanity, we stand baffled before an unfathomable mystery, that the human mind cannot comprehend. The more we reflect upon it, the more amazing does it appear. How wide is the contrast between the divinity of Christ and the helpless infant in Bethlehem's manger! How can we span the distance between the mighty God and a helpless child? . . . Looking upon Christ in humanity, we look upon God, and see in Him the brightness of His glory, the express image of His person" (*Signs of the Times,* July 30, 1896).

"Was the human nature of the Son of Mary changed into the divine nature of the Son of God? No; the two natures were mysteriously blended in one person—the man Christ Jesus. In Him dwelt all the fullness of the Godhead bodily. . . .

"This is a great mystery, a mystery that will not be fully, completely understood in all its greatness until the translation of the redeemed shall take place. . . . But the enemy is determined that this gift shall be so mystified that it will become as nothingness" (letter

280, 1904, quoted in *The Seventh-day Adventist Bible Commentary,* vol. 5, p. 1113).

"It is a mystery that One equal with the eternal Father should so abase Himself as to suffer the cruel death of the cross to ransom man; and it is a mystery that God so loved the world as to permit His Son to make this great sacrifice" (*Signs of the Times,* Oct. 24, 1906).

"The work of God's dear Son in undertaking to link the created with the Uncreated, the finite with the Infinite, in His own divine person, is a subject that may well employ our thoughts for a lifetime" (*Review and Herald,* Jan. 11, 1881).

The Full Deity of Christ

"If men reject the testimony of the inspired Scriptures concerning the deity of Christ, it is in vain to argue the point with them; for no argument, however conclusive, could convince them. . . . None who hold this error can have a true conception of the character or the mission of Christ, or of the great plan of God for man's redemption" (*The Great Controversy,* p. 524).

"In Christ, divinity and humanity were combined. Divinity was not degraded to humanity; divinity held its place, but humanity by being united to divinity, withstood the fiercest test of temptation in the wilderness" (*Review and Herald,* Feb. 18, 1890).

"As a member of the human family He was mortal, but as a God He was the fountain of life to the world. He could, in His divine person, ever have withstood the advances of death. . . . The eternal Word consented to be made flesh! God became man" (*Review and Herald,* July 5, 1887).

Christ "walked this earth as the Eternal Word" (*Fundamentals of Christian Education,* p. 400).

"He was God while upon earth, but He divested Himself of the form of God, and in its stead took the form and fashion of a man. . . . He was God, but the glories of the form of God He for awhile relinquished. . . . He bore the sins of the world, and endured the penalty which rolled like a mountain upon His divine soul" (*Review and Herald,* July 5, 1887).

"'I and my Father are one.' The words of Christ were full of deep meaning as he put forth the claim that he and the Father were of one substance, possessing the same attributes" (*Signs of the Times,* Nov. 27, 1893).

"Yet the Son of God was the acknowledged Sovereign of heaven, one in power and authority with the Father" (*The Great Controversy,* p. 495).

"Christ was God essentially, and in the highest sense" (*Review and Herald,* Apr. 5, 1906).

"In Christ is life, original, unborrowed, underived. 'He that hath the Son hath life' (1 John 5:12). The divinity of Christ is the believer's assurance of eternal life" (*The Desire of Ages,* p. 530).

"With solemn dignity Jesus answered, 'Verily, verily, I say unto you, Before Abraham was, I AM.' Silence fell upon the vast assembly. The name of God, given to Moses to express the idea of the eternal presence, had been claimed as His own by this Galilean Rabbi. He had announced Himself to be the self-existent One, He who had been promised to Israel, 'whose goings forth have been from of old, from the days of eternity'" (*ibid.,* pp. 469, 470).

"The world's Redeemer was equal with God. His authority was as the authority of God. He declared that he had no existence separate from the Father. The authority by which he spoke, and wrought miracles, was expressly his own, yet he assures us that he and the Father are one" (*Review and Herald,* Jan. 7, 1890).

"Jehovah, the eternal, self-existent, uncreated One, Himself the Source and Sustainer of all, is alone entitled to supreme reverence and worship" (*Patriarchs and Prophets,* p. 305).

"Jehovah is the name given to Christ" (*Signs of the Times,* May 3, 1899).

"In His superadded humanity consists the reason of Christ's appointment. God has committed all judgment unto the Son, for without controversy He is God manifest in the flesh" (*Review and Herald,* Nov. 22, 1898).

The Eternal Preexistence of Christ

"Christ was God essentially, and in the highest sense. He was with God from all eternity, God over all, blessed forevermore" (*Review and Herald,* Apr. 5, 1906).

Upon His ascension, "Christ was indeed glorified, even with the glory which He had with the Father from all eternity" (*The Acts of the Apostles,* pp. 38, 39).

"The name of God ["I AM"], given to Moses to express the idea of the eternal presence, had been claimed as His own by this Galilean Rabbi. He had announced Himself to be the self-existent One" (*The Desire of Ages,* pp. 469, 470).

"The Word existed as a divine being, even as the eternal Son of God, in union and oneness with His Father. From everlasting He was the Mediator of the covenant, the one in whom all nations of the earth, both Jews and Gentiles, if they accepted Him, were to be blessed. 'The Word was with God, and the Word was God.' Before men or angels were created, the Word was with God, and was God. . . . Words spoken in regard to this are so decisive that no one need be left in doubt. Christ was God essentially, and in the highest sense. He was with God [the Father] from all eternity, God over all, blessed forevermore.

"The Lord Jesus Christ, the divine Son of God, existed from eternity, a distinct person, yet one with the Father. . . . This was no robbery of God. . . .

"There are light and glory in the truth that Christ was one with the Father before the foundation of the world was laid. This is the light shining in a dark place, making it resplendent with divine, original glory" (*Review and Herald,* Apr. 5, 1906).

"Christ is the pre-existent, self-existent Son of God. . . . In speaking of His pre-existence, Christ carries the mind back through dateless ages. He assures us that there never was a time when He was not in close fellowship with the eternal God" (*Signs of the Times,* Aug. 29, 1900).

"Here Christ shows them that, although they might reckon His life to be less than fifty years, yet His divine life could not be reckoned by human computation. The existence of Christ before His incarnation is not measured by figures" (*Signs of the Times,* May 3, 1899).

"From the days of eternity the Lord Jesus Christ was one with the Father; He was 'the image of God,' the image of His greatness and majesty, 'the outshining of His Glory'" (*The Desire of Ages,* p. 19).

"In it [God's Word] we may learn what our redemption has cost Him who from the beginning was equal with the Father" (*Counsels to Parents and Teachers,* p. 13).

Only One Equal With God Could Atone for Human Sin

"Not one of the angels could have become surety for the human race: their life is God's; they could not surrender it. The angels all wear the yoke of obedience. They are the appointed messengers of Him who is the commander of all heaven. But Christ is equal with God, infinite and omnipotent. He could pay the ransom for man's freedom. He is the eternal, self-existing Son, on whom no yoke had come; and when God asked, 'Whom shall I send?' He could reply, 'Here am I, send me.' He could pledge Himself to become man's surety; for He could say that which the highest angel could not say,—I have power over my own life, 'power to lay it down, and . . . power to take it again'" (*Youth's Instructor,* June 21, 1900).

"Man could not atone for man. His sinful, fallen condition would constitute him an imperfect offering, an atoning sacrifice of less value than Adam before his fall. God made man perfect and upright, and after his transgression there could be no sacrifice acceptable to God for him, unless the offering made should in value be superior to man as he was in his state of perfection and innocency.

"The divine Son of God was the only sacrifice of sufficient value to fully satisfy the claims of God's perfect law. The angels were sinless, but of less value than the law of God. They were amenable to law. They were messengers to do the will of Christ, and before him to bow. They were created beings, and probationers. Upon Christ no requirements were laid. He had power to lay down his life, and to take it again. No obligation was laid upon him to undertake the work of atonement. It was a voluntary sacrifice that he made. His life was of sufficient value to rescue man from his fallen condition" (*Review and Herald,* Dec. 17, 1872; later published in *The Spirit of Prophecy* [1877 ed.], vol. 2, pp. 9, 10).

"Christ alone could open the way, by making an offering equal to the demands of the divine law" (*Review and Herald,* Dec. 17, 1872).

"In dying upon the cross, He transferred the guilt from the person of the transgressor to that of the divine Substitute, through faith in Him as his personal Redeemer. *The sins of a guilty world,* which in figure are represented as 'red as crimson,' *were imputed to the divine Surety"* (manuscript 84a, 1897, cited in *The Seventh-day Adventist Bible Commentary,* vol. 7A, p. 462).

"Justice moved from its exalted throne, and with all the armies of heaven approached the cross. There it saw One equal with God bearing the penalty for all injustice and sin. With perfect satisfaction Justice bowed in reverence at the cross, saying, It is enough" (*General Conference Bulletin,* Fourth Quarter 1899, vol. 3, p. 102).

"Justice demanded the sufferings of a man. Christ, equal with God, gave the sufferings of a God. He needed no atonement" (*Review and Herald,* Sept. 21, 1886).

"Christ bore our sins in His own body on the tree. . . . What must sin be, if no finite being could make atonement? What must its curse be if Deity alone could exhaust it? The cross of Christ testifies to every man that the penalty of sin is death" (letter 23, 1873, in *Our High Calling,* p. 44).

"No sorrow can bear any comparison with the sorrow of Him upon whom the wrath of God fell with overwhelming force. Human nature can endure but a limited amount of test and trial. The finite can only endure the finite measure, and human nature succumbs; but the nature of Christ had a greater capacity for suffering; for the human existed in the divine nature, and created a capacity for suffering to endure that which resulted from the sins of a lost world" (manuscript 35, 1895, in *That I May Know Him,* p. 64).

Only One Who Is God Can Be an Effective Intercessor or Advocate With God

"The reconciliation of man to God could be accomplished only through a mediator who was equal with God, possessed of attributes that would dignify, and declare Him worthy to treat with the Infinite God in man's behalf, and also represent God to a fallen world. Man's substitute and surety must have man's nature, a connection with the human family whom He was to represent, and, as God's ambassador, He must partake of the divine nature, have a connection with the Infinite, in order to manifest God to the world, and be a mediator between God and man" (*Review and Herald,* Dec. 22, 1891).

"Christ as High Priest within the veil so immortalized Calvary, that though He liveth unto God, He dies continually to sin and thus *if any man sin, he has an Advocate with the Father.* He arose from the tomb enshrouded with a cloud of angels in wondrous power and glory,—*the Deity and humanity combined"* (manuscript 50, 1900, quoted in *The Seventh-day Adventist Bible Commentary,* vol. 7A, p. 485).

"Jesus became a man that He might mediate between man and God. He clothed His divinity with humanity, He associated with the human race, that with His long human arm He might encircle humanity, and with His divine arm grasp the throne of Divinity" (letter 121, 1897, cited in *The Seventh-day Adventist Bible Commentary,* vol. 7A, p. 487).

"The completeness of His humanity, the perfection of His divinity, form for us a strong ground upon which we may be brought into reconciliation with God. It was when we were yet sinners that Christ died for us. We have redemption through His blood, even the forgiveness of sins. *His nail-pierced hands are out-reached toward heaven and earth. With one hand He lays hold of sinners upon earth, and with the other He grasps the throne of the Infinite, and thus He makes reconciliation for us.* Christ is today standing as our Advocate before the Father. He is the one Mediator between God and man. *Bearing the marks of His crucifixion, He pleads the causes of our souls"* (letter 35, 1894, quoted in *The Seventh-day Adventist Bible Commentary,* vol. 7A, p. 487).

"Jesus could give alone security to God; for He was equal with God. He alone could be a mediator between God and man; for He possessed divinity and humanity. Jesus could thus give security to both parties for the fulfillment of the prescribed conditions. As the Son of God He gives security to God in our behalf, and as the eternal Word, as one equal with the Father, He assures us of the Father's love to usward who believe His pledged word. When God would assure us of His immutable counsel of peace, He gives His only begotten Son to become one of the human family, forever to retain His human nature as a pledge that God will fulfil His word" (*Review and Herald,* Apr. 3, 1894).

The Personality and Deity of the Holy Spirit

"The Comforter that Christ promised to send after He ascended to heaven, is the Spirit in all the fullness of the Godhead, making manifest the power of divine grace to all who receive and believe in Christ as a personal Saviour. There are three living persons of the heavenly trio; in the name of these three great powers—the Father, the Son, and the Holy Spirit—those who receive Christ by living faith are baptized, and these powers will co-operate with the obedient subjects of heaven in their efforts to live the new life in Christ" (*Special Testimonies,* Series B, No. 7, pp. 62, 63 [1905], quoted in *Evangelism,* p. 615).

"The prince of the power of evil can only be held in check by the power of God in the third person of the Godhead, the Holy Spirit" (*Special Testimonies,* Series A, No. 10, p. 37, quoted in *Evangelism,* p. 617).

"We need to realize that the Holy Spirit, who is as much a person as God is a person, is walking through these grounds" (manuscript 66, 1899; from a recorded talk given to the students at the Avondale School and cited in *Evangelism,* p. 616).

"The Holy Spirit is a person, for He beareth witness with our spirits that we are the children of God. When this witness is borne, it carries with it its own evidence. At such times we believe and are sure that we are the children of God. . . .

"The Holy Spirit has a personality, else He could not bear witness to our spirits and with our spirits that we are the children of

God. He must also be a divine person, else He could not search out the secrets which lie hidden in the mind of God. 'For what man knoweth the things of a man, save the spirit of man which is in him? even so the things of God knoweth no man, but the Spirit of God' " (manuscript 20, 1906; cited in *Evangelism,* pp. 616, 617).

"The eternal heavenly dignitaries—God, and Christ, and the Holy Spirit—arming them [the disciples] with more than mortal energy . . . would advance with them to the work and convince the world of sin" (manuscript 145, 1901, cited in *Evangelism,* p. 616).

"We are to co-operate with the three highest powers in heaven,—the Father, the Son, and the Holy Ghost,—and these powers will work through us, making us workers together with God" (*Special Testimonies,* Series B, No. 7, p. 51, cited in *Evangelism,* p. 617).

Compilers' note: We observe a telling similarity of expression when Ellen White, using the language of Colossians 2:9, applies this language to all three members of the Godhead: "The Father is all the fullness of the Godhead," "The Son is all the fullness of the Godhead," and the Holy Spirit is "all the fullness of the Godhead" (*Evangelism,* pp. 614, 615).

The Oneness or Unity of the Godhead

"The unity that exists between Christ and His disciples does not destroy the personality of either. They are one in purpose, in mind, in character, but not in person. It is thus that God and Christ are one" (*The Ministry of Healing,* p. 422).

"The Godhead was stirred with pity for the race, and the Father, the Son, and the Holy Spirit gave themselves to the working out of the plan of redemption" (*Counsels on Health,* p. 222).

"Christ, the Word, the only begotten of God, was one with the eternal Father,—one in nature, in character, in purpose,—the only being that could enter into all the counsels and purposes of God" (*Patriarchs and Prophets,* p. 34; compare *The Great Controversy,* p. 493).

"The Jews had never before heard such words from human lips, and a convicting influence attended them; for it seemed that divinity flashed through humanity as Jesus said, 'I and my Father are one.' The words of Christ were full of deep meaning as he put forth the claim that he and the Father were of one substance, possessing the same attributes" (*Signs of the Times,* Nov. 27, 1893).

"To save the transgressor of God's law, Christ, the one equal with the Father, came to live heaven before men, that they might learn to know what it is to have heaven in the heart" (*Fundamentals of Christian Education,* p. 179).

"The only way in which the fallen race could be restored was through the gift of his Son, equal with himself, possessing the attributes of God" (*Review and Herald,* Nov. 8, 1892).

"The Son of God shared the Father's throne, and the glory of the eternal, self-existent One encircled both" (*Patriarchs and Prophets,* p. 36).

"The world's Redeemer was equal with God. . . . The authority by which he spoke, and wrought miracles, was expressly his own, yet he assures us that he and the Father are one" (*Review and Herald,* Jan. 7, 1890).

"The Word existed as a divine being, even as the eternal Son of God, in union and oneness with his Father. From everlasting he was the Mediator of the covenant, the one in whom all nations of the earth, both Jews and Gentiles, if they accepted him, were to be blessed. 'The Word was with God, and the Word was God.' Before men or angels were created, the Word was with God, and was God" (*Review and Herald,* Apr. 5, 1906; *Selected Messages,* book 1, p. 247; *Evangelism,* p. 615).

"That the transgressor might have another trial, that men might be brought into favor with God the Father, the eternal Son of God interposed himself to bear the punishment of transgression. One clothed with humanity, who was yet one with the Deity, was our ransom" (*Review and Herald,* Feb. 8, 1898).

"'Search the Scriptures.' John 5:39. This injunction is from the eternal Son of God" (*Youth's Instructor,* Aug. 31, 1887).

"It was poverty that as He passed to and fro among the subjects He came to save, scarcely a solitary voice called Him blessed, scarcely a solitary hand was stretched out in friendship, and scarcely a solitary roof proffered Him shelter. Then look beneath the disguise, and whom do we see?—Divinity, the Eternal Son of God, just as mighty, just as infinitely gifted with all the resources of power, and He was found in fashion as a man" (*Manuscript Releases,* vol. 15, pp. 25, 26; *1888 Materials,* p. 28).

"Christ, the author of man's salvation [was] the eternal Son of God" (*Review and Herald,* Aug. 8, 1878).

"The Lord Jesus Christ, the divine Son of God, existed from eternity, a distinct person, yet one with the Father. . . . This was no robbery of God" (*Review and Herald,* Apr. 5, 1906).

"There are three living persons of the heavenly trio; in the name of these three great powers—the Father, the Son, and the Holy Spirit—those who receive Christ by living faith are baptized, and these powers will co-operate with the obedient subjects of heaven in their efforts to live the new life in Christ" (*Evangelism,* p. 615).

"We are to co-operate with the three highest powers in heaven,—the Father, the Son, and the Holy Ghost,—and these powers will work through us, making us workers together with God" (*ibid.,* p. 617).

"The eternal heavenly dignitaries—God, and Christ, and the Holy Spirit—arming them [the disciples] with more than mortal energy, . . . would advance with them to the work and convince the world of sin" (*ibid.,* p. 616).

"Had the Father come to our world and dwelt among us, humbling Himself, veiling His glory, that humanity might look upon Him, the history that we have of the life of Christ would not have been changed. . . . In every act of Jesus, in every lesson of His instruction, we are to see and hear and recognize God. In sight, in hearing, in effect, it is the voice and movements of the Father" (*That I May Know Him,* p. 338).

Bibliography for Section Three

Anderson, Godfrey T. *Spicer: Leader With the Common Touch.* Washington, D.C.: Review and Herald Pub. Assn., 1983.

Andreasen, M. L. "Christ, the Express Image of God." *Review and Herald,* Oct. 17, 1946, p. 8.

———. "The Spirit of Prophecy." Chapel address at Loma Linda, California, Nov. 30, 1948. Quoted in Russell Holt, "The Doctrine of the Trinity in the Seventh-day Adventist Denomination: Its Rejection and Acceptance," p. 20. Term Paper, Seventh-day Adventist Theological Seminary, 1969.

Bainton, Roland H. *Hunted Heretic: The Life and Death of Michael Servetus, 1511-1533.* Boston: Beacon Press, 1953.

Bates, Joseph. *The Autobiography of Elder Joseph Bates.* Battle Creek, Mich.: Seventh-day Adventist Publishing Association, 1868; reprint, Nashville: Southern Pub. Assn., 1970.

Berkhof, Louis. *History of Christian Doctrine.* London: Banner of Truth, 1969.

Bourdeau, D. T. "We May Partake of the Fullness of the Father and the Son." *Review and Herald,* Nov. 18, 1890.

Burt, Merlin. "Demise of Semi-Arianism and Anti-Trinitarianism in Adventist Theology, 1888-1957." Research paper, Andrews University, 1996. Ellen G. White Research Center, Andrews University.

Butler, G. I., to J. H. Kellogg, Apr. 5, 1904. Kellogg-Butler Correspondence Collection, Adventist Heritage Center, Andrews University, Berrien Springs, Michigan.

Calvin, John. *Institutes of the Christian Religion.* 2 vols. Library of Christian Classics. Edited by John T. McNeill. Philadelphia: Westminster, 1960. Vols. 20, 21. The reference (I. xiii. 29) is to Calvin's book I, chapter 13, section 29 [vol. 20, p. 159, in the LCC edition].

Canale, Fernando L. *A Criticism of Theological Reason: Time and Timelessness as Primordial Presuppositions.* Andrews University Seminary Doctoral Dissertation Series. Berrien Springs, Mich.:

Andrews University Press, 1983. Vol. 10.

———. "Doctrine of God," in *Handbook of Seventh-day Adventist Theology*. Ed. Raoul Dederen. Seventh-day Adventist Bible Commentary Reference Series. Hagerstown, Md.: Review and Herald Pub. Assn., 2000. Vol. 12, pp. 105-159.

Conkin, Paul K. *American Originals: Homemade Varieties of Christianity*. Chapel Hill: University of North Carolina Press, 1997.

Cottrell, R. F. "The Doctrine of the Trinity." *Review and Herald,* June 1, 1869.

Cullman, Oscar. *Immortality of the Soul; or, Resurrection of the Dead? The Witness of the New Testament*. New York: Macmillan, 1958.

Dederen, Raoul. "Reflections on the Doctrine of the Trinity." *Andrews University Seminary Studies* 8 (January 1970): 1-22.

Dick, Everett N. *William Miller and the Advent Crisis,* 1831-1844. Ed. Gary Land. Berrien Springs, Mich.: Andrews University Press, 1994.

Doctrines and Discipline of the Methodist Episcopal Church. New York: Carlton and Porter, 1856.

"Fifteenth Meeting." *Review and Herald,* June 14, 1946.

Froom, LeRoy Edwin. *The Coming of the Comforter*. Washington, D.C.: Review and Herald Pub. Assn., 1928, rev. ed. 1949.

———. *Movement of Destiny [MOD]*. Washington, D.C.: Review and Herald Pub. Assn., 1971.

Fudge, Edward W. *The Fire That Consumes: A Biblical and Historical Study of Final Punishment*. Houston: Providential Press, 1982.

———. and Robert A. Peterson. *Two Views of Hell: A Biblical and Theological Dialogue*. Downers Grove, Ill.: InterVarsity Press, 2000.

Gane, Erwin R. "The Arian or Anti-Trinitarian Views Presented in Seventh-day Adventist Literature and the Ellen G. White Answer." M.A. thesis, Andrews University, 1963.

Gonzalez,, Justo L. *Christian Thought Revisited: Three Types of Theology*. Nashville: Abingdon, 1989.

———. *History of Christian Thought. From the Protestant Reformation to the Twentieth Century*. Nashville: Abingdon, 1975. Vol. 3.

Hatch, Nathan O. *The Democratization of American Christianity*. New Haven: Yale University Press, 1989.

Himes, Joshua V. "Christian Connection" [1833]. In *Encyclopedia of Religious Knowledge*. Ed. J. Newton Brown. Brattleboro, Vt.: Brattleboro Typographic, 1838. Pp. 362, 363.

Hogan, Richard M., and John M. LeVoir. *Faith for Today: Pope John Paul II's Catechetical Teachings*. New York: Doubleday, 1988.

Holt, Russell. "The Doctrine of the Trinity in the Seventh-day Adventist Denomination: Its Rejection and Acceptance." Term Paper, Seventh-day Adventist Theological Seminary, 1969.

Kellogg, J. H. *The Living Temple*. Battle Creek, Mich.: Good Health Pub. Co., 1903.

———. to G. I. Butler, Oct. 28, 1903a. Adventist Heritage Center, Andrews University, Berrien Springs, Michigan.

Knight, George R. *Search for Identity: The Development of Seventh-day Adventist Beliefs*. Hagerstown, Md.: Review and Herald Pub. Assn., 2000.

Liechty, Daniel. *Sabbatarianism in the Sixteenth Century: A Page in the History of the Radical Reformation*. Berrien Springs, Mich.: Andrews University Press, 1993.

Loughborough, J. H. "Questions for Bro. Loughborough." *Advent Review and Sabbath Herald,* Nov. 5, 1861.

Maxwell, C. Mervyn. Review of *Movement of Destiny,* by LeRoy Edwin Froom. *Andrews University Seminary Studies* 10 (January 1972): 119-122.

Miller, William. *William Miller's Apology and Defence*. Boston: J. V. Himes, 1845. Reproduced in *1844 and the Rise of Sabbatarian Adventism: Reproductions of Original Historical Documents*. Ed. George R. Knight. Hagerstown, Md.: Review and Herald Pub. Assn., 1994.

Moon, Jerry. "M. L. Andreasen, L. E. Froom, and the Controversy Over *Questions on Doctrine*." Term paper, Andrews University, 1988.

Moore, A. Leroy. *Adventism in Conflict: Resolving Issues That Divide Us*. Hagerstown, Md.: Review and Herald Pub. Assn., 1995.

Mustard, Andrew G. *James White and SDA Organization: Historical Development, 1844-1881*. Andrews University Seminary Doctoral Dissertation Series. Berrien Springs, Mich.: Andrews University Press, 1988. Vol. 12.

Olmstead, Clifton E. *History of Religion in the United States*. Englewood Cliffs, N.J.: Prentice-Hall, 1960.

Olson, Roger E. *The Story of Christian Theology: Twenty Centuries of Tradition and Reform*. Downers Grove, Ill.: InterVarsity Press, 1999.

"Monarchianism," "Modalism," "Sabellianism," and "Trinity." *Oxford Dictionary of the Christian Church*. 2nd ed. Oxford: Oxford University Press, 1983.

Pelikan, Jaroslav. *The Christian Tradition: A History of the Development of Doctrine*. Chicago: University of Chicago Press, 1971-1989. 5 vols.

Pinnock, Clark. "Conditional View." In *Four Views on Hell*. Ed. William Crockett. Grand Rapids: Zondervan, 1992.

Pipkin, J. Wayne, and John H. Yoder. *Balthasar Hubmaier, Theologian of Anabaptism*. Scottdale, Pa.: Herald Press, 1989.

Seventh-day Adventists Answer Questions on Doctrine [QOD]. [By LeRoy Edwin Froom, W. E. Read, and Roy Allan Anderson.] Washington, D.C.: Ministerial Department of the General Conference of Seventh-day Adventists. Washington, D.C.: Review and Herald Pub. Assn., 1957.

Robinson, Dores Eugene. *Story of Our Health Message*. 3rd ed., rev. and enl. Nashville: Southern Pub. Assn., 1943, 1965.

[Servetus] Serveto, Michael. *On the Errors of the Trinity*. In *The Two Treaties of Servetus on the Trinity*. Ed. Earl Morse Wilbur. Cambridge: Harvard University Press, 1932.

Seventh-day Adventists Believe . . . : A Biblical Exposition of 27 Fundamental Doctrines. [Principal author, P. Gerard Damsteegt.] Silver Spring, Md.: Ministerial Department of the General Conference of Seventh-day Adventists, 1988.

Seventh-day Adventist Encyclopedia. 1996 ed.

Smith, Uriah. "In the Question Chair." *Review and Herald*, Mar. 23, 1897.

———. *Looking Unto Jesus.* Battle Creek, Mich.: Review and Herald Pub. Assn., 1898.

———. *The State of the Dead and the Destiny of the Wicked.* Battle Creek, Mich.: Seventh-day Adventist Pub. Assn., 1873.

———. *Thoughts on the Book of Daniel and the Revelation.* Battle Creek, Mich.: Review and Herald, 1882.

Snyder, C. Arnold. *Anabaptist History and Theology: Revised Student Edition.* Kitchener, Ontario, Canada: Pandora Press, 1997.

Spear, Samuel T. *The Bible Doctrine of the Trinity.* Bible Students' Library, No. 90 (March 1892): 3-14. Reprinted from the New York *Independent,* Nov. 14, 1889.

Stott, John R. W., and David Lawrence Edwards. *Essentials.* London: Hodder and Stoughton, 1988.

Unruh, T. E. "The Seventh-day Adventist Evangelical Conferences of 1955-1956." *Adventist Heritage* (Winter 1977).

Verduin, Leonard. "Luther's Dilemma: Restitution or Reformation?" In *Essays on Luther.* Ed. Kenneth A. Strand. Ann Arbor, Mich.: Ann Arbor Publishers, 1969. Pp. 73-96.

Waggoner, Ellet J. *Christ and His Righteousness.* Oakland, Calif.: Pacific Press Pub. Assn., 1890; reprint, Riverside, Calif.: Upward Way, 1988.

Waggoner, Joseph H. *The Atonement.* Oakland, Calif.: Pacific Press Pub. Assn., 1884.

White, Arthur L. *Ellen G. White.* Washington, D.C.: Review and Herald Pub. Assn., 1985. Vol. 1.

White, Ellen G. "An Appeal to the Ministers." *Review and Herald,* Aug. 8, 1878.

———. *Counsels on Health.* Mountain View, Calif.: Pacific Press Pub. Assn., 1923.

———. *Counsels to Parents and Teachers.* Mountain View, Calif.: Pacific Press Pub. Assn., 1913.

———. *Counsels to Writers and Editors.* Nashville: Southern Pub. Assn., 1946.

———. *The Desire of Ages: The Conflict of the Ages Illustrated in the Life of Christ.* Mountain View, Calif.: Pacific Press Pub. Assn.,

1898, 1940.
———. *Early Writings*. Washington, D.C.: Review and Herald Pub. Assn., 1906.
———. Ellen G. White Comments. *The Seventh-day Adventist Bible Commentary*. Vol. 5, p. 1113.
———. *1888 Materials*. Washington, D.C.: Ellen G. White Estate, 1987. 4 vols.
———. *Fundamentals of Christian Education*. Nashville: Southern Pub. Assn., 1923.
———. *The Great Controversy Between Christ and Satan During the Christian Dispensation*. Oakland, Calif.: Pacific Press Pub. Assn., 1888.
———. *The Great Controversy Between Christ and Satan: The Conflict of the Ages in the Christian Dispensation*. Mountain View, Calif.: Pacific Press Pub. Assn., 1911, 1950.
———. Manuscript 131, 1897.
———. *Manuscript Releases*. Silver Spring, Md.: Ellen G. White Estate, 1993. Vol. 15.
———. *The Ministry of Healing*. Mountain View, Calif.: Pacific Press Pub. Assn., 1905.
———. *Patriarchs and Prophets, The Story of,* or *The Great Conflict Between Good and Evil as Illustrated in the Lives of Holy Men of Old*. Oakland, Calif.: Pacific Press Pub. Assn., 1890.
———. "'Search the Scriptures.' John 5:39." *Youth's Instructor,* Aug. 31, 1887, par. 1.
———. *Selected Messages From the Writings of Ellen G. White*. Washington, D.C.: Review and Herald Pub. Assn., 1958, 1980. 3 vols.
———. *Special Testimonies,* Series B, No. 7. N.p., 1906.
———. *Spritual Gifts*. Battle Creek, Mich.: Seventh-day Adventist Pub. Assn., 1858-1864. 4 vols.
———. *Steps to Christ*. Mountain View, Calif.: Pacific Press Pub. Assn., 1956.
———. *Testimonies for the Church*. Mountain View, Calif.: Pacific Press Pub. Assn., 1948. 9 vols.

———. "The First Advent of Christ." *Review and Herald,* Dec. 17, 1872.

———. "The Truth Revealed in Jesus." *Review and Herald,* Feb. 8, 1898.

———. "The Word Made Flesh." *Review and Herald,* Apr. 5, 1906.

———. To the Teachers in Emmanuel Missionary College, Sept. 22, 1903 (letter 211, 1903).

———. To Brother and Sister Hastings, Mar. 24-30, 1849 (letter 5, 1849). In *Manuscript Releases.* Vol. 5, p. 200.

———. In *Youth's Instructor,* Aug. 4, 1898.

White, James. "Christ Equal With God." *Review and Herald,* Nov. 29, 1877.

———. In *Day-Star,* Jan. 24, 1846.

———. *Sketches of the Christian Life and Public Labors of William Miller.* Battle Creek, Mich.: Seventh-day Adventist Pub. Assn., 1875.

Whitney, Seymour B. "Both Sides." *Review and Herald,* Feb. 25, Mar. 4, 1862.

Wilbur, Earl Morse. *A History of Unitarianism. Socinianism and Its Antecedents.* Cambridge: Harvard University Press, 1945. Vol. 1.

———. *A History of Unitarianism. In Transylvania, England, and America.* Cambridge: Harvard University Press, 1952. Vol. 2.

Wilcox, F. M. "The Message for Today." *Review and Herald,* Oct. 9, 1913.

SECTION FOUR

The Doctrine of the Trinity and Its Implications for Christian Thought and Practice

Glossary for Section Four

Abba—the Aramaic word for Father.

Alter ego—literally a second I or self.

Athanasius—church leader and thinker from Egypt who played the major role in the triumph of Trinitarian teaching at and after the Council of Nicaea in A.D. 325. He was the major opponent of Arius, the champion of the idea that Christ was not eternally preexistent with the Father.

Atonement—a technical theological term mainly employed to explain the reasons behind or the meaning of the death of Christ as a saving event in the plan of salvation.

Celestial—a word used to refer to heaven.

Council of Constantinople—an important church council that met in A.D. 381. The participants reaffirmed the doctrine of the Trinity and clarified the doctrine of the Holy Spirit.

"Extraterrestrial"—a being who comes to the earth from outer space.

Governmental Model—a name given to a theory or model of the atonement that emphasizes that Christ died to demonstrate heavenly justice. It holds that Christ died so that God could maintain moral order in the universe while at the same time freely forgiving sinners.

"Great Controversy" Theme—a concept that reflects the biblical theme that there has been a cosmic struggle going on in the universe between the forces of Christ and Satan since Satan (then known as Lucifer) rebelled in heaven and sought to take Christ's place in the governance of creation.

Justifying grace—the work of God's grace that forgives the sinner and reckons him or her as completely perfect for Christ's sake.

Legalistic—the basic idea that a person can be reconciled to God by perfect obedience to the law of God. The legalist understands such law obedience as creating merit that obliges God to reward the person with salvation. It is opposed to the classic Protestant belief in salvation by grace through faith alone, not by works of the law.

Maranatha—an Aramaic expression used by Paul in 1 Corinthians 16:22 and translated "O Lord, come."

Moral Influence Model—a name given to the theory or model of the atonement that claims that we should primarily understand the death of Christ as a demonstration of God's love, not as a substitute to satisfy divine justice.

Nicene—a term used to refer to the famous Council of Nicaea in A.D. 325 at which the basic idea of the Trinity doctrine triumphed over the ideas of Arius and his followers. The term also applies to the thought of the major proponents of the Trinity before and after the council.

Objective Models—an expression employed by theologians to refer to theories or models of the atonement that emphasize what God needed to do for sinners to make provision for their forgiveness.

Satisfaction Model—a name given to the model of the atonement that claims that the death of Christ was needed to satisfy God's nature of justice. In satisfying justice, He or His death had made provision for the forgiveness of sinners.

Scenario—the basic outline or plot of a play or opera.

Subjective Models—an expression employed by theologians to refer to theories or models of the atonement that emphasize the appropriate response of the sinner to the death of Christ or the desired effect that it would have on them.

Substance—a technical word used by Christian thinkers since the fourth century A.D. to refer to the essential nature of a thing or being. It was used to express the concept that Christ possessed the same substance or divine nature as that of the Father.

Substitutionary—a term employed in theological discussions about the meaning of Christ's death. The basic concept conveyed by this expression is that Christ suffered the penalty of God's justice as a substitute for sinners. His death satisfies the demands of divine justice so that sinners can be declared forgiven.

Vindicating Judgment—the idea that God has an investigative phase of final judgment, not to inform Himself about the worthiness or guilt of those judged, but to demonstrate that He has acted in a totally fair manner in deciding the destiny of each person who stands before His judgment bar.

Chapter 15

WHY THE TRINITY IS IMPORTANT:

—PART I—

The Love of God and the Deity of Christ

INTRODUCTION

Having surveyed the biblical evidence for the Trinity (the "what" of the doctrine) and the historical development of the doctrine (the "how" of the teaching), we now turn our attention to the question of "why" the doctrine is crucial for Christians to accept. In other words, if the doctrine is true, "so what?"

Key Components of Trinitarian Teaching

Before we proceed any further, let's review the fundamental elements of the doctrine.

The Trinity doctrine teaches that the Godhead consists of three divine Persons—the Father, Son, and Holy Spirit. They are not three Gods, but three divine Persons who are one in nature (same essence or substance), character, and purpose. Each has eternally pre-existed—that is, there has never been a time in eternity past when They did not coexist, and there will never be a time when They will cease to exist.

While the three divine Persons are one, They have taken different roles or positions in the Godhead's work of creation, redemption, and the loving administration of the universe. The Father has assumed overall leadership, the Son has subordinated Himself to the leadership of the Father, and the Spirit is voluntarily subordinate to both the Father and the Son.

The Son is the fully divine second person of the Godhead who, while retaining His full deity, laid aside the trappings or prerogatives of His divine power and became fully human in the Incarnation. The Spirit acts as the personal, divine representative of the Trinity on earth. The Holy Spirit is just as much divine as the Father and the Son and is fully personal.

These are the main convictions that Christians have confessed as the biblical truth about the Holy Trinity.

The "Why" or the "So What" of the Trinity

What follows in this chapter and the next two are (1) the most important theological reasons as to why a believer would find the Trinity an essential doctrine and (2) some practical implications that flow forth from these theological reasons. In other words, the "why" or "so what" of the Trinity includes important—even essential—theological implications that arise out of serious reflection on the love of the Father, the full deity of the Son and the Spirit, the personhood of the Spirit, and the essential oneness of nature shared by all Three.

A Perspective on Doctrine

Doctrine, however right it may be intellectually, is not very helpful unless it can plainly demonstrate some very practical theological implications.

We can best set forth the issue with the following questions: Is it really important to be doctrinally right on the issues stirred up by the Trinity? Could someone lose their soul if they denied the doctrine? Is this doctrine essential to a clear understanding of the very nature of God, the meaning of the death of Christ on the cross, and the victory of both God and His people over sin, temptation, and death?

Before we begin sustained reflection on the issues at hand, we offer the following perspective.

While doctrine is important for Christian experience, being doctrinally correct is not an *absolute* requirement for salvation. We must admit that all of us have been off the mark doctrinally. Each of us has held some pretty immature theological convictions in the past. The stark truth is that we have some growth and clarity yet to gain in our understanding of God. Thus, if salvation were based on absolutely perfect doctrine, we would all be doomed.

Yet having admitted the above, we must also acknowledge that false doctrine and bad theology can greatly contribute to diminished spiritual experience, mainly because of depressing or distorted views of God.

I am sure that many of us have had the experience of receiving bad referrals on a prospective employee, business partner, or significant other. They tend to create doubts that lead to distrust. And distrust is a major roadblock to any productive friendship or business relationship. When, however, such allegations prove to be false and we get the real truth about the person in question, it allows great progress in developing satisfying and productive fellowship or partnerships.

We can compare sound doctrine to a good background check on God. You question whether we need to run one on God? The answer is yes!

The challenge is quite simply that there has been so much bad information spread abroad by God's enemies that a person might be better served if he or she did some pretty thorough checking up on the truthfulness or falsity of any claims made about Him.

For Seventh-day Adventists such a background check would be consistent with our understanding of the great controversy theme. This compelling scenario portrays a universe wracked by a great struggle over the nature of God and His love. It pictures the God of the universe openly inviting us to ponder carefully the truth about His nature and ways of running things. His key means of communicating the truth about His nature and character are the Bible and His self-revelation in the person of Jesus.

So our question is: Are there issues involved in the doctrine of the Trinity that could help us get to the heart of what we really need to know about God? Furthermore, can such knowledge give special help to us to survive the final stages of the great controversy?

We would humbly submit that the Trinity is an absolutely foundational and essential doctrine that clarifies gross misconceptions about God, His nature, and character. And what the Trinity reveals will make it easier for us to be reconciled to Him and be more effective servants in our witness to and for Him.

The Primary Issue

As we completed the survey of the biblical evidence for and against the doctrine of the Trinity in chapter 7, we gave some careful attention to the issue of God as the embodiment of love. The doctrine of the Trinity claims that the Godhead consists of three coeternal divine persons who have lived in a mutually supportive and submissive love relationship for all eternity. This claim, if true, speaks volumes to us about the Godhead's essential nature.

Furthermore, not only is the fundamental nature of God involved in this revelation of triune love, but what He has had in mind for those whom He has created in His image is at stake.

If God is love (1 John 4:8) in the very essence of His nature and He has made us in His image and "according to" His "likeness" (Gen. 1:26, 27), then this ought to tell us that the very core of what it means to be human is found in living in social/spiritual relationships that are loving, trusting, and submissive to God and our fellow human beings.

Maybe we could put the issue like this: if the gist of God's nature is eternal, infinite, and relational love, and He has made us in His image, *then the very heart of what it means to live is to participate in loving relationships!* In other words, really and truly to exist is to live in outward-oriented love, not in inward-directed, self-focused gratification.

The first practical implication is that if the very nature of the God-created universe is one of outflowing love, then any attitudes or actions destructive to genuine, Godlike (lawful) love relationships become suspect. And those attitudes and actions that build satisfying, productive relationships are what we should pursue.[1]

This, however, raises a very serious issue: Can sinful humans truly know what constitutes a legitimate, other-oriented love relationship? The great adversary, Satan, has claimed that the only way to find love and true happiness is to make self and self-gratification the major goal of life.

Who is right? We would suggest that God, in His Trinitarian self-revelation, has claimed that He created us to reflect the love that supernaturally resides in His very being as an eternally loving God who is one in three. Furthermore, the triune love found in God is not self-oriented, and thus strongly implies that we will find our greatest joy and satisfaction in living for and serving others.

Now, we believe that all Christians would acknowledge that God's way of love is the best. In fact, it is the only way to go. The next consideration, however, is the fact that we humans simply do not naturally want to live like that. Our very nature, in conflict with the heart of God's nature of self-sacrificing relationships, constantly pushes us to live like the devil—all out for self! What does the Trinity say to this terrible predicament that we find ourselves caught in?

Who Alone Can Redeem?

The biblical story tells us that in God's original creation He invested humanity with the natural ability to love and live like the Trinity. But humans have rebelled and now live more demonically than lovingly. How then has God reacted to the tragic turn of events?

The great news from our Maker is that not only has He created us in an amazing act of overflowing love (He wanted to widen the circle of Trinitarian love), but He has now determined to redeem us in an awesome outpouring of self-sacrificing love. It is at the very essence of this sacrificial love where the truth of the Trinity receives its greatest acid test and most startling, moving revelation.

God has to confront the issue of angelic and human rebellion, a type of sin totally against the grain of His heart of eternal love. What is He to do?

The compelling story line of the Bible is that the triune God has chosen to love us in a way that creates the only possible path for reconciliation and redemption. It manifests a redemptive scenario that can restore other-directed relationships with Himself and in the process establish a relational orientation that will once again enable human beings to live in love with one another.

While God does not love our sin and sinfulness, His very nature of love has instinctively impelled Him to reach out in redemptive mercy, not to lash out in a hot flash of righteous justice. And He has done all of this in ways intended to restore our status as His infinitely valued sons and daughters. His goal is to savingly change us into His image through the healing of our sinful histories and natures that have so bedeviled our existence (and His).

Once more we ask, How is He to accomplish all of this? Is He to act with righteous force and purge the universe of its rebellion? Yes, He could have done that, but He has not chosen such a quick fix. The biblical narrative strongly suggests that His way has been the path of patient, long-suffering appeals and demonstrations of His eternal love. The heart of His plan has been sacrificially to give His own divine Son to come and be one with us as a man to show us what godly love is really all about. The climax of the Son's mission was to live and die in such a way that we could be forgiven, reconciled, and ultimately healed of the disease of sin.

Christ Alone Is Able to Redeem

But did the sacrificial gift have to be the person of His very own Son? Could the agent of reconciliation have been an angel or some other unfallen being from some other world who has always loved God and remained loyal?

Such questions incited the ancient debates of the fourth century A.D. over the divine nature of Christ. Athanasius, the major advocate for the full deity of Christ at Nicaea, took a firm stand against Arius by affirming that the only one who could effectively redeem and heal the world was none other than God Himself. No created or derived being (angelic or otherwise) was deemed able to pull off this great mission.

But why is it that only the unique Son of God would be capable of such a mission? Why is Jesus the only being who could fully reveal what God is like? What follows are answers flowing from the very core of the Trinitarian nature of the Godhead!

Only God Can Reveal God

Only one who is God in the fullest sense of the word can effectively show us what God is like (John 14:8-11; 1 Cor. 1:21-24). And since Jesus was fully one in nature and character with the Father, He could demonstrate the truth about God. Not only does it "take one to know one," but it takes one who really knows about deity by nature to give a truly credible revelation of what God is like. No created god, semigod, or god of some derived divine nature would be sufficiently equipped to do the job. Only a divine "insider" can really show humanity the truth about God.

Only God Can Make the Sacrifice

The deeper question, however, swirls around the issue of why it is that only a member of the Godhead (Jesus was chosen) could offer a fully effectual, saving sacrifice for sin. Here we need to move with the utmost care and clarity. We need to remind ourselves that we are on the borders of heavy truth shrouded in profound mystery.

First of all, we need to admit that in a literal sense, true deity is naturally immortal and cannot experience death. This simple, biblical truth (1 Tim. 6:14-16) explains one of the reasons for the necessity of the Incarnation (Heb. 2:9, 14-18). Only dependent, mortal human nature could be subject to death. And in the experience of the Incarnation, Jesus took on human nature and died.

But once more we pose the question Why was it that only one who is fully divine would be capable of offering the sacrifice of an atoning death? Why would this be true if Christ in His deity was incapable of death?

Jesus the Only Atonement Maker

It appears that the answer has a number of fascinating facets:

1. The very union of divinity with humanity in Christ's incarnate nature suggests that though divinity did not literally die, it as good as died in the following sense. Christ's deity, along with His humanity, self-sacrificially consented to death at every step of the way to the cross. And in so doing the very nature of Christ's human

death became invested with the infinite value of eternal love.

An illustration from the death of Abraham Lincoln might prove helpful. From a purely personal human point of view, his death was no more tragic than that of any other murder victim. But from the perspective of his value to the nation, his death was a much greater tragedy. The value invested in the life and character of Lincoln, by virtue of his office as president and his acts as the healer of the nation's wounds in the Civil War, invested his death with much greater significance than that of any other ordinary citizen. And Christ, the one who was by divine nature endowed with the offices of Creator and Redeemer, is the only being of sufficient value and virtue to offer an effectually saving sacrifice for sin.

Ellen White, following the same theme as Athanasius and the early Trinitarian writers, put it this way: "The divine Son of God was the only sacrifice of sufficient value to fully satisfy the claims of God's perfect law. The angels were sinless, but of less value than the law of God. . . . His [Christ's] life was of sufficient value to rescue man from his fallen condition" (*The Spirit of Prophecy,* vol. 2, p. 10).

"Christ is equal with God, infinite and omnipotent. He could pay the ransom for man's freedom. . . . He could say that which the highest angel could not say,—I have power over my own life, 'power to lay it down, and . . . power to take it again'" (*Youth's Instructor,* June 21, 1900).

2. Only a love that resided in a member of the Godhead was capable of effectually judging sin. We could phrase the issue of sin's judgment this way: The fully divine love of Christ possessed not only innate value, but also the power to conquer sin. And why is this so? A possible clue lies in the very nature of what sin is.

When we really boil it all down, we can safely say that sin involves the nature and actions of creaturely "un-love." You might ask, "What in the world are you speaking about when you use the term 'un-love'"?

The very nature of godly righteousness is the manifestation of love. The law of God is a concrete expression of His nature of love (Matt. 22:36-40; Rom. 13:8-10; 1 John 5:2, 3). It defines, in vivid commands, the very way that beings filled with divine love will think and act. And that which goes contrary to God's express law acts contrary to the love of God. Thus sin is thinking and acting in not only an unlawful but in an unloving manner.

To put the issue another way, sin could come into existence only because of the very nature of God's love. The fact that God's love requires free choice makes it possible for sin to exist. The very God-given freedom essential to the exercise of love allows for sinful disobedience. Yet when sin takes advantage of God's love-borne freedom and goes against His very nature, it can manifest itself only as the selfishly chosen attitudes and actions of un-love. Thus sin becomes a human creation that feeds off God's love and becomes an intensely perverse twisting of divine love. Sin simply cannot exist without God's nature of love, but is a perversely parasitic development.

Most certainly God is not in any sense sin's author. It is the mysterious, perverse brainchild of Satan, and nothing can ever fully explain it. But without God's granting the right to choose things contrary to His nature of love, there could be no such thing as sin. God could have played it safe and preprogrammed us not to sin. But then we would have been a bunch of robots doing God's will only by instinct. Yes, God took a highly chancy route when He created beings in the image of His own loving nature. But could He have done it any other way if He truly wanted a race of beings who could freely and responsively relate to Him in love?

Therefore, since we can understand sin only as that which is totally at loggerheads with God's love (freely choosing the unloving attitude and action), then it must be true that only one who is eternal, divine love in nature would be equipped to expose, define, and destroy sin and its author. Only the knowledgeable power of divine love residing in Christ—in whom "dwells all the fullness of the Godhead bodily" (Col. 2:9)—has the power to unveil and judge its parasitic alter ego. The upshot of these facts is that the death of Christ on the cross was—in principle—the judgment and defeat of sin.

This judging and destruction of sin through the divine power of Christ has two important consequences:

a. Christ's life and death revealed divine love in a way never before seen in the history of the universe. And it is such loving and merciful justice that reaches out in waves of spiritual and moral influence to give sinners repentance for sin. Such repentance is inspired not only by Christ revealing the enormity of sin, but also results from a deeper appreciation of God's offer of a mercy that we really don't deserve. So Jesus' revelation of love in His perfect life and atoning death changes our attitudes toward sin and God so that we are enabled to respond to His offer of mercy and new life. But the Son's judgment of sin by His life-and-death demonstration of love enables God to do one more important act:

b. The perfect obedience of Christ to the law and His bearing the penalty of the broken law for us allows God to forgive repentant sinners. He grants forgiveness to the repentant sinner for Christ's sake. That is, because of what God's love has secured in the life and death of Christ, God is able to secure our forgiveness by declaring that all that belongs to Christ is now accounted as ours. We are given new histories (Christ's life is now ours), new legal standing, and powerful motives of God's love to live like and for Him from henceforth. And all of this has been obtained on the basis of what the love of God has wrought out, not what some mere human creature has accomplished. The justifying merits of Christ are the manifestations of God's righteousness, not those of some creature!

This understanding of God's way of forgiveness and justifying grace is inextricably bound up with His divine love. Only the love that resides in the fully divine Christ could secure such a righteousness. What has proven to be quite interesting is that over the centuries anti-Trinitarian and Unitarian religious traditions have always fallen into legalistic views of salvation. In other words, only when the sinner has been good and obedient can such a person be deemed to be forgiven. But when Trinitarian clarity comes, Trinitarian movements have a strong tendency to give a renewed emphasis to forgiveness or justification by grace through faith alone.[2]

Judaism, Islam, the Jehovah's Witnesses, and early nontrinitarian Adventism all have tended to lack a clear doctrine of justifying grace based solely on the merits of God's divine righteousness. It was only when Seventh-day Adventism began to emerge out of its non-Trinitarian understandings of Christ's divinity that it began to find clarity on justification by grace through faith alone. In fact, it seems to be a law of sacred history that until believers gain greater insight to the full deity of Christ, salvation by grace through faith alone does not fare too well.

The benefits of Christ's full deity do not end, however, with the manifestation of justifying grace. His deity also guarantees a powerful experience of new life for the believer in transforming grace.

3. The necessity of a divine sacrifice also arises from the fact that only a being who naturally possesses immortality can offer everlasting life to those who take advantage of the saving power of His atoning death.

The new life from Christ includes conversion to a life of love in time and a never-ending life at the Second Coming. Thus His death not only cancels sin and destroys the power of death, but Christ's divine love enables us to be restored in our characters.

4. We call the great work of character restoration sanctifying or life-changing grace. Not only is the full deity of Christ absolutely essential to His offer of forgiving or justifying grace, but it also provides the power of transforming grace. Sin has so profoundly deranged God's creation that the only being who can put it right is none other than the original active agent of Creation—the divine Son of God!

Jesus the great Creator becomes the great physician of the human soul ravaged by the raging infection of sin! Flowing out of His righteous life and atoning death, His healing powers are so powerful that not one desperate soul need despair that he or she cannot be healed.

Possibly still another metaphor besides that of healing could also explain the issue of transforming love. That would be the metaphor of the comforting presence of a strong parent with a weak and fearful child. When a little boy, I was desperately afraid of the dark. When I would have to go on an errand at night, I imagined all sorts of evil ogres lurking in the shadows. But somehow, when my strong father was along, all seemed safe and secure. When the mighty God, the powerful Jesus, is by our side in the struggle with the demonic forces of darkness, we need not fear.

5. Furthermore, not only was the full deity of Christ necessary for Him to forgive sin and transform our characters, but His divine nature assures us that He is always there for us as our Redeemer. That is, the divine Christ is a constantly available and effective advocate, intercessor, or mediator between humanity and God. Yet the One who is divine is also Himself "the Man" (1 Tim. 2:5, 6, NKJV).

It is a concept beautifully expressed in the metaphor of the "surety." This reassuring term projects the idea of a person who unceasingly stands for another, particularly in cases of debt. The guarantor will make sure that the debt will be paid if the one who has incurred it should fail. Bible-believing writers have often used the wonderful description of Christ as the sinner's "substitute and surety" to picture Him as our mediating advocate before the Father. Yes, there is One who stands for us, whose plenitude of infinite love is in our favor! What a fully sufficient Savior we have in Christ!

Once more, Ellen White has expressed this theme in a way that closely resembles the classic fourth-century A.D. Trinitarian confessions:

"The reconciliation of man to God could be accomplished only through a mediator who was equal with God, possessed of attributes that would dignify, and declare Him worthy to treat with the Infinite God in man's behalf, and also represent God to a fallen world. Man's substitute and surety must have man's nature, a connection with the human family whom He was to represent, and, as God's ambassador, He must partake of the divine nature, have a connection with the Infinite, in order to manifest God to the world, and be a mediator between God and man" (*Review and Herald,* Dec. 22, 1891).

But Christ is no longer physically present with us to do this work. How then can He effect such changes and bring such comfort from so far away? We find the answer in the work and person of the mighty agency of the third person of the Godhead, the powerful Holy Spirit. It is to this issue that we turn our attention in the next chapter.

ENDNOTES

[1] We will discuss more of the practical, ethical implications of God's love in the final chapter of this section.

[2] A possible exception to this tendency is Roman Catholicism. I would suggest that the reason for this exception is twofold: (1) the Trinity doctrine is almost a philosophical dead letter in the Roman tradition (on the books, but not really utilized theologically); (2) the intercessory work of Jesus has been just about totally obliterated by the practical emphasis on the intercession of Mary and the saints. In other words, human intercessors have virtually displaced the divine/human person of Jesus.

Chapter 16

WHY THE TRINITY IS IMPORTANT:
—PART II—
The Holy Spirit and the Triune Oneness of the Godhead

INTRODUCTION

Certainly the Holy Spirit has received less notice in theology and practical Christianity than has the Father or the Son. Yet that is most likely just the way the Holy Spirit would have it. His business has never been to call attention to His own being or person. Rather, His greatest delight comes when He lovingly places the focus of His ministry on highlighting the Father through His representation of the Son. It is in this ministry that we can truly speak of the Spirit as the heavenly "Comforter" (KJV) or "Helper" (NKJV).

Could the Holy Spirit, however, truly and effectively carry out His ministry if He were only some sort of created celestial Internet, not the mighty third person of the eternal Godhead?

And finally, what theological implications could the triune oneness or profound unity of the Godhead have for our understanding of salvation and the security of God's governance of the universe? We turn first to the person and work of the Holy Spirit.

The Holy Spirit as the Divine and Personal Agent of Salvation

Closely related to the issues of Christ's divine person and nature are those involving the Holy Spirit's deity, person, and work. The classic Trinitarian convictions have consistently held that only a being who is fully God could rightly represent the Father and the Son to the human race. Furthermore, only the fully divine Spirit could effectively make the work of Christ a saving fact in the human heart.

The Full Deity of the Spirit

The Bible text witnessing most persuasively to the practical necessity of the full deity of the Holy Spirit is 1 Corinthians 2:7-12: "We speak the wisdom of God in a mystery . . . which none of the rulers of this age knew. . . . But God has revealed them to us through His Spirit. For the Spirit searches all things, yes, the deep things of God. For what man knows the things of a man except the spirit of the man which is in him? Even so no one knows the things of God except the Spirit of God. Now we have received, not the spirit of the world, but the Spirit who is from God, that we might know the things that have been freely given to us by God" (NKJV).

This passage plainly claims that we can know God only through the Spirit of God, who is now His authoritative representative on earth, the revelation of His love and saving power. Thus it only makes sense that if the Holy Spirit is to rightly represent both the divine Father and the Son, then He must also be fully divine Himself. Once more, it not only "takes One to know One," but it demands a being of the same essential kind or nature to reveal that kind to some other kind. In other words, only a being who is fully divine, who wholly shares the eternal nature of divine love, can adequately communicate such love to a world woefully destitute of divine knowledge and doomed to death.

Carefully ponder a number of other "only" implications of the full deity of the Holy Spirit:

1. Only the Holy Spirit of God could bring the converting and convicting power of the great love of God to fallen humanity. Only One who has been eternally bound up with the heart of self-sacrificing love in the Father and the Son can fully communicate such love to lost human beings.

2. Only the Holy Spirit, who fully shares the adopting heart of God, inflamed with love for His lost children, can impart to His estranged human children "the Spirit of adoption by whom we cry

out, 'Abba, Father.' The Spirit Himself bears witness with our spirit that we are children of God" (Rom. 8:15, 16, NKJV).

3. Only One who has worked with the Son in creation would be equipped to re-create souls ravaged by the destructive forces of Satan and sin (Rom. 8:10, 11). The re-creative function of the Spirit is closely connected with the work of bearing spiritual fruit. Thus, only the divine Spirit, who works with Christ the vine (John 15:1-11), is competent to produce in God's people the "firstfruits of the Spirit" (Rom. 8:23).

Furthermore, the issue of the "fruit of the Spirit" takes on clearer meaning when it becomes apparent that all of these discrete fruits (joy, peace, long-suffering, kindness, etc.) are but manifestations of the one all-encompassing "fruit" of love (see Gal. 5:22-24).

4. Only the Holy Spirit who sustained Christ through the horror of Gethsemane and Calvary can fully comfort us through our own dark valleys and frightful nights of the soul.

5. Only the Spirit, who fully knows the heart of our great high priestly Intercessor, can adequately represent the comforts and impart the blessings of Christ's constant intercession on our behalf before the Father of love.

6. Only the Spirit who inspired the prayers of Jesus can effectually help in our weaknesses. "For we do not know what we should pray for as we ought, but the Spirit Himself makes intercession for us with groanings which cannot be uttered. Now He who searches the hearts knows what the mind of the Spirit is, because He makes intercession for the saints according to the will of God" (Rom. 8:26, 27, NKJV).

7. Only One who can be fully in tune with the heart of Jesus' incarnate ministry, and yet at the same time be able to be everywhere at once (the omnipresence of God), could transmit the redeeming presence of Christ to the entire world. The only being who could do such a thing is the ever- and all-present Holy Spirit.

The Personhood of the Spirit

In chapter 4 we outlined the biblical evidence for the fully divine personality of the Holy Spirit. Why is this issue so critical? Do we really sense the power in the statement that the Spirit of Christ is the manifestation of the personal presence of Christ to us?

Is not a lover's personal presence the heart of the power of love? Can there really be an effectually redeeming love that does not ultimately manifest itself in personal presence? Does the thought of the Holy Spirit as being some sort of celestial Internet bring any thrill of personal anticipation to your soul? Thank God that the Holy Spirit is the divine person communicating, rather than some sort of impersonal electronic network!

I most vividly recall the joy of communicating, via electronic means, with my fiancée when we were temporarily separated by seemingly interminable miles and days. But blessed as such electronic channels were, they proved ultimately not to be a very satisfying substitute for actually being with her! If the only hopes of love that I could have aspired to in those days were an e-mail or phone relationship, I would have been "of all men most miserable" (1 Cor. 15:19, KJV)! Thank God, the Holy Spirit is an effective, personal presence of the Bridegroom to the bride.

How many have experienced the technically competent but impersonal services of medical personnel who lack what we call a good bedside manner. Yet when Christ comes to comfort us in all of our sin-related stresses and illnesses, His bedside manner is powerfully and personally ministered to us through the person of His Holy Spirit representative on earth.

Furthermore, when God calls upon us to serve, witness for, and do mighty acts for God, it is the power and guidance of the personal Spirit that strengthens us and provides courage, vision, and wisdom. Thus only the Holy Spirit, the heavenly Comforter, can truly heal the sick human soul and direct our witness and service in the world.

THE ONENESS OF THE GODHEAD AND ITS THEOLOGICAL SIGNIFICANCE

God's Oneness and the Unity of the Universe

The world is full of terrible divisions and deep fractures. Wrenching alienation between individuals, people groups, religions, and nations has ripped the social fabric.

Furthermore, based on the concepts that undergird the great controversy theme, a sense of intuitive distrust pervades the larger universe when it comes to the issue of how God meets the crisis called sin. Does the oneness of the Godhead have anything to say to these troubling dilemmas?

Triune Unity Promises a Unified Universe

If the divisions that disturb the tranquillity of our world and the cosmic concerns of the intelligent universe have any chance of being healed, it will have to come from the reconciling efforts of the Godhead. We say this because the doctrine of the Trinity holds that the profound unity of nature, character, and purpose of the Godhead provides the only sure basis for hope that anything can ever heal the alienation of the created order.

Wayne Grudem expresses the issue this way: "If there is not perfect plurality and perfect unity in God himself, then we have no basis for thinking there can be any ultimate unity among the diverse elements of the universe either" (Grudem, pp. 247, 248).

The alienation that has ripped apart God's universe has its source in the horrific phenomenon of sin. The core of the issue is this: Does the Godhead have within Their nature of infinite love the resources to reconcile the disruptions that sin has caused?

Christ's Death Brings Reconciliation

We would suggest that the heart of the Christian response to the above question revolves around the atoning death of Christ. Can the death of Christ truly bring full reconciliation? We are convicted that it can, and the crux of the issue has to do with God's judgment of sin that He manifested through our divine Lord's substitutionary sacrifice.

Many Christians, however, have expressed deep misgivings about the whole concept of Christ offering a sacrifice of substitution to satisfy God's nature of justice. They argue that such a view is not only morally questionable, but that it makes God resemble some angry ogre intent on taking out His wrath on an unwilling third party. What is the truth of this issue?

If we are to have a fair assessment of the concept of Christ's death, understood in terms of an act of sacrificial substitution that satisfies God's justice, it will be necessary to provide some background on the various explanatory models Christianity has used to explain the meaning of the cross. Thus we invite the reader's careful attention to the following lines of thought.

The Models of the Atonement

Thinkers who have deeply reflected on the meaning of Christ's death have come up with a number of classic theories or models with which to illustrate the meaning of, or to make sense of, Christ's death. In other words, such models seek to answer the question of why Christ had to die.

While all of these models have proven helpful to our understanding of the atonement, not any one of them (or even all of them put together) can exhaust the mysterious depths of God's redeeming act of sacrificial love. Yet they do help us to gather our thoughts in a more focused way as we think about the meaning of Christ's death.

The most influential models fall into two basic categories: "subjective" and "objective."

Subjective Models: What the term "subjective" attempts to communicate is that the death of Christ mainly seeks to demonstrate differing aspects of God's redeeming love so that they will produce a change in the minds and hearts of rebellious sinners.

The most well known of the subjective models is the "moral influence" theory. It contends that Christ died to show the lengths to which God would go in manifesting love for the sinner. God loved us so much that He would give His Son to die so that He could express His love in solidarity with sinners in their terrible plight. We know of no one who would disagree with this point.

What, however, makes the theory controversial is what it denies, not what it affirms. It sees no need for the death of Christ to satisfy God's nature of justice as a prerequisite to His offer of forgiveness. The moral influence advocates claim that God's love freely or gratuitously forgives sin, and there was no prior need for divine justice to be satisfied in the execution of a just penalty for sin.

The theory's proponents state that the necessity for Christ's death appears in God's desire to demonstrate love, not the loving satisfaction of justice through paying the penalty for sin. Thus they deem Christ's death to be only a demonstration of love, not the loving execution of divine justice.

Another well-known subjective model is the governmental theory. It also affirms that Christ's death displays God's love and that it was not necessary for Christ to die as a substitute to satisfy God's personal wrath, or justice. Let's be very clear about this model—it does not deny the need for Christ to die, but simply claims that God did not require the cross to satisfy the just wrath residing within His own nature of love.

This model goes on to claim that God illustrates His love through a manifestation of His public justice. What the death of Christ establishes is that God is willing to suffer as much as He has to in order to maintain governmental order in the universe.

Furthermore, the theory argues that Christ's death clearly shows that if sinners persist in sin, they will have to pay the consequences of an executionary death. Thus, out of love, God warns sinners of the results of clinging to sin and reminds us that He will maintain justice in His universe in which He presides as moral governor.

What both of the subjective models hold in common is that the death of Christ was (1) a saving necessity and (2) a clear demonstration of God's love, but then they proceed to an important qualification: (3) the Father did not need Jesus' death to satisfy God's personal nature of justice or revulsion against sin. Thus the death of Christ demonstrates the greatness of divine love and warns against sin's deadliness. The advocates of each subjective model, however, have expressed deep reservations about any real need for the death of a substitute whose sacrifice would satisfy God's nature of loving justice.

Objective Models: These concepts of the atonement present explanations of the death of Christ that hold that God in His love needed to take certain actions in order to ensure that the provisions for human salvation were fully consistent with the justness and mercy of divine love. Thus these models demand more than a demonstration of love. They strongly claim that love must act in a way that fully satisfies justice before God can offer mercy to sinners.

Therefore, the expression "objective" refers to what God's nature of love did for us, not to a change in how we would respond to God within ourselves. Objectively, God had to demonstrate His love in the death of Christ through first judging sin. It is then, on the basis of His just judgment of sin, that God can offer us the fruit of His love. Thus He provided a merciful forgiveness for our sins consistent with His nature of justice. In other words, the death of Christ objectively changed the human status before God, not just our mental state or attitude toward Him.

The most well known of the objective models is the so-called satisfaction theory. It basically states that God's love offered Christ as the sinners' substitute in order to pay their just penalty for sin (eternal death). In the course of this substitutionary sacrifice, Christ's death satisfied divine justice.

The satisfaction model does not deny any of the positive claims of the subjective models, but only disagrees with what they deny. It clearly teaches that God's love cannot manifest itself in mercy unless it first fully meets the justice of His love by the substitutionary payment of the penalty for sin.

The satisfaction model has had numerous well-known proponents. Martin Luther, John Calvin, John Wesley, and Ellen G. White are among the most familiar to Protestant and Seventh-day Adventist Christians.

An Appraisal of the Models

Now the reader might ask, What do all of these atonement models have to do with the divine unity of the Godhead? And what might our understanding of the death of Christ have to do with His full deity and His equality with the Father and the Holy Spirit?

As already pointed out, all of the advocates of the various models affirm the positive truth of the subjective models. All agree that divine love needs an extraordinary demonstration by none other than God Himself. And as we have urged in the previous chapter, only a fully divine Christ could effectively reveal the complete nature of God's love to an alienated world.

The crucial question, however, is Did Christ need to die to meet the requirements of God's loving justice? Was the satisfaction of divine justice a necessary demand of God's love before He could offer His merciful forgiveness to sinners?

We would urge that God's loving justice did need to be satisfied by Christ's death as a penalty for sin.

The whole basis for this contention arises out of what we mean by God's love. We contend that the Bible's and Ellen White's understanding of divine love includes a perfect balance of two complementary components—justice and mercy! God's love manifests itself in the justice of His law and His wrath against sin, not just in a gratuitous (free) offer of forgiving mercy. All agree that God demonstrated His love through His willingness to forgive sinners. But the question that seems most urgently to demand an answer is What do we mean when we speak of God's wrath? Can there be any such thing as a "just wrath" in God's nature of love?

Many find themselves confused by the word "wrath." It provokes visions of God having a bad temper or fit of revenge against sinners. But such a view terribly misses the point of God's justice. We would propose that God's wrath refers to that aspect of His love that can do no other than have an allergic reaction to sin. That is, when God's love confronts whatever is contrary to His just nature, His nature cannot ultimately abide anything that opposes His core nature of just love!

Yet God's revulsion is against sin, not sinners. Thus when God's just love confronts sin, it is then that its merciful side comes into play. God's loving mercy simply will not allow Him to give up on those held in sin's grip without a vigorous offer of redemption. And He provides it through Christ's merciful sacrifice for our sins.

Thus His death has provided mercy in a manner fully consistent with divine justice. Christ our substitute satisfied God's just wrath, enabling Him to be both "just and the justifier of the one who has faith in Jesus" (Rom. 3:26, NKJV). Therefore in the death of Christ we have not only a demonstration of God's justice, but a fully just satisfaction of it so that there can be a fully just offering of divine mercy.

Who Is the Substitute?

Now the key question that confronts the satisfaction model is Who would be an acceptable candidate for the office of atoning substitute? Here we find the oneness of the Trinity's divine nature coming into play.

We have already established that whoever this substitute would be, it could not be a human being or some other creature. Only one who is fully God could both demonstrate divine love and judge sin capably in all of its horror. If we claim that it could be some created being (the Arian version of the Son of God) or some being who possessed only some sort of derived deity (the semi-Arian view of the Son of God), then we have the odd situation of God being dependent on some creature to demonstrate His love and satisfy His justice. Such a picture conjures up visions of a creature begging God for mercy or God demanding justice from some creaturely victim. And finally, God would be taking out His wrath on an innocent third party, raising the question of the entire justice of such an act.

If, however, the sacrificial victim is both fully God and truly human, such as we find in Jesus Christ, then we have a new set of possibilities. Think of it this way:

The death of the God/man, Jesus, is not merely the death of a human or an extraterrestrial creature, but it is also the death of God! As we pointed out earlier, Christ's death did require His deity; not that His deity literally died, but that it was there in full unity with His human nature. His deity fully consented to His death as a sacrifice for sin. The deity of Christ died a proverbial "thousand deaths" in the death of His humanity!

The offering of Isaac by Abraham provides a touching illustration of the truth we are seeking to clarify (see Gen. 22). God brought to bear on Abraham the greatest test imaginable. "Take now your son, your only son Isaac, whom you love, and go to the land of Moriah, and offer him there as a burnt offering" (Gen. 22:2).

No one but God will ever be able fully to know the pain that wrenched the great patriarch's heart! While Abraham was completely obedient to God in his astounding test, the grace of God spared him the actual execution of his "only son." But for all practical purposes Abraham did sacrifice his son and died a thousand deaths himself in the process.

And thus it was with the deity of Christ: His deity, so bound up with and blended with His humanity, fully shared in the mental anguish of Christ's death so that we can truthfully say that God died for us.

The Godhead Suffers the Penalty

And yet, when we say that God died, does this refer only to the deity of the Son? Most certainly not! Because of their profound unity of triune oneness in nature, we can acknowledge that the Father and the Holy Spirit were also profoundly present and in solidarity with Christ's atoning death. It is this deep and penetrating truth that the apostle Paul expresses: "Now all things are of God, who has reconciled us to Himself through Jesus Christ . . . that is, that God was in Christ reconciling the world to Himself" (2 Cor. 5:18, 19, NKJV).

So who is the substitute? Was it simply the man Christ Jesus? Absolutely not! Did it include the man Christ Jesus? Most certainly! Was that all that was included in the substitutionary death? Certainly not! Christ's humanity was so bound up with His full deity that when He died we can truly say that the entire Godhead "was in Christ" and suffered His atoning death.

The deity of Christ is the full deity of the entire triune Godhead. And this amazingly unified self-sacrifice judged sin in such a way that it made complete provision for the salvation of the whole human race.

Therefore we can truthfully say that God, in satisfying His nature of loving justice, did not take His wrath out on an innocent third party or some unwilling victim. Rather, in Christ He has met the needs of justice through His own willingly given divine self-sacrifice. Is there any injustice revealed in such a substitutionary satisfication of God's justice? And is not such a sacrifice the very essence of triune love for all eternity? It is a love that is mutually self-submissive, self-sacrificing, and overflowing with creative and redemptive consequences to the created beings of the universe.

Furthermore, what has been substituted is not moral character, but the fulfillment of legal requirements reflecting God's own nature of love. And once more we hold that God's love involves an outflowing demand for both justice and mercy. And if one is denied, the other becomes meaningless, dissolving God's love into some sort of mushy mercy or untempered wrath.

Both Ellen White and John Stott have powerfully expressed this truth: "Through Jesus, God's mercy was manifested to men; but mercy does not set aside justice. The law reveals the attributes of God's character, and not a jot or tittle of it could be changed to meet man in his fallen condition. God did not change His law, *but He sacrificed Himself, in Christ, for man's redemption*" (White, *The Desire of Ages,* p. 762; italics supplied).

"In order to save us in such a way as to satisfy himself, God through Christ substituted himself for us. Divine love triumphed over divine wrath by divine self-sacrifice" (Stott, p. 159).

The great truth of the Holy Trinity and the atoning death of Christ speaks eloquently that God has, in His Son, borne the penalty of sin as our substitute and made an infinitely valuable and powerful provision for the full reconciliation of the entire human race. And if God can make such effective provision for the sin-alienated human race, it assures us that He can also heal the larger divisions of the universe.

The Judgment and the Vindication of God

One of the most pressing philosophical problems that all religions wrestle with is that of evil. Many individuals have also struggled with this challenging issue. The basic question involves how a good God, who claims to be the loving Creator, can allow so much evil, suffering, and injustice to spoil the happiness and joy of earth's inhabitants.

Once more we would suggest that the doctrine of the Trinity makes a vital contribution to this discussion.

The heart of the Christian answer to the issue of evil and the injustice of so much suffering is that the ultimate source of the evil and suffering afflicting the world is sin. Yet according to the Christian understanding of sin and evil, the present experience of suffering is not the whole story. Christians do believe that there will come a day when evil will be eradicated and wrongs righted. But who will get the job done?

Here is where the Trinity reveals profound truth. The solution to the problem of evil has and will continue to come from none other than God Himself in the person and work of His Son. He has thrust Himself into the battle against suffering and evil. And how has He involved Himself? Through sending His very own divine Son as a solution to the horrid blot that evil has spread across creation. No mere creature could fully supply the answer—only God in Christ could.

Put another way, God has not dispatched the angel Gabriel, neither a mere human being, nor some unfallen extraterrestrial from another world. But He has sent His Son to be the point person in the battle with evil. Thus God has not passed the problem along to any finite being (natural or supernatural) to solve, but in His divine Son He has taken full responsibility.

The Trinity and the Great Controversy Theme

We would strongly submit that the work of the divine Jesus, in the setting of the great controversy, provides the only satisfying explanation of the existence of evil and its ultimate eradication from the universe.

Sin erupted into God's heaven through the mysterious and inexplicable rebellion of Lucifer. God bore long with Lucifer, but finally had to banish him from the heavenly courts.

Now many have questioned why God did not immediately destroy Lucifer and the angels who joined him in his uprising. The great controversy answer is that God settled in for the long-haul solution rather than a quick fix. He knew that the unfallen beings of heaven and the rest of the universe did not then fully understand all the issues involved with Satan's disaffection. If He had immediately destroyed Satan, then these beings would serve Him more out of fear rather than out of rationally informed love.

But the sin emergency did not catch the Holy Trinity off guard. They had conceived a plan in which God would send His very own Son to our world to meet Satan in hand-to-hand combat. Through His life, teachings, and especially His death, Christ has defeated Satan, atoned for sin, and exposed him for the liar and murderer that he really is.

While Satan emerged fully defeated in his temptations of Christ and alienated from the affections of the unfallen beings, other issues still remained to be clarified. They involved the disposition of sin and the salvation of the penitent sinners, questions that could be answered only in a process of judgment.

And who is the key figure in this vindicating judgment? None other than the Lord Jesus Himself. The Son of God Himself, as both Savior and Judge, will demonstrate in each phase of judgment that He has behaved in ways completely consistent with His love in His dealings with each and every individual case. The cases of both the redeemed and those finally lost will all testify that God, in Christ, has acted in a manner that will fully justify His final eradication of evil and His salvation of the redeemed.

Most likely the major reason there were still issues to be settled after the atoning death of Christ* comes from the fact that Satan had originally accused God of being unjust in requiring obedience to His law of love. Satan argued that God's justice must be swallowed up by mercy. When Satan was able to seduce human beings to sin he then argued that God must not extend mercy to them. Since Satan did not receive mercy and God banished him from heaven, he claimed that God should not show any mercy to Adam and Eve. Thus he turned around his original argument and went on to claim that justice must swallow up mercy.

The devil has continued to use both lines of argument whenever it suits his purposes. But when we come to the great crisis of the cross, God confronted Satan with a powerful argument: Christ's death perfectly manifested both justice and mercy. In the death of Christ, as our substitute, God has provided a perfect exhibition of mercy filled with unflinching justice. Yet this justice, conditioned by mercy, has allowed God to forgive sins for Christ's sake. At the same time, Christ's death demonstrated a perfect justice profoundly permeated with mercy. God has thus met both of Satan's objections to His love, and Christ has triumphed. Therefore, why did the controversy continue?

The answer seems to revolve around the question of how God's treatment of sin and sinners would play out after the cross. This is especially crucial when Satan, after Calvary, now goes back full force to his original argument—mercy must completely swallow up justice and the death of Christ does away with the law altogether.

Yes, it would seem superficially that Christ's death was such a telling and profound manifestation of merciful love that quite possibly God would now lean toward the mercy side of things in applying the effects of the atonement to each human case. But would God's mercy cause Him to go soft on sin and evil?

What the judgment will demonstrate (in all of its phases—pre-Advent, millennial, and at the end of the millennium) is that God has not gotten out of balance. The investigation of all cases, both those of the redeemed and the lost, will fully substantiate that Christ's divine love will be consistently and fairly applied.

Thus when the whole conflict ends, God will be able to banish evil and all of its proponents from the universe. Perfect love will finally vanquish evil, vindicate the faithful, and fully support God as the rightful moral governor of the universe. Then and only then will full and harmonious unity return.

The final question is Who is it that will have achieved the great victory over evil? It will be clearly seen that God, in Christ, pulled it off through the power of infinite, divine love. And this love is the very heart of the triune God's nature. At last the intelligent beings of the entire universe will be unified under the governance of the Holy Trinity. One pulse of harmony will beat throughout the vast creation, and all will declare that the Godhead is love!

---

*What follows is a condensation of Ellen White's explanation of the essential issues at stake in the great controversy found in the book *The Desire of Ages,* pp. 761-763.

Chapter 17

PRACTICAL IMPLICATIONS AND CONCLUSIONS

As we bring this biblical, historical, and theological study to a conclusion, some practical and ethical considerations are in order. Certainly, if a doctrine is as important theologically as we sense the Trinity is, it must have some vital implications for our daily Christian life.

We have already suggested a number of practical, salvational insights that reside in the very nature of God's trinitarian nature and self-revelation. But what about such matters as prayer, praise, and worship?

To Whom Should the Church Pray?

The oneness in nature and character of the three persons of the Godhead raises the very useful question of prayer, praise, and worship. To whom should we direct our petitions and adoration in personal devotions and corporate worship?

Most certainly the ordinary method of prayer is to follow the example of our Lord in His great prayer and His practice of reverent address to the Father (see Matt. 6:9-13 and Luke 11:2-4). It is our great privilege to address our adoration, petitions, and praise to the Father in the name of the Son, always conscious that the Holy Spirit transmits our earthly communiques with "groanings which cannot be uttered" (Rom. 8:26, NKJV).

We do, however, have instances in Scripture in which God's servants have directed prayerful appeals to the Son of God. Stephen, in his final breaths, prayed directly to Jesus—"Lord Jesus, receive my spirit" (Acts 7:59, NKJV). Paul also addressed the "Lord Jesus Christ," declaring, "O Lord, come" (using the Aramaic "Maranatha," 1 Cor. 16:22, NKJV). John the revelator ended his book with a prayer: "Come, Lord Jesus!" (Rev. 22:20, NJKV).

But what about direct prayer to the Holy Spirit? While we have no clear example of or direct command to pray to the Spirit in Scripture, doing so does have, in principle, some implicit biblical support. If the Spirit is indeed divine and personal and He interacts in all sorts of direct personal ways (bringing conviction, healing, transforming grace, granting gifts, etc.), it only seems logical that God's people can pray directly to and worship the Holy Spirit.

We would express the issue this way: The normal pattern of prayer is to the Father, in the name of the Son, with the knowledge that the "groanings" of the Holy Spirit expedite our prayers. In personal and corporate instances of prayer, however, it seems best to pray to the most relevant person of the Godhead. For instance, it would seem to be most appropriate to pray directly to the Holy Spirit for spiritual gifts and witnessing power for the church. Prayers to Jesus would include those of confession, penitence, and forgiveness, and pleas for His soon return.

In sum—if the persons of the Godhead are truly one in nature, character, and purpose, then it seems only logical and practical to address appropriate petitions and praises to any one of the heavenly Trio at any given time and situation.

Ethical Implications

While space limitations do not permit an extended discussion of the ethical implications of Trinitarian teaching, we will suggest some of the most important principles for Christian attitudes, actions, and relationships.

Earlier we argued that if the gist of God's triune nature is eternal, infinite, and relational (social) love, and that we are made in His image, then the very heart of what it means to live is to do so through loving relationships! In other words, if the essence of God's nature is relational love, then the very nature of human existence should also reflect such satisfying and loving relationships.

But what do we mean by "love relationships"? If reality is truly defined by the nature of the Trinity, then we can come to only one conclusion: To really exist is to live in outward-oriented love, not inward-directed, self-focused gratification. Paul portrays this when he declared: "Therefore if there is any consolation in Christ, if any comfort of love, if any fellowship of the Spirit, if any affection and mercy, fulfill my joy by being like-minded, having the same love, being of one accord, of one mind. Let nothing be done through selfish ambition or conceit, but in lowliness of mind let each esteem others better than himself. Let each of you look out not only for his own interests, but also for the interests of others" (Phil. 2:1-4, NKJV).

Most certainly this principle, so powerfully evident in the Trinity's very nature and actions, would preclude all destructive pursuits of rank or gratification of appetite, position, fame, and power.

We see none of these pernicious characteristics in the manifestations of the Holy Trinity. Instead, we find constant self-submission before, and outward flowing love toward, one another. The Son submits Himself to the lordship of the Father in the Incarnation, and the Spirit is submissive (even to the point of almost obliterating His personal identity) to both the Father and the Son, doing Their bidding in a self-sacrificial manner.

The reader, however, may ask: What about the Father? Do we find Him manifesting such self-sacrificial, mutual submission? What is self-sacrificial about headship?

Perhaps the only way that we can answer such a question is to put it to Christian leaders and parents. Here is what they will say: "One of the most awesome privileges, yet weighty burdens in the world, is social and family leadership. Yes, such leadership does give one a certain prominence, but it also brings with it a mighty burden of care and responsibility." This is certainly what the Father bore as He assumed His role as the chief leader of the great plan of creation and redemption.

Without doubt those sent forth to do the bidding of their leaders bear special, unique burdens—but those who send them also endure great agony as they feel concern for the ones sent. Every heartache and woe that afflicted our Lord in His incarnate experience struck the loving heart of the Father. The great Father God sacrificed Himself in an amazing sense as He "was in Christ reconciling the world to Himself" (2 Cor. 5:19, NKJV). Only in this type of self-denying love can we have any sense of communal harmony and joy.

The Home and the Church

This last point leads to some vital considerations for God's two key social institutions—the family and the church. Both have come under severe attack, especially in recent times. Does the Trinity have anything to contribute to our understanding of the importance and proper functioning of society's two fundamental units?

If God's very nature of mutually submissive love unfolds in the family arena of the "heavenly trio," then we have the essence of what makes the marriage institution work. If we, like the Trinity, would self-sacrificially study the interests of our marriage partner first, how much happier the world would be. We would also be able more fully to discover the truth that as we study the happiness of others, we truly find life's deepest and most satisfying joys.

But what about the church? Once again, if the very nature of existence flows forth from God's social nature, then we can begin to glimpse more of the privileges of church membership. The church, along with the family, provides the most important arenas for the exercise and manifestation of mutually edifying love. Here we have two wonderful settings in which to learn and experience the blessings of mutual encouragement, thoughtful service, sharing, worship, and the vital lesson of patience.

In fact, the blessings and challenges of participating in both marriage and church fellowship are so crucial to learning and exercising God's love that I have often wondered if anybody could possibly make it to heaven without the benefits of being in them. Most certainly large numbers of single persons will enter heaven, and some people, because of extreme circumstances, will have to go to heaven without benefit of church participation. But they will be the exceptions, not the rule.

Where but in the church and family will we be more directly called upon to put our Christian practice and attitudes into concrete action? Most certainly the workplace and other social situations do challenge us. But my experience has been that the church and the home are the places that expect the most from us. If you can make it as a truly selfless, loving Christian in the home and the church, you can pretty well do so anywhere. Your family and fellow church members usually know the real you. And the key to vibrant Christian success in both arenas is the prevailing power of outwardly flowing love that "considers others better than" ourselves.

I know that what we have outlined above flies in the face of the highly individualistic attitudes so prevalent in Western culture. But if the profoundly loving nature located in the very social nature of God Himself means anything, it indicates that life finds its deepest levels of fulfillment only when we live as beings in social units. Only in such social situations permeated with the love of the triune God can we experience the most fulfilling parts of life. Radical individualism is not where the action is in a universe created for loving relationships.

Gender and Leadership

Many have wondered if the doctrine of the Trinity has anything to contribute to the more recent debates over the role of women in ministry. Some have argued that Christ's subordination to the Father provides an example of the lesser role that females would take in both marriage and church relationships. More specifically, others have argued that Christ's subordination to the Father is eternal and thus strongly suggests that women should always, in all social venues, be under male leadership.

Quite possibly the fact of Christ's subordination to the leadership of the Father may suggest some clues about leadership role in the church and the family. But the Bible only compares the husband's leadership role to that of Christ's in the church, not to that of the Father over the Son during the Incarnation (Eph. 5:22-29).

And even with the model of Christ, the bridegroom leader of the church which is the bride, every husband should remember that his leadership role in the family is one of profoundly self-sacrificing service. Any husband who wants to claim some sort of domineering leadership role over his wife should carefully ponder the thought of the apostle Paul: "Husbands, love your wives, just as Christ also loved the church and gave Himself for her" (verse 25, NKJV).

But what about women and leadership roles in the church? If anyone wants to argue on the basis of Christ's alleged eternal subordination to the Father in the experience of the Trinity, we find no convincing biblical evidence that Christ's subordination has been from all eternity. His subordination was only temporary. Furthermore, the scriptural evidence is that the subordination of Christ to the Father and the Holy Spirit to both the Father and the Son is merely for the practical purposes of creation and redemption among those otherwise equal in their shared divine nature. And finally, Revelation 22:1 speaks of the throne of God as the "throne of God and of the Lamb" (NKJV). The powerful implication is that They shall share the throne of the universe as fully equal partners.

We would therefore suggest that the Trinity provides no compelling clues, one way or the other, when it comes to the issue of what sort of leadership roles each gender should receive in the church. We must decide the issue on other biblical principles.

Many other ethical issues also cry out for Trinitarian analysis. For instance, how does the gratification of sexual fulfillment fit into God's ideal of love as mutual submission? If sexual love locates its core meaning in the Trinity's experience of mutually expressed love for the respective members of the Godhead and their creatures, do such considerations have anything to say to us about certain forms of sexual perversion (such as masturbation)? What does Trinitarian love have to teach us when it comes to healing nurture, especially in modern medical practice that has become all too technical and impersonal?

These and many other issues must possibly wait for another book, but not for your thoughtful and prayerful reflection.

Conclusions and Appeal

Having shared the most appealing and convincing evidence from the Bible to support the Trinitarian view of God, we would now strongly suggest that while the Bible does not use the exact term "Trinity" to describe the Godhead, the core meaning of the Trinitarian terminology and concepts reflect the basic biblical view of God. The God revealed in Scripture consists of three divine Persons who have existed for all eternity in a profound unity, or oneness of nature, purpose, and character. The most striking implications of this divine unity have arisen out of the affirmation that Christ is just as fully God as is the Father and that the Holy Spirit shares the same nature and is a person.

Furthermore, we have discovered that the essential nature of Their divine unity is one of dynamic creative outflowing and self-sacrificing love. This love has most movingly and ardently revealed itself in the incarnation of Christ Jesus, the eternal Son of God. In His amazing demonstration of self-sacrificing love, the good news of God's mercy and justice revealed itself in victory over temptation, in death that provided forgiveness through the satisfaction of divine justice, in resurrection that leads to eternal life, and in heavenly intercession that makes the whole accomplishment of incarnate love always and directly available to the whole world.

The incarnation of the Son, however, did not end God's communication of His love to the world. At the ascension of Christ, the Father and the Son dispatched the third person of the Godhead, the Holy Spirit, to be Their unique, divine, yet earthly agent of conviction, conversion, comfort, and empowerment for those who respond to God's saving initiative in Christ.

We then gave a historical overview of how God's people have developed their thinking about God and how it has repeatedly arrived at Trinitarian convictions. These convictions developed out of deep Bible study, the experience of God's love in salvation, prayerful reflection, worship, and the knowledge of God's power experienced in Christian witness and service.

Finally, we have sought to lay out the compelling theological and practical aspects of selected ethical implications of God's Trinitarian self-revelation. We have suggested that the doctrine of the Trinity contains principles absolutely essential to the most foundational doctrines and ethical principles of the gospel.

The Trinity's extraordinary and vital contribution to the teachings of the gospel has finally led us to rest our case. There is certainly more that we could say, but we desire to close with this:

We are convinced that the doctrine of the Trinity is not just a minor quibble over some peripheral doctrine or dubious moral issue. The truth contained in this profound doctrine forms the essential basis for the very heart of what is unique to Christianity. Out of our insights to the Trinity emerges our very understanding of the greatest of all biblical notions—God is love.

Such love is defined not just by feeling or human experience—but by none other than the Creator and Redeemer God of the universe Himself. And the definitions of love that really count are those that reside in the very core or substance of God's eternal triune nature.

Such love, however, has not simply lain dormant in God's inner being. To the contrary, it has revealed itself in the ways that He has created the world, redeemed it from sin, and has continually sought to reestablish His moral rulership over the universe. If the universe's moral governance is not based on the justness of His love, then all creation is in deep trouble.

Without the creative and redemptive initiatives that have their source in God's freely manifested and bestowed love, the universe will ultimately sink into moral, social, and physical anarchy. Therefore, only the love that abounds in God's triune nature can establish the moral principles that make life orderly and meaningful. Not only do we owe our existence and salvation to God, but we are utterly dependent upon Him for any semblance of moral order (either now or in the world to come).

But His love is not just about tender, merciful sentiment and moral order. The Triune manifestation of love has a flinty side to it—justice. Sin has forced the justice aspect of love to confront the unspeakable horror of evil's invasion of a universe created by expansive, divine love. And the question persists: Is there any solution to this indescribable terror?

We would answer in the affirmative: God's love is not only tender, relational, and personal, but it is also just and sovereign. The latter concepts comfort us with the fact that God will not allow sin and its horrible fruit of evil and suffering to afflict the universe forever.

While the wheels of His justice have ground slowly, they will ultimately grind to a satisfying finality. He has vanquished evil's terrors by finally taking care of the emergency Himself. In the person of His beloved Son, God has come and met sin and its attendant terrors head-on. God did not delegate the solution of the sin problem and all its resulting suffering to some creaturely surrogate.

The concept of the Trinity is simply too foundational, too essential, too biblical, and finally too precious to the very nature of our understanding of God to relegate it to a side issue. We urge a renewed commitment to the truth of the Triune Godhead and the "heavenly Trio's" awesome vision of a loving and benevolent human existence.

In a word, the Trinitarian understanding of God points us to the exalted experience of making Him central to all of our worship, moral formation, service, and witness to the world. Our prayer is that one day soon, we may all be able to stand before the eternal throne and shout " 'Give glory to Him' for the 'hour of His judgment has' passed, and all is well with the universe. Even so, Maranatha!"

Bibliography for Section Four

Grudem, Wayne. *Systematic Theology.* Grand Rapids: Zondervan Pub. House, 1994.

Stott, John R. W. *The Cross of Christ.* Downers Grove, Ill.: InterVarsity Press, 1986.

White, Ellen G. *The Desire of Ages.* Mountain View, Calif.: Pacific Press Pub. Assn., 1898.

———. *Review and Herald Articles* (facsimile reprint). Washington, D.C.: Review and Herald Pub. Assn., 1962. 6 vols.

———. *The Spirit of Prophecy* (facsimile reproduction). Washington, D.C.: Review and Herald Pub. Assn., 1969. 4 vols.

———. *Youth's Instructor Articles* (facsimile reproductions). Washington, D.C.: Review and Herald Pub. Assn., 1986.

Index

Scriptural Index

ACTS

ROMANS

1 CORINTHIANS

2 CORINTHIANS

GALATIANS

EPHESIANS

PHILIPPIANS

COLOSSIANS

1 THESSALONIANS

1 TIMOTHY

TITUS

HEBREWS

1 PETER

2 PETER

1 JOHN

JUDE

REVELATION